To President Barack Obama,
who inspired me to rise up and tell these unsung
stories of American individualism, exceptionalism,
and entrepreneurship.

ALSO BY MICHELLE MALKIN

Culture of Corruption: Obama and His Team
of Tax Cheats, Crooks, and Cronies

Unhinged: Exposing Liberals Gone Wild

In Defense of Internment: The Case for Racial
Profiling in World War II and the War on Terror

Invasion: How America Still Welcomes Terrorists,
Criminals, and Other Foreign Menaces to Our Shores

WHO BUILT THAT

Awe-Inspiring Stories
of American Tinkerpreneurs

MICHELLE MALKIN

THRESHOLD EDITIONS / MERCURY INK

New York   London   Toronto   Sydney   New Delhi

Threshold Editions/Mercury Ink
An Imprint of Simon & Schuster, Inc.
1230 Avenue of the Americas
New York, NY 10020

First Threshold Editions/Mercury Ink paperback edition January 2016

THRESHOLD EDITIONS and colophon are trademarks of
Simon & Schuster, Inc.

GLENN BECK is a trademark of Mercury Radio Arts, Inc.

For information about special discounts for bulk purchases,
please contact Simon & Schuster Special Sales at 1-866-506-1949
or business@simonandschuster.com.

The Simon & Schuster Speakers Bureau can bring authors
to your live event. For more information or to book an event,
contact the Simon & Schuster Speakers Bureau at 866-248-3049
or visit our website at www.simonspeakers.com.

Interior design by Jaime Putorti

Manufactured in the United States of America

10   9   8   7   6   5   4   3   2   1

Library of Congress Cataloging-in-Publication Data is available.

ISBN 978-1-4767-8494-6
ISBN 978-1-5011-3083-0 (pbk)
ISBN 978-1-4767-8495-3 (ebook)

The great glory of the Americans is in their wondrous contrivances—
in their patent remedies for the usually troublous operations of life.
—ANTHONY TROLLOPE, 1863

So I suppose all those great works built themselves!
—GEORGE WESTINGHOUSE,
RESPONDING TO NEWSPAPER ATTACKS ON HIS ENTERPRISE, 1907

CONTENTS

PART III: BFFs: DYNAMIC DUOS OF AMERICAN BUSINESS

PART IV: PAST, PRESENT, FUTURE

INTRODUCTION

Many of you know me as that angry brown lady on cable TV who's always yelling at liberals. The truth is, I am so much more than just the Angry Brown Lady on Cable TV. My kids, for example, know me as the angry lady who's always yelling at *them*—to do their (non–Common Core) homework, pick up their underwear, eat their vegetables, and enter the No-Whine Zone.

But I do have a softer side. Really.

At home, I'm a geek mom who loves to watch the Science Channel's *How It's Made* and ABC's *Shark Tank*. *Popular Science,* and *Popular Mechanics* are my airplane reading must-haves. I may be the only wife in America who was thrilled when her husband gave her a quadcopter for Christmas. And in high school, I was named "Class Braintrust," which is the politically correct way of saying Queen of the Nerds. My two "action shots" in the yearbook showed me studying in the library and staring intently at lab equipment in my Advanced Placement Chemistry class, which increased my nerd factor by several orders of magnitude.

**CLASS
BRAINTRUST**
Michelle Magla-
lang and Joe Duffy
Runners-up
Rupal Patel and
Eric Schreiner

Here is another confession: I am a tinkerer-wannabe. Among my
contrivances gone wrong:

- a modified Weber grill that exploded and nearly burned my
  eyebrows off,
- a soda-bottle submarine that sank like a concrete block in
  the bathtub, and
- a cache of defective PVC marshmallow shooters clogged up
  with sticky-sweet ammunition.

Each of these endeavors remains the subject of family mockery. But
yes, I'm proud of my discards. In failure, after all, lies progress. In mis-
adventure lies enlightenment. Disappointment and dead ends induce
turnarounds. Turnarounds yield new and endless paths toward improvement and success. I agree wholeheartedly with Don J. Whittemore of the American Society of Civil Engineers, who wrote in 1896:
"The Scrap Heap—that inarticulate witness of our blunders, and the
sepulchre of our blasted hopes; the best, most humiliating, legacy we

are forced to leave to our successors—has always, to me, been brimful of instruction."

As an abysmal flop at even the most modest engineering and manufacturing projects, I believe I am uniquely equipped to write a book celebrating unsung American inventors and entrepreneurs who've actually succeeded. Who better than an obsessive geek tinkerer-wannabe to tell the stories of these unappreciated geniuses and business phenoms? My reverence for makers and risk-takers is unabashed and unbridled. Call me a sideline technophile, innovation groupie, and a lifelong fan girl of the American Dream. Of all the books I've written, this one has led me on the most joyful journey through American history. I've shared every research tidbit and discovery with my family, started my own little collection of nineteenth-century artifacts of American invention (thanks for the inspiration, Glenn Beck!), and interacted with some of the most fascinating and brilliant people I've ever met in more than two decades as a journalist and author.

When I first thought of writing *Who Built That*, though, I must admit I was still in Angry Cable TV Lady mode. In 2010, Vice President Joe Biden had boasted that "every single great idea that has marked the twenty-first century, the twentieth century and the nineteenth century has required government vision and government incentive." Yes, he really did say "every." My poor family heard me rant about this for weeks.

That same year, President Obama opined that the proper role of private entrepreneurs was to fulfill "the core responsibilities of the financial system to help grow our economy"—as opposed to fulfilling their own happiness, pursuing their own personal and professional ambitions, or providing for their own families. Next, Obama argued that "at a certain point you have made enough money." Then, in the fall of 2012, Republicans got their electoral butts kicked. How could this happen after Obama got caught on the campaign trail openly denigrating American entrepreneurs? Let me remind you of what he said: "If you've got a business—you didn't build that. Somebody else made that happen."

The Obama campaign and its media defenders argued that his remarks were taken "out of context" by critics. But here's what he said immediately preceding that infamous sound bite, straight from the White House transcript:

> Look, if you've been successful, you didn't get there on your own. You didn't get there on your own. I'm always struck by people who think, well, it must be because I was just so smart. There are a lot of smart people out there. It must be because I worked harder than everybody else. Let me tell you something—there are a whole bunch of hardworking people out there. [Applause.]
>
> If you were successful, somebody along the line gave you some help. There was a great teacher somewhere in your life. Somebody helped to create this unbelievable American system that we have that allowed you to thrive. Somebody invested in roads and bridges. If you've got a business—you didn't build that. Somebody else made that happen.

The context makes Obama's contempt for private entrepreneurial achievement even clearer. His intent was to humiliate and shame those who reject collectivism. The president's message: *Innovators are nothing special. Their brains and work ethics are no different from anyone else's. They owe their success to taxpayers and public school teachers and public roads and bridges.* Pushing to raise taxes even higher on wealthy Americans, Obama brazenly stoked you-think-you're-so-smart resentment of business owners and placed government at the center of every American success story.

This government-built-that version of America is anathema to how our Founding Fathers envisioned, pioneered, practiced, and enshrined the "progress of science and useful arts" in Article I, Section

8, Clause 8, of the Constitution. They understood that the ability of brilliant, ambitious individuals to reap private rewards for inventions and improvements benefited the public good. From colonial times through the nineteenth-century Age of Progress, our political leaders and judiciary supported the most generous protections for entrepreneurial patent-holders. Mainstream culture celebrated never-satisfied rags-to-riches capitalists.

"Profit," however, is now treated as a profanity in today's class-warfare-poisoned discourse. Those who seek financial enrichment for the fruits of their labor and creativity are cast as greedy villains, selfish barons, and rapacious beasts—and so are the wealthy investors who support them. During the 2012 U.S. presidential campaign, candidates and operatives in *both* political parties derided private equity and venture capitalism as "vulture capitalism." President Obama routinely indicted "millionaires and billionaires" as public enemies (before jetting off to raise money from them in Hollywood and Manhattan).

Anticapitalism saboteurs organized wealth-shaming protests at corporate CEOs' private homes in New York and in private neighborhoods in Connecticut. *New York Times* columnist Paul Krugman (a former high-paid adviser to corrupt energy company Enron) whipped up hatred against the "plutocrats" in solidarity with the Occupy Wall Street mob. Krugman mocked business leaders who objected to political persecution as "a small but powerful group of what can only be called sociopaths." Democratic strategist Donna Brazile publicly endorsed an incendiary protest slogan embraced by so-called progressives: "The tree of life is dying. Prune the top 1% and feed the roots!" And in 2011, New York State lawmakers received threatening mail from a disgruntled state government worker saying it was "time to kill the wealthy" if they didn't renew the state's tax surcharge on millionaires: "If you don't, I'm going to pay a visit with my carbine to one of those tech companies you are so proud of and shoot every spoiled Ivy League [expletive] I can find," the death threat read.

Class-warfare attacks continue to proliferate in Washington and

Hollywood—even as private venture capital has grown from "the pilot light of American industry" to its "roaring glass furnace," as San Francisco financier Thomas Perkins put it. These "vultures" are visionaries whose private funds have nurtured job-creating powerhouses—including many cutting-edge companies in the knowledge industry used by "progressive" propagandists to disseminate their anticapitalist message to the masses.

Apple, Intel, and Microsoft? Venture capital helped fund that.

Facebook, Google, Skype, YouTube, PayPal, and Instagram? Thank private venture capital, not government-coerced redistribution of wealth.

American venture capital and American innovation over the past quarter-century are inextricably linked. In *The Money of Invention*, business professors Paul Gompers and Josh Lerner noted, "By the end of 2000, venture-backed firms that had gone public made up over 20 percent of the total number of public firms in existence in the United States. And of the total market value of public firms ($8.25 trillion), venture-backed companies came in at $2.7 trillion—over 32 percent."

Private venture-financed firms are the center of the nation's most innovative sectors: biotechnology, computer services, industrial services, and semiconductor industries. In fact, America's much-maligned venture capitalists "create whole new industries and seed fledgling companies that later dominate those industries." From San Francisco venture capitalist Tom Perkins's $100,000 investment in a few biochemists came Genentech—the multibillion-dollar biotech giant that produced blockbuster, life-saving drugs including Herceptin (breast cancer); Rituxin (non-Hodgkins lymphoma and rheumatoid arthritis); and Avastin (for several types of cancer). An MIT profile notes that in its first three decades, Kleiner Perkins "made more than 475 investments, generating $90 billion in revenue and creating 275,000 jobs" and "funded 167 companies that later went public, including Amazon, AOL, Genentech, Google and Netscape."

In January 2014, Tom Perkins wrote a passionate letter to the *Wall Street Journal* decrying the "progressive war on the American 1 percent," which he likened to "fascist Nazi Germany" and "its war on its 'one percent,' namely its Jews." He called on the left to stop demonizing "the rich," and he condemned the Occupy Wall Street movement's "rising tide of hatred." Perkins was no crony capitalist or privileged elitist. He started out at the bottom at Hewlett-Packard, founded his own separate laser company on the side, and then teamed up with fellow entrepreneur Eugene Kleiner to establish one of the nation's oldest and most important venture capital firms, Kleiner Perkins Caufield and Byers. A hands-on dynamo, Perkins immersed himself in the science and technology of the companies in his portfolio. He even accompanied them on sales calls. He poured his heart and soul into the business of business.

Perkins achieved great wealth for himself, his partners, and his clients—and the world is a better place for it. But because he dared to compare the seething resentment of modern progressives to Kristallnacht and Nazi Germany, the visionary investor was condemned by liberal journalists and commentators as "nuts" and a "rich idiot." His cowardly former colleagues at the venture capital firm he founded threw him under the bus. Perkins apologized for the Kristallnacht analogy, but he bravely refused to back down from his message defending the "creative 1 percent."

After the public backlash, Perkins repeated the theme of his letter: "Any time the majority starts to demonize a minority, no matter what it is, it's wrong. And dangerous. And no good ever comes from it."

He also chastised those who bemoan "income inequality," including his erstwhile "friends" Al Gore, Jerry Brown, and Barack Obama: "The 1 percent are not causing the inequality. They are the job creators. . . . I think Kleiner Perkins itself over the years has created pretty close to a million jobs, and we're still doing it." The venture capitalist then delivered his most stinging and effective rebuke to the wealth-shamers: "It's absurd to demonize the rich for being rich and for doing what the rich do, which is get richer by creating opportunity for others."

Amen! The demonization of the one percent will not stop until the 99 percent truly comprehend how much marvelous progress and opportunity they enjoy as a result of the nation's makers and creators. Their stories need to be told early and often. Plenty of general-interest books have been written about U.S. inventions and inventors. But few of these history lessons emphasize the unique ingredients that created our country's fertile climate for technological progress and entrepreneurship. Foremost among these are profit motive, intellectual property rights, individual risk-taking, venture capital, our unique patent system, and an unwavering belief in American exceptionalism.

My mission for this book, which I wrote for my kids and yours, is to fight the wealth-shamers with enlightenment and inspiration. *Who Built That* is a treasury of stories about my favorite American heroes of the one percent. They got rich, made other people richer, and made the world a safer, brighter, more comfortable, and happier place to live. My personal obsession has always been with the mundane things we take for granted. That's why I picked the makers of ordinary, everyday items that make modern life modern—toilet paper, the bottle cap, glass bottles, the disposable razor, root beer, wire rope, the alternating current (AC) motor, air-conditioning, and durable flashlights.

I call the heroes of *Who Built That* "tinkerpreneurs." These underappreciated inventors and innovators of mundane things changed the world by successfully commercializing their ideas and creating products, companies, jobs, and untold opportunities that endure today. They enlisted some of the nation's very first venture capitalists—private profit-seekers, not government funders—to help them succeed. They secured patents, met payroll, made lots of money, and bettered the lives of their countrymen while bettering their own. These tireless capitalists devoted their lives to improving their designs and products. They were self-made and largely self-taught.

The stars of *Who Built That* have common traits:

1. mechanical ability from an early age;
2. stubborn practicality and dedication to making and selling useful things;
3. willingness to expand their creative orbits as widely as possible to get the job done;
4. relentless work ethic and insatiable commitment to continual self-improvement;
5. a deep and abiding respect for intellectual property, fair play, and the rule of law;
6. strong faith and perseverance through failure and adversity; and
7. reverence for America's special role as a beacon of freedom and opportunity.

In my research and interviews, I came to appreciate another key lesson of American tinkerpreneurship: Character counts. Integrity matters. These stories involve some of the most honest, loyal, and humble people I've encountered in my lifetime. You'll meet eighty-three-year-old Maglite flashlight inventor and CEO Tony Maglica, who opened up his heart and factory floor to me, while workers of all backgrounds embraced him everywhere we went. You'll discover the intrepid sacrifices that George Westinghouse and Nikola Tesla, Edward Libbey and Michael Owens, and Willis Carrier and Irvine Lyle made for each other and for their companies. You'll learn about the fierce family ties that bound the Scott brothers and the Roeblings.

The pioneers in *Who Built That* gave glory to God, their families, colleagues, and America's free enterprise system. Of course, they benefited from the help of others. We *all* stand on the shoulders of our Founding Fathers. But these successful tinkerpreneurs deserve the ultimate credit for the fruits of their individual minds and the untold by-products of their labor. And yes, President Obama, they *were* smarter and more hardworking than everyone else, including you and me.

Perhaps the most remarkable discovery I made was how much natural overlap occurred among the lives of the men and women whom I chose to profile. The quintessential American stories you are about to read breathe life and color into eighteenth-century philosopher and political economist Adam Smith's famous free-market theory:

> Every individual is continually exerting himself to find out the most advantageous employment for whatever capital he can command. It is his own advantage, indeed, and not that of the society, which he has in view. . . . *He generally, indeed, neither intends to promote the public interest, nor knows how much he is promoting it . . . he intends only his own gain, and he is in this, as in many other cases, led by an invisible hand to promote an end which was no part of his intention.* Nor is it always the worse for the society that it was no part of it. By pursuing his own interest he frequently promotes that of the society more effectually than when he really intends to promote it. [Emphasis added.]

Without ever intending to do so, colonial paper-makers paved the way for the Scott brothers' toilet paper and paper towel products, which enhanced public hygiene during the deadly influenza epidemics of the early twentieth century and continue to provide comfort and convenience today.

Inventive giants George Westinghouse and Nikola Tesla, who together harnessed the power of Niagara Falls and electrified the world, unknowingly influenced air-conditioning pioneer Willis Carrier.

The technology of Carrier and his business partner, Irvine Lyle, catalyzed the movie industry, malls, skyscrapers, and development of the American South, Southwest, and West. Carrier and Lyle also improved the manufacturing processes of textile mills, printing presses, life-saving drugs, and King Camp Gillette's disposable razor.

Gillette's mentor was bottle-cap innovator William Painter, whose tiny, cork-lined metal tops ushered in the era of safe, cheap packaging for beverages, processed foods, and pharmaceuticals.

Painter's breakthrough came in tandem with the independent tinkerpreneurial efforts of glass bottle industry leaders Edward Libbey and Michael Owens, whose partnership yielded breakthroughs in the production of lightbulbs and kerosene lamps, bottle-making, standardization of pharmaceutical packaging, mass-manufacture of flat glass and auto glass, and the invention of fiberglass.

Wire rope engineer John Roebling and his family, who built the Brooklyn Bridge, spearheaded the industrial age of iron and steel-cable suspension bridges, and supplied the wires used for telegraphs, telephones, cable cars, airplanes, electricity, mining, and oil drilling.

These connections sprang up organically, not from top-down regulations or government policy. No federal Department of Innovation is responsible for the tinkerpreneurs' success. No Ten-Point White House Action Plan for Progress can lay claim to the boundless synergies of these profit-earning capitalists. Here is the marvel we take for granted: The concentric circles of American innovation in the free marketplace are infinite. This miracle repeats itself millions of times a day through the voluntary interactions, exchanges, and business partnerships of creative Americans and their clients, customers, and consumers. I'll show you how just a small handful of tinkerpreneurs profoundly revolutionized and improved every aspect of our lives—from the bathroom to the kitchen to the office, to the food and drinks we consume and the medicines and medical devices that prolong our lives.

After delving into the stories of these awe-inspiring American makers and risk-takers, I know, dear readers, that you will agree:

We owe *them*, not the other way around.

PART I

ENGINEERS OF PROSPERITY

We had faith and enthusiasm in our enterprise,
with loyalty to each other and to a common cause.
—EDWARD T. MURPHY, CARRIER CORPORATION

1.

MAGLITE'S TONY MAGLICA:

Torchbearer of the American Dream

"Tony."

The spry eighty-three-year-old CEO's name is embroidered in cursive on a slightly rumpled, short-sleeved lab coat. Underneath the industrial gray uniform, his baby-blue-plaid dress shirt is unbuttoned at the collar and his cuffs are casually rolled up. His dark slacks hang loosely on a weathered but fit frame. On his feet are bright white New Balance sneakers, made in the U.S.A. His shoes need to be comfortable, because he traverses his 450,000-square-foot factory floor dozens of times over the course of his twelve-hour workday, six days a week, beginning at the crack of dawn and ending after most of his eight hundred employees have clocked out.

Tony looks like a cross between Albert Einstein and Mark Twain, with a much better barber. His olive skin is offset by a neat head of silver curls, fluffy sideburns, and a perfectly trimmed mustache. He's intense, but not intimidating. He's proud, but not arrogant. He's larger than life, but stubbornly down to earth. His deceptively mundane inventions and innovations are synonymous with engineering excellence and economical value.

Like the products he made famous around the world, Tony is tough, durable, handsome, beloved, long-lasting, and lit from within.

Sitting across from Tony Maglica in the glass-encased meeting room of his Ontario, California, headquarters, I am in complete awe of the man who invented the revolutionary Maglite flashlight and founded a billion-dollar business that grew from a tiny garage. Yet I feel right at home. Within minutes of meeting each other, we are talking about his family and I need a Kleenex. "Michelle, I owe everything to my mother," Tony says with a catch in his voice. We both wipe our eyes. He hands me a genealogy book titled *O Zlarinskim Obiteljima Jurcan I Maglica*—a story of the Jurcan and Maglica families' lives in Zlarin, which seamlessly transports us back to the Great Depression and the formative childhood years that ignited his enduring passion for life, liberty, and the American Dream.

War, Hunger, and Hardship on the Isle of Zlarin

"Zlato" means gold in Croatian. The sun-washed island of Zlarin, the "Golden Island," sits in the Sibenek archipelago of the Adriatic Sea one mile south of Croatia's Dalmatian coast. Cars are banned on the three-square-mile territory to preserve its tranquil habitat, which boasts exotic red coral, sandy beaches, thick pine trees, and lush olive groves. Despite these ample resources, life on the tiny Mediterranean island of about three hundred inhabitants was filled with hardship and deprivation. Large families, whose ancestors came from mainland Croatia in the thirteenth century, would rise as early as 2:00 a.m., trudging several miles, along with their donkeys, through rocky hills to till their fields. Many islanders owned vineyards, but a devastating plant disease called *Peronospora* blighted the wine farms at the beginning of the twentieth century.

Generations of Zlarin men sought work as fishermen and sailors, often leaving their one-room stone cottages by the tender age of twelve. The wives stayed behind, harvesting and hand-making what they could to feed and clothe their children, who helped grind cornmeal and gathered figs, lentils, and wild berries. Several families would share a single kettle, hanging from the ceiling beams, to boil cabbage. It would take from midafternoon until almost midnight for each family to have its turn. To pass the time as they tended the fire, the relatives entertained each other around the hearth with treasured Zlarin songs, poems, and fables about sea creatures and fairies (called "vile and the vidine") that roamed the hills and snatched up children.

The women and kids plastered the walls of their stone homes with pictures of the sailing ships and steamers that their male relatives worked on around the world. The men slaved away as crewmen, stokers, oilers, and coalmen in order to send money home. Many drowned at sea or fell victim to crime or disease in faraway foreign ports.

Tomicahad Maglica (née Jurcan), Tony's mother, came from a small hamlet known as Borovica on the interior of the island. The topography consisted of pristine pools, caves, and a sandy mixture of chalk and dolomite that could be sold as clay soap. Borovica residents worked as field laborers and fishermen. The Jurcans' early homes on Zlarin were one-room huts made of dry stone walls, fortified with stone slabs. In the most crowded cottages, some family members slept on straw mattresses in the cellar, crammed in next to wine kegs and olive oil casks. Both Tomicahad's great-grandfather and grandfather were seamen who left home at young ages. Her grandfather later found work at a restaurant in New York City. Several of Tomicahad's loved ones fought in the resistance movement against fascism during World War II.

The family of Jerko Maglica, Tony's father, had lived on the easternmost part of the island, known as Ruza, dating back to the fifteenth century. Jerko had two brothers, Ive and Joso. Their father, Ante, who had been lame since childhood, was the village crier ("*kredar*"). He would announce news from the church or shout out the merchandise arriving from boats that came from the Croatian mainland (pots, tureens, baskets, and fish traps) or the Italian ports of Puglia, Abruzzi, and Marche (lentils, beans, and wheat). Local villagers said Ante's cries "could make the fish jump," but he remained mired in debt. His crier's job paid pennies. Much of the time, he received no wages at all, but was compensated instead with a bit of fish for lunch or a small carafe of wine.

By pooling family funds, the Maglicas managed to cobble enough ship fare ("pasaj") to sail to America. Third-class or "steerage" class tickets on the bottom deck ranged from ten to twenty-five dollars, which took months if not years for many poor families to raise. The brothers departed from Antwerp, Belgium, where an estimated 2 million European immigrants boarded the famed Red Star Line from 1873 to 1935. Among the most famous passengers of the ocean liner to freedom (which was founded in Philadelphia in 1871 by Quaker businessman Clement Griscom): Irving Berlin and Albert Einstein. After sailing the world to settle their father's debts, brother Ive settled in New York in the late 1920s to work as a stoker for a gasworks plant. Joso and Jerko joined him soon after and found work as dockers.

In November 1930, as the Great Depression raged, Jerko and wife, Tomicahad, welcomed the birth of their only son, Ante "Tony" Maglica, in the longshoremen's district of Manhattan's Lower West Side. Some six thousand people in the city were out of work and on the streets at the time, desperately selling apples for a nickel apiece.

With Jerko barely able to earn a living, Tomicahad decided to return to Zlarin with toddler Tony.

At first, Tomicahad survived as a subsistence farmer on a meager plot of family land. Tony was poor, but happy. As World War II erupted and closed in on the islanders, however, misery and famine encroached. Tony recalled watching his mother and her twin sister, Nata, depart Zlarin in a small rowboat, fighting strong winds and risking their lives to get to the mainland to trade any items of value they could scrape together for food. "They would be gone for days and I would be alone," Tony told me. "My mother left me with one can of flour and told me to make it last a week." With tummy grumbling, Tony would mix the flour with water and heat it into a barely edible paste. Each day, he'd climb the roof of his home to keep watch for the boat. Each night, he'd look out at the stars illuminating the Adriatic Sea. As time ticked away and the can of flour dwindled to nothing, Tony's mother and aunt would finally return. The boy greeted them with a mixture of relief and anticipation. "My mother brought back beans, which I would beg her to boil right away. I never grew tired of those beans! I still love them today," he says with a twinkle in his eye.

Young Tony was resourceful and creative. He took apart clocks, carved chess pieces out of wood, and built cradles and stone shelters for his family. Tomicahad and her sister, meanwhile, tore apart their homes—stripped the bed sheets, emptied the kitchen of plates and utensils, rustled up religious artifacts and furniture—for bartering. "My mother, God rest her soul, even pulled out one of her own gold-filled teeth to trade for food," Tony reminisces with a pained face as if it were yesterday. She motivated him to work and study hard, to squander nothing, and to relish every opportunity. Tony's education was rudimentary; as a teen, he apprenticed as a locksmith and shipyard worker.

The Axis annexation and occupation of Zlarin, first by the Italians and then by the Germans, brought fear and death to Tony's village.

Croats who had joined the antifascist resistance movement, including at least one of Tomicahad's relatives, were thrown into Italian concentration camps. Mass terror took the form of daily raids, deportations, and ethnic cleansing. Islanders were executed randomly. Still visibly shaken after all these years, Tony tells me he "hid in the forest" for hours at a time, trembling as "planes dropped bombs from the sky."

Another time, Tony, his mother, and their friends and neighbors were rounded up by German soldiers wielding machine guns. The islanders were lined up in the village square. "I thought we were going to be shot. I thought that was it." A local priest apparently talked the bloodthirsty occupiers out of a massacre. But other Croatian villagers were not so lucky. In Dalmatia, forty inhabitants were slaughtered by Italians in May 1942 after several dozen telegraph poles near Sibenek had been sabotaged by resistance fighters. Axis forces opened up an artillery barrage on civilians in the town of Primosten after they revolted against Italian sailors. Clamping down on resistance movement revolts, Germans executed nearly 270 Croats in the mainland village of Lipa.

Through it all, Tomicahad held on to hope that she and Tony would survive. She encouraged him relentlessly to pursue his dreams of returning to his birthplace—the land of the free and the home of the brave. In 1950, with Communists overtaking Croatia, Tony made it back to New York. He returned to America at the dawn of the postwar economic boom. Tony brought the mechanical skills he had honed in Zlarin. Most important, he carried Tomicahad's spirit of perseverance and optimism burning within him.

"Without His Maglite®, He Would Have Been Buried Alive"

Back at the sprawling headquarters of Mag Instruments, Tony leads me to a large, memento-filled room on the second floor. I'm immediately drawn to a long glass case featuring typewritten, signed letters and battered Maglite flashlights of all sizes. The stylish, sturdy torches had been run over, submerged in water, or caught in flames.

And yet, like Tony himself, his inventions endured in the face of crushing adversity.

The surviving Maglite products on display at Tony's headquarters represent just a few of the countless "amazing stories" the company has collected from first responders, soldiers, sportsmen, and ordinary housewives. The testimonials could fill an entire museum.

A police officer from New Caney, Texas, wrote:

Dear Maglite,

On December 4, 1992, one of my men was involved in a shooting incident & the Maglite® that he was carrying on duty saved his life. My officer was responding to a family violence call in progress in the city adjoining ours. Upon arrival to the residence, the officer was advised that the subject in the house had a rifle. He then requested more officers at this location & while waiting, the officer & his sergeant took up a position by the residence's front door, & tried to get the subject inside the house to give up his weapon & surrender.

The sergeant kicked the front door of the house, allowing the officer to shine his flashlight down the hallway of the residence, [where he saw] the subject at the end of the hallway pointing a high powered rifle at him. He then backed out of the house & took up a defensive position at the edge of the doorway in front of the sergeant. The subject crawled up the hallway & fired a shot from the rifle at the officer. If not for the fact that [the] officer's flashlight was in direct contact with the bullet first & took the impact of the bullet, I might be delivering a funeral speech for him instead of writing you this letter.

Enclosed you'll find the picture of the flashlight that is being held as evidence. Once again I thank you for a well-built flashlight. It saved my officer's life.

A Santee, California, firefighter took time out of his busy day to send his thanks:

> *I'm a firefighter and many of us, as you know, use Maglite® flash-*
> *lights to see our way in the heavy smoke of a fire. While at work one*
> *day and after one of the fire engines had moved, I noticed a three-*
> *cell Maglite® flashlight on the floor. Looking closely at where it was*
> *lying, I noticed that it was in the tire tracks of the fire engine. I called*
> *one of my coworkers over and we could see where the tire track from*
> *the outside dual tire was not complete. We picked up the Maglite®*
> *flashlight and we could see where it had been pressed into the concrete*
> *floor. To our amazement, there were only two small indentations on*
> *the Maglite® flashlight from the floor. The light still worked and the*
> *body of the Maglite® flashlight was not even bent. Needless to say, we*
> *were impressed. Thank you for making such a good product.*

A cop from Weber City, Virginia, related his story:

> *On May 4, 2001, in the early morning hours of 4 a.m., I found a*
> *house engulfed in flames. I entered the side door of the residence. The*
> *smoke was so heavy that you couldn't see your hand in front of your*
> *eyes. I placed my Maglite® on the floor by the door. I crawled down*
> *the hall to the kitchen, where I found a person passed out. I took the*
> *person and stood up then proceeded to exit the residence. I lost my bear-*
> *ings. I dropped to the floor. I was very disoriented from the heat and*
> *the smoke. As I lay on the floor, I looked around and there by the door*
> *I could see the Maglite® showing me the way out of that inferno.*
>
> *I want to take this opportunity to thank you with all my heart for*
> *this great flashlight that saved the life of the victim and myself. You*
> *have a great product. Again, thank you.*

A soldier who served during Operation Desert Storm thanked Tony for his donation of Maglite products to the U.S. military:

In response to your items & letter that you supplied to my troops here in Saudi Arabia: The accessory packs & bulbs have really come in handy. They allowed our troops to walk around at night & not be detected. They have out-performed the bulky & larger military lights. They are really nice they strap right to our web gear & are easy to get at.

Again, I want to thank you for your support to my troops while in Desert Storm. All of my troops want to thank you. Thank you for your support. God Bless You.

A New York City office worker who escaped the World Trade Center 1 during the 9/11 terrorist attacks wrote:

A quick story: On Sept 11, 2001, 35 of my fellow workers [and I] were working 6 levels under the World Trade Center in NYC. At approximately 8:55 AM that morning, we were given a heads up that a plane had crashed into the adjacent North Tower (we had been previously involved in the 1993 bomb blast).

We ran 7 stories up the fire exit to the street level and escaped with our lives. We were unaware that one of our coworkers was left in the bathroom. The lights went out. Totally black 7 stories underground, except for his Maglite®. The technician, who has bad eyesight and bad hearing, made his way up the stairs and out of the building as the second plane hit the south side of the south tower, directly above the fire exit.

He barely made it across the street as the building began to collapse—steel, glass, people raining down on him. Without his Maglite®, he would have been buried alive. Thank you.

And another worker who survived the 9/11 attack on the World Trade Center 2 Tower shared his emotional experience:

I am a Licensed Electrical Contractor in NY City. I am a survivor of the massive terrorist attack on the World Trade Center complex. We

are the house electricians for the lease owners of the Trade Center. I,
along with one colleague, was trapped in 7 WTC at the very time that
the 1st tower imploded. Just prior, 4 seconds, to the debris that was
WTC #2, the first tower to fall, my colleague & I were in the lower
lobby of 7 WTC along with several different personnel from several
different agencies—OEM, FDNY, NYPD, etc. We ran to safety in cor-
ridor that connected the lower lobby to the loading dock. When the
tower hit ground, the smoke, soot & powdered debris not only filled
the lobby & loading dock, but the enclosed corridor where we, about
25 people, were trapped.

Breathing was our greatest concern. There was no visibility. Panic
occurred. One of the others screamed that we are all professionals.
"Stop screaming. Does anybody know a way?" My colleague and I did.

At that time I reached into my trusty and sturdy briefcase for 2
Mini Maglite® flashlights given to me as presents. These two 2 Mini
Maglite® flashlights allowed me to shine a light onto the wall that led
us to the Washington Street exit of 7 WTC.

Approximately 25 people followed us to safety. This note to you at
Maglite® is to let you know that the convenience of your product was
essential to our escape from what was and is the ultimate disaster.

I will never be without these 2 Mini Maglite® flashlights as long as
I continue to live. I do not have the serial number of the units, however
I will now take these out of service, in memoriam to all of our brothers
& sisters lost to the monstrous attack of the cowards among all of us.
I will purchase a larger version of your product for my trusty briefcase
to hold.

Long Live the USA and their fantastic manufacturers. The lives
of several are intact because of your product. Letting you know this is
therapy for me.

"$150 and Twenty English Words"

Long before he was saving other people's lives, Tony Maglica had to save his own. He started at the bottom. Rock bottom. After arriving back in the U.S., he took a job at a sweatshop sewing clothes. The piecework paid fifty cents an hour. He worked hard to assimilate, teaching himself English from a dictionary. The Croatian community in New York City was tight-knit and maintained the culture and customs of the "old country." Maglica's father and uncles established a "social society" of Zlarinians who helped each other out. But economic opportunity beckoned from outside the Big Apple slums. With his wife and young child in tow, the ambitious twenty-year-old tinkerer packed up a rusted, bald-tired 1947 Studebaker and headed West. He summed up his possessions for the journey: "$150 and twenty English words."

Machinist positions abounded in Colorado. The manufacturing sector around Denver boomed alongside the defense industry. By the mid-1950s, manufacturing had surpassed agriculture as the top economic driver in the state. Tony found work here and there, but some employers doubted his ability to comprehend schematics because of his Croatian accent. He also aroused the ire of union shop leaders who complained when he worked through mandated breaks or completed more pieces than his colleagues.

"Why were they so angry that I wanted to work? I came here to work!" Tony exclaims to me. Determined, not defeated, Tony packed up the Studebaker again after a few years and headed with his family to California, where the promise of three-dollar-an-hour jobs beckoned. The journey was literally uphill, with Tony often forced to push his broken-down car through the Rocky Mountains.

In Long Beach, California, Douglas Aircraft's largest plant pumped out parts and planes for the U.S. military during World War II. At its peak production, workers could build a plane in an hour. After the war, Douglas produced both military transports and passenger aircraft before merging with McDonnell Aircraft. Maglica applied for a job at Douglas, but was once again rejected over his limited English proficiency.

"One man I spoke to would not even shake my hand," Tony tells me softly. "I'll never forget that."

Undaunted, he secured work operating a lathe at Long Beach–based Pacific Valve Company and at A.O. Smith Water Products Company, a water heater manufacturer that had converted to production of landing gear, propellers, bomb casings, and atomic bomb project parts during World War II. When Tony learned that other workers at A.O. Smith had set up their own home shops to do contract work on the side, he decided to strike out on his own. In 1955, he rented a tiny garage in working-class South El Monte, whose motto is "City of Achievement."

"This is where it all started," Tony tells me, pointing to an old black-and-white photo of the garage, more of a shed, with bars on its narrow window slits, at 2218 Merced Ave. Another photo shows his young daughter, Jenny, standing at a Logan lathe adorned with a pile of metal shavings. Tony had scrimped and scraped together $125 as a down payment on the $1,000 machinery.

To hook up the lathe, he once reminisced, "I had to disconnect the stove and run fifty feet of cable to the garage. I worked the night shift at my job, because that shift paid better, and worked on this little lathe in my garage during the day. It was job-shop work, very competitive, and the hardest part was getting paid. I've always had to be economical. Even when my business began to get successful, I didn't have an air-conditioned room and expensive machines. I modified the machines I had."

The superior quality of Tony's precision tool work won him several loyal aerospace and defense clients. He contributed critical parts for U.S. missiles and satellites. Tony worked harder, faster, and longer than other contractors to get a job done. He slept in the garage on his workbench to meet deadlines.

And he was never satisfied.

In 1960, just five years after he established his one-man Maglica Machine Shop, Tony filed an application for his first patent on a machine tool device. Accompanied by three pages of meticulously detailed sketches, the document certainly put to rest any questions about Tony's ability to communicate. "There are a number of important considerations in operating machine tools on a profitable basis," he explained, "and two of the most important are set-up time and accuracy," particularly for smaller lot sizes. To avoid time-consuming disassembly and reassembly of work piece machinery, Maglica invented a rotatable lathe tool holder for threading, facing, form, and cut-off tools. The tool holders that existed before his improvement were expensive, difficult to manipulate, and "[did] not firmly hold tool holders and cutting tools to the extent required by the close tolerances presently practiced in the fabrication of components for missile and weapons systems." Tony's special tool table featured a piston, expansion chamber, cylinder body, and pressure fluid that could be moved, aligned, and readjusted based on which of several tools built into it was needed for a work piece.

Obsessed with both the aesthetics of industrial design and the cost efficiency of the manufacturing process, Maglica continued to patent improvements on precision tool devices and incorporated Mag Instrument in 1974. Work poured in as his reputation for fine craftsmanship and integrity grew. A few years later, while fulfilling orders for a long-defunct flashlight parts manufacturer, a proverbial bulb flashed in Tony's head and the era of Maglite dawned.

"Let There Be Light"

Before Tony Maglica came along, flashlights were ugly, flimsy objects. They were called "flash lights" because the carbon filament bulbs were inefficient and could not produce a steady stream of light. Made of cheap plastic, they broke easily and required frequent replacement.

Like Tony, the inventor of the original electric hand torch, Conrad Hubert (born Akiba Horowitz), was an Eastern European immigrant and serial entrepreneur. After arriving in America in 1891, he opened up a cigar shop, restaurant, jewelry store, and novelty shop. Hubert worked with fellow inventor and battery specialist Joshua Lionel Cowen, the eighth of nine children of Eastern European Jewish immigrants, to market lighted knickknacks such as electric tie tacks. Cowen had created an "electric flowerpot" illuminated with a slender, battery-operated tube with a lightbulb on one end. The novelty item flopped, but Hubert continued to tinker with the lighting system, which he believed held great commercial promise. Cowen sold the patent rights to Hubert and moved on to other projects, establishing the famous Lionel Train Company in 1902. Hubert, meanwhile, was fashioning the first portable flashlights out of crude paper and fiber tubes. He hired engineer/inventor David Missell, a battery expert, to help him perfect and patent the portable, tubular lamps. They marketed the devices to police officers, and the torches became a national sensation. In 1906, Hubert went on to found the Ever-Ready Battery Company, which advertised the flashlights using the biblical phrase "Let There Be Light."

Dissatisfied with the state of flashlight design by the late 1970s, Tony innovated a strong, sleek torch of anodized aluminum powered by D-cell batteries. The anodized aluminum, an alloy of aluminum, magnesium, and silicon, resists corrosion inside and out. After extensive research and design experimentation, Tony came up with a better flashlight that sported "a pushbutton switch instead of a slide switch, and an adjustable beam, so you could go from flood to spotlight," he explained. Tony described how he added "contacts inside that are self-cleaning—when you push the button, the contact revolves and scrubs against the other part. It takes the oxidation off the metal, so you get a better connection." The torch's three seams are sealed with O-rings for water resistance. U.S. Patent 4,286,311, filed by Tony in 1978 and approved by the Patent Office in August 1981, ushered in a new age of heavy, rugged flashlights with powerful beams.

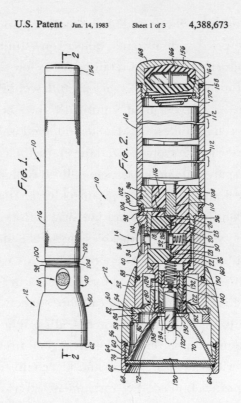

U.S. Patent   Jun. 14, 1983   Sheet 1 of 3   4,388,673

Tony's obsession was and remains: quality, quality, quality. "Why would you want to be associated with something that wasn't the best?" Tony put it bluntly.

Mag Instrument initially targeted the public safety sector, and as the ever-increasing mountain of letters of gratitude at the company headquarters shows, Tony won fiercely loyal clients among police officers, firefighters, and other first responders. But consumers embraced it, too, as much more than a tactical device. It became a household necessity. Admirers dubbed his torch "engineered light" and a "work of art that works." Industrial design expert Jennifer Garrett explained why she kept one in her designer purse: "The light is bright and focusable, the power use is efficient (batteries last amazingly long), the construction is solid, they double as weapons and hammers, and they come in an array of sizes and colors. What more could you ask for?"

As important as the design and function of each and every Maglite
flashlight is the price and customer value. Tony stubbornly insisted
on keeping production costs and retail prices as low as possible. Distributor prices for the company's legacy incandescent flashlights have
remained steady or even declined. Until 2013, the wholesale price of
a standard, 2 D-cell incandescent Maglite remained under twenty dollars, just as it was when it revolutionized the marketplace in 1979. Tony
also included a spare bulb in the tail cap of his flashlights and offered
limited lifetime warranties on his products. Over the next decade,
Tony took the consumer goods sector by storm with the successive introduction of the Maglite® Rechargeable Flashlight System™, the Mini
Maglite® AA flashlight, and the Solitaire® single AAA-Cell flashlight.
Tony noted in his patent application for the miniature flashlight that
no one before him had applied optical improvements and variable
light dispersion to small, handheld torches. His bright beams of light
became a staple not just on the belts of police and firefighters, but in
millions of American homes, purses, and key chain holders. *Fortune*
and *Money* magazines ranked Mag Instrument® products among the
top one hundred products that "America makes best." Former CEO of
Apple Computer Gilbert F. Amelio told the *Wall Street Journal* that his
company aimed to be "essentially the Maglite® of computers."

With success came competition, of course. And while imitation
may be the best form of flattery in some instances, for an inventor, it
can be the worst form of theft. Maglica came too far and worked too
hard to sit back and watch his intellectual property be stolen from him.
He made a principled decision to fight patent infringers every step of
the way as they flooded the market with their inferior knockoffs.

"We have worked hard to earn our reputation," Maglica explained.
"We must protect it."

Maglite first won a pivotal case in 1978 against American retailers
selling foreign ringers. The company made the stores rid their shelves
of the imitations and forced them to stock the real deal. Several years
later, a jury awarded the company $3.1 million in a copyright infringe-

ment lawsuit against Streamlight, Inc., which had been selling inferior rip-offs. Scores of companies around the world tried to do the same. In 1989, the U.S. International Trade Commission blocked importation of all foreign infringers who had attempted to steal Tony's small aluminum flashlight and component designs. Overseas, the company won rare design protections in Japan after an Osaka court banned Asahi Electric Corporation from making and selling Maglite look-alikes. The Japanese judicial body ordered Asahi to destroy all the remaining imitations and ordered payment of compensatory damages. Mag Instrument is proud of its aggressive patent and trademark stance. The company explains that Tony views his hard-fought and hard-won battles as integral not only to the success of Mag Instrument, but also to the success of a free enterprise system:

> Mr. Maglica believes that all American manufacturers benefit from the aggressive defense of intellectual property rights against any and all infringers. By protecting its technical innovations and its trademarks, an American manufacturer protects the American workforce that makes and sells the products that embody those technologies and bear those marks.

To date, Maglite has spent more than $100 million battling intellectual property thieves and their enablers. The company has never lost a lawsuit.

As Tony and I watch his newest products roll off the assembly line, he says resolutely: "You have to defend what is yours and what is right."

Keeping the American Dream American

Design anthropologist Dori Tunstall has dubbed Tony's Maglite "the Jason Bourne of flashlights." "It will still work after being twenty thousand feet underwater, run over by a semi truck, washed in two cycles of laundry, and dropped into vats of acid. What is most remarkable is that the flashlight is unabashedly 'Made in America.'" After relocating to his current headquarters in Ontario, California, in 1982, where he now employs close to eight hundred highly paid, skilled workers, Tony insisted on state-of-the-art, U.S.-based automation to maintain high quality and competitive costs. He doesn't just build flashlights in America. He builds many of the machines that build those flashlights. And he boosts other American businesses by using their products— like the aluminum from Kaiser Aluminum, which supplies miles of aluminum tubing every year for Maglite's famed cases.

Tony has continued to improve and perfect his designs over the last thirty-five years, securing some two hundred other patents as his lamps have evolved from using xenon and krypton incandescent bulbs to LEDs. He leads me to an empty lab room where he had been developing new, revolutionary incandescent bulb parts. The machinery is dormant. The U.S. Environmental Protection Agency forbade him from producing the bulbs in the wake of the government's incandescent bulb ban that went into effect in 2014. The federal ban, passed as a top-down energy conservation measure, has sent thousands of jobs to China, decreased consumer choices, caused more environmental headaches because of the mercury content of compact fluorescent light (CFL) alternatives, and stifled innovation by private enterprise. He had planned to hire more workers to make the new products. Those plans are off. "That was such a shame," Tony tells me, shaking his head. "Such a waste."

Agitated, Tony takes his glasses off for a moment and rubs his eyes. "Government doesn't innovate. People like me do. Government doesn't create jobs. We do. What is happening to our country, Michelle? I came here with nothing. If I can do it, anyone can! This is America!"

From day one, Tony vowed to manufacture products that were 100 percent American. "Politicians always talk about supporting American manufacturing. I have done it," Tony says. We stroll his factory floor, where employees call out cheerful greetings and come right up to give their boss a hug. He tells me he refused to grant licenses to foreign companies and he refused to move his facilities to Mexico as so many other southern California companies were doing. When Mag Instrument needed a certain battery clip, it refused to import the part from China. Tony designed his own clip and spent $1 million tooling up his plant to manufacture the parts in-house and in-country.

The company "puts its money where its mouth is." And its mouth is where Tony's heart is. Maglite has defiantly refused to outsource workers because, as the company explains:

> For one, it would offend against his faith in the American free-enterprise system, and against the spirit of giving back. Mr. Maglica knows that Mag Instrument got where it is by being an American company. And he deeply believes that Mag Instrument could not have happened anywhere but in America—that nowhere else but in the U.S.A. could somebody who started with as little as he had ever build from scratch a company such as Mag Instrument has become.
>
> To "outsource" flashlight manufacturing jobs would also offend against Tony Maglica's commitment to quality. . . . His approach to continuous product improvement entails walking the factory floor—observing, teaching, listening to suggestions, praising what is done right and correcting what is not. . . . Mr. Maglica knows the difference between good quality and great quality, and he knows what makes that difference—an abiding commitment to real, true product excellence. Further, he understands that quality is not a goal but a process; not an endpoint but a dogged, relentless pursuit—all day, every day.

Mag Instrument's entire line of products is manufactured in the U.S. But because Maglites require a minuscule number of tiny parts that are only produced outside the country, the state of California forbids

Tony from carrying the label "Made in the U.S.A." Every other state, plus federal law, allows Maglites to bear that label. But only in California is 99 percent American not American enough. Tony mounted a challenge to the archaic, arbitrary, and capricious law, but the politicians didn't listen.

No matter. To anyone who knows Tony's story, the red, white, and blue that runs through his veins is unmistakable.

Tony firmly believes the fate of Maglite and the fate of American manufacturing are inextricably linked, which is why he won't give up on his workers or leave crazy California. In what little spare time he has, Tony lends his philanthropic support to U.S. law enforcement, the U.S. military, and the land of his ancestors back in Croatia. He has donated tens of thousands of his products to aid rescuers during the Oklahoma City bombing, Hurricane Katrina, the 9/11 terrorist attacks, and the Japanese tsunami in 2011.

At eighty-three, he hasn't taken a vacation in more than a decade and doesn't plan to any time soon.

"Michelle, I still believe in the American Dream," Tony the torchbearer tells me as we sit in his sun-bathed company cafeteria eating lunch, surrounded by employees from all walks of life.

"As long as I'm alive, I will never give up."

2.

THE WIZARDS OF COOL:

Air-Conditioning Innovators Willis Carrier and Irvine Lyle

No. 808,897.

PATENTED JAN. 2, 1906.

W. H. CARRIER.
APPARATUS FOR TREATING AIR.
APPLICATION FILED SEPT. 16, 1904.

Fig. 1.

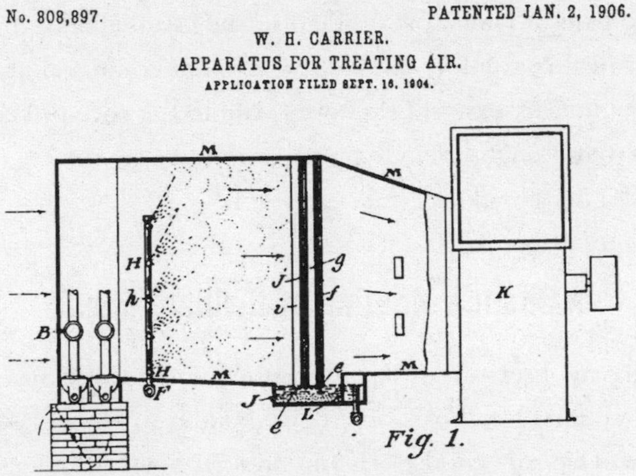

The first car I ever owned was a rinky-dink 1993 Toyota Tercel. It was factory white with a stick shift—and little else. As a penny-pinching young journalist in Los Angeles, my sweat-drenched daily commute through the stifling San Fernando Valley in that bare-bones buggy reminded me of what a luxurious marvel air-conditioning really is.

Every perfectly chilled home, office, movie theater, mall, factory, hospital, and lab owes its existence to the pioneers of "manufactured weather": Willis Carrier and Irvine Lyle. These early-twentieth-century inventive giants brought air-conditioning to the market and to the masses. Willis Carrier was the scientist-tinkerpreneur whose lifelong stream of epiphanies and experiments fueled historic technological advances in heating, refrigeration, and air-conditioning. Irvine Lyle was the creative salesman who imagined countless new commercial applications for Carrier's work—and successfully turned those ideas into a multibillion-dollar business through relentless promotion, pitches, networking, advertising, and outreach.

From Hollywood to the pharmaceutical industry to textiles and tobacco to the retail industry to the military to homeowners, there isn't a sector of the American economy that Carrier and Lyle didn't help transform. Their zealous focus on helping businesses provide better products at lower cost resulted in the invaluable by-products of increased health, comfort, and happiness. Air-conditioning changed *everything*, but Carrier and Lyle stayed true to the core tinkerpreneurial values that brought them together in the first place.

A Chance Meeting of Brilliant Minds

Willis Carrier's preparation for a prolific and practical inventive life began in western New York, on a dairy farm near the Quaker village of Angola. The only child of Duane and Elizabeth Carrier was born in the fall of 1876, the centennial year of America's founding. His ancestors came from New England pioneer stock. Young Willis showed promising mechanical aptitude early on. After he had done his farm chores, Willis would tinker on a perpetual motion machine. Or tackle math problems he made up for himself. Or create his own games to amuse himself, including imagining a zoo of mechanized animals. He assembled the family farm thresher and "worked geometry in the snow." From his aunt Abbey, he also learned how a well pump worked. He never forgot when she explained how "the atmosphere exerts a pressure of about fifteen pounds per square inch." It whetted his appetite for learning about the miracles and mysteries of air.

His father, Duane, was a teacher and merchant who had once aspired to be a doctor. But Willis credited his mother, Elizabeth, for his relentlessly curious mind. She fixed alarm clocks, toured a paper mill, and provided Willis with problem-solving skills that would serve him (and the two-hundred-plus industries that his company would later support) well. Carrier described how his mom helped him understand fractions after he came home angst-ridden from school at age nine:

> My mother told me to go to the cellar and bring up a pan of apples. She had me cut them into halves, quarters, and eighths, and add and subtract the parts. Fractions took on meaning, and I was very proud. I felt as if I'd made a great discovery. No problems would be too hard for me after that—I'd simply break them down to something simple and then they would be easy to solve.

Mrs. Carrier died when Willis was eleven years old, but he carried her pragmatic Yankee spirit from that day forward both in words and in deeds. "Figure out things for yourself," she urged. And self-reliant Willis did just that. The economy was in a slump during Willis's high school years. He rose at five in the morning, every morning, to help his father milk twenty-four cows. He delivered the milk, rushed home for breakfast, walked a mile to get to school, excelled at all his classes, and then rushed home to do more cow-milking. After winning a scholarship to Cornell University, he continued to balance a rigorous academic schedule and athletic activities (boxing, cross-country, crew) with more work, including lawn-mowing, furnace-tending, and table-waiting. With a college friend, Carrier invented the first student "co-op" laundry in the nation. Those co-ops remain ubiquitous on college and university campuses today.

On another college campus, at the University of Kentucky, Joel Irvine Lyle was also thriving as a scholar-athlete. Lyle played varsity football for the school and joined Sigma Chi (the social fraternity) and Tau Beta Pi (the honor society for engineers). A farm boy, football star, fraternity brother, and natural-born salesman, Lyle graduated in 1896 with a degree in mechanical engineering and earned a master's in the same subject five years later. He was hired by the Buffalo Forge Company upon graduation.

Willis Carrier graduated from Cornell in 1901, five years after Lyle. His alma mater, established by self-taught tinkerpreneur Ezra Cornell in 1865, emphasized technical innovation and applied science. The son of Quaker merchants, Cornell worked at his father's pottery business at six, on a farm at twelve, and as a carpenter at seventeen. Cornell had made his fortune as a pioneer in the telegraph industry—first by designing and patenting a plow (personally approved by telegraph inventor Samuel Morse) to dig trenches for laying telegraph cable underground. After he researched electricity and magnetism at the U.S. Patent Office and Library of Congress, Cornell concluded that he needed to fix faulty cable insulation problems by stringing the cables on glass-insulated poles above ground. Morse hired him to string up the overhead line between Washington and Baltimore, through which the telegraph inventor delivered his famous "What hath God wrought?" message.

An intrepid capitalist, Cornell took a large part of his pay in stock and became Western Union's largest stockholder. He used his fortune to construct his namesake university, which was the first in the nation to establish an electrical engineering department. Willis Carrier earned his degree in mechanical engineering at Cornell, but in the spirit of his school's entrepreneurial founder, the farm boy from Angola would answer without hesitation when opportunity knocked. Though he had never heard of the company before, Carrier accepted a job offer from the Buffalo Forge Company instead of applying to famed General Electric as he had originally planned. Buffalo Forge, cofounded by a Cornell grad, made blacksmith's forges, upright drills, steam engines, heaters, dust collectors, blowers, and bandsaws.

In June 1901, while riding public transportation on his way to a meeting with the company, Carrier asked a stranger for help finding

Buffalo Forge's office. The young man turned out to be J. Irvine Lyle, who was also headed to the headquarters to discuss an office transfer from the Syracuse branch to the New York City office. By chance or fate, Carrier and Lyle boarded the same Broadway streetcar that day to get to Buffalo Forge's Mortimer Street building. They parted ways, but the two bright, ambitious engineers would be meeting again soon enough. There were problems to solve and fish to catch. As Carrier famously explained of his practical approach to research, inventing, and business: "The 'catch' must be edible or I don't try for it. I only fish for edible fish and test for useful data."

Indeed, long before the idea of "comfort air" for humans became the norm, Carrier and Lyle's work targeted industrial factories and plants. Their first project focused not on helping sweaty people, but on fixing sweaty paper.

Printing, Crown Caps, Razors, and Tobacco

The spring and summer seasons of 1902 were scorchers in New York City. Families flocked to public baths. Slum-dwellers slept out on their stoops and unleashed fire hydrants for relief. "MANY ARE HEAT STRICKEN IN SUDDEN TORRID WAVE," the *Brooklyn (N.Y.) Daily Eagle* reported in late May of that year. President Theodore Roosevelt escaped from the sweltering Washington, D.C., swamp to the cooler confines of his Sagamore Hill beach home on Oyster Bay, New York. And businesses of all sizes grappled with the deleterious effects of high temperatures and high humidity on their goods and machinery.

At the Sackett & Wilhelms Printing Plant in Brooklyn, workers struggled with the muggy air's damage to its multicolor printing jobs. The Fifth Avenue shop produced show cards, business cards, pamphlets, and illustrations of all kinds. A team of thirty-five employees operated the plant's twenty-five steam-power presses and forty hand presses at all hours to meet grueling deadlines. One of the company's most im-

portant clients was *Judge* magazine, a leading, Republican-leaning sa-
tirical publication that featured bold four-color chromolithographic
covers, political cartoons, and artistic spreads. (The magazine's most
famous cartoonist: Theodor "Dr. Seuss" Geisel, who was hired at age
twenty-three as a writer and artist in the late 1920s. Another famous
Judge alumnus, Harold Ross, left in 1925 to found *The New Yorker.*) Renowned for its fine color work, Sackett & Wilhelms found that the heat
wave ruined its print runs. Paper is "hygroscopic," meaning it retains
moisture from its surrounding environment through absorption or ad-
sorption. Humidity caused the paper to shrink and expand and warp.
The colors bled together. Haywire weather resulted in disastrous ink
realignment and required costly reprints or cancellations. Additional
heat was generated by the lights, the steam engines, the presses, the
workers, and leakage from outside.

As temperatures spiked, a consulting engineer for the print shop
sought help from Irvine Lyle at Buffalo Forge's New York City office.
Lyle forwarded the project to that fellow he had met on a Buffalo
streetcar the previous fall, Willis Carrier, who had quickly made a
name for himself at the company by initiating experiments to improve
the firm's design and installation of heating, drying, and forced draft
systems. Unsatisfied with the industry's traditional "rule of thumb"
guesstimates, Carrier systematically constructed tables of heater data
to make it easy for engineers to figure out how much heat air would
absorb when it was circulated over steam-heating coils. Carrier's bosses
wisely supported his research and allowed him to establish an in-house
industrial lab.

Now, his task was to fix the hot mess at Sackett & Wilhelms. Just as
his mother had taught him to do as a child with apples and fractions,
Willis Carrier broke down the problem into digestible pieces. He
needed to conquer the four factors that define air-conditioning: control of the temperature, humidity, cleanliness/purity, and effective distribution of air. Previous tinkerpreneuers had used fans, snow, and ice

to try to cool air in enclosed spaces. But no one had yet succeeded in both reducing the air's humidity and holding moisture content steady at a specific level. Sackett & Wilhelms needed a system to maintain an indoor temperature of seventy degrees F in winter and eighty degrees F in summer, with relative humidity of 55 percent kept constant year round. Carrier decided to adapt Buffalo Forge heating machinery for the new cooling apparatus. Instead of steam, he would circulate cold water through a set of heating coils. Carrier pored over U.S. Weather Bureau tables that Lyle sent over to aid him in constructing a system to dehumidify the air. From the data, he chose dew-point temperatures that would maintain the right amount of moisture for the air in the printing plant. (Dew point is a measure of atmospheric moisture. The higher the dew point, the more moisture is present in the air.)

By July 17, 1902, as New York sweated out the heat wave, Carrier had drawn up plans for what would be the world's first scientific air-conditioning system. Two sections of pipes (the evaporator coils) were used for cooling and dehumidifying. One drew cold water up from an artesian well; the other was attached to a faster-cooling ammonia refrigerating machine. ASHRAE (the American Society of Heating, Refrigerating and Air Conditioning Engineers) explained the basic operating principles:

> The air is cooled by blowing it over a set of cold pipes called an evaporator coil. This works just like the cooling that happens when water evaporates from your skin. The evaporator coil is filled with a special liquid called a refrigerant, which changes from a liquid to a gas as it absorbs heat from the air. The refrigerant is pumped outside . . . to another coil where it gives up its heat and changes back into a liquid. This outside coil is called the condenser because the refrigerant is condensing from a gas back to a fluid just like moisture on a cold window. A pump, called a compressor, is used to move the refrigerant

between the two coils and to change the pressure of the refrigerant so that all the refrigerant evaporates or condenses in the
appropriate coils.

The energy to do all of this is used by the motor that runs
the compressor. The entire system will normally give about
three times the cooling energy that the compressor uses. This
odd fact happens because the changing of refrigerant from a
liquid to a gas and back again lets the system move much more
energy than the compressor uses.

Carrier engineer Margaret Ingels marveled at the scope of her bosses'
breakthroughs as she documented the new system's components:
"Taken together, their cooling effect totaled 54 tons, the equivalent
of melting 180,000 pounds of ice in a 24-hour day. The installation
was indeed a milestone in man's control of his indoor climate!" It was
an important trial, but not an unqualified success. The retrofitted
equipment was not optimal. Carrier turned his attention to leaks of
moisture-bearing air in the coils' gaps and uneven distribution of the
treated air through the jerry-rigged parts. Eventually, Carrier and Lyle
would initiate in-house construction of their own air ducts of the highest quality. Always striving to do better, Carrier and Lyle also turned
to lowering costs of the system for the customer by recycling the water
drawn from the artesian well. A year later, they replaced the compressor at Sackett & Wilhelms and Lyle reported back to Buffalo Forge
that "the cooling coils which we sold this company have given excellent
results during the past summer."

Lyle pulled out all the stops to spread the word about Carrier's
new air-conditioning system. He presented technical papers before
the American Society of Heating and Ventilating Engineers and the
American Society of Refrigerating Engineers. He gave speeches and
helped write product brochures and manuals. He arranged for Buffalo Forge to form a new, wholly owned subsidiary called the Carrier
Air Conditioning Company to manufacture and sell the conditioners.

Lyle aggressively courted new clients and provided stellar customer service. Inside the company, he served as a father figure—networking and nurturing camaraderie among his fellow engineers. An industry journal at the time gave due credit:

> Those in a position to know give to J. I. Lyle the credit for a large measure of the commercial success of the Carrier Air Conditioning Company, for he standardized the Carrier designs for the various applications and to him was also due the company's broad and liberal policy both in dealing with its customers and in the spreading of reliable information regarding the subject of air conditioning.

Carrier, meanwhile, tooled, retooled, tested and retested, pondered, and dwelled on the difficulties of humidity control. His obsessiveness was legendary. A paradox of supreme pragmatism and comical absent-mindedness, the tinkerpreneur would often neglect to eat meals or forget that there were people around him. He drew technical diagrams on tablecloths at restaurants. He once jetted off on a business trip only to discover that his suitcase contained nothing but a handkerchief. While he seemed to walk with his head in the clouds, Carrier's brilliant mind was grounded in solving the most practical problems of mechanical engineering.

It was in the midst of a literal evening fog, while standing on a train platform in Pittsburgh, that Willis Carrier was struck by a moment of inventive clarity whose impact is still felt today in every aspect of our daily, modern lives. Here's how he described his thought process during the "flash of genius" incident:

> Here is air approximately 100 percent saturated with moisture. The temperature is low so, even though saturated, there is not much actual moisture. There could not be at so low a temperature. Now, if I can saturate air and control its temperature at

saturation, I can get air with any amount of moisture I want in it. I can do it, too, by drawing the air through a fine spray of water to create actual fog. By controlling the water temperature I can control the temperature at saturation. When very moist air is desired, I'll heat the water. When very dry air is desired, that is, air with a small amount of moisture, I'll use cold water to get low temperature saturation. The cold spray water will actually be the condensing surface. I certainly will get rid of the rusting difficulties that occur when using steel coils for condensing vapor in the air. Water won't rust.

This was, as his industry heirs recognize, "an insight so counterintuitive that it still dazzles." Carrier realized in that foggy moment that he could dry air by *wetting* it—passing it through water and using the spray as the condensing surface. The discovery would make possible the controlled manufacture of air with specific amounts of moisture in it. The trick, as *American Heritage* magazine explained, "was to chill the water first and then spray it into a chamber. With a huge number of tiny droplets, a cold mist would cool and dehumidify the air much more efficiently than any set of coils and would yield a reproducible result." After the air was misted, it was blown through a chamber with baffles to separate the water droplets from the saturated air. The mist also helped cleanse and purify the air of dust, providing revolutionary improvements in both human health and personal comfort. Carrier received a patent for his "Apparatus for Treating Air" in 1906 and would receive more than eighty other patents over his lifetime of engineering improvements and additions.

While taking care to protect their patent rights, Carrier and Lyle interacted closely with the scientific community, sharing knowledge and opening up their offices for demonstrations. These exchanges yielded more benefits for the industry and consumers everywhere. Carrier continued to search for a better coolant. After dielene, he experimented with methylene chloride, CH_2Cl_2, which he dubbed

"Carrene-1." After DuPont chemist Thomas Midgely unveiled a new class of cheaper, nonflammable refrigerants, the chlorofluorocarbon Freons, Carrier reached out to discuss his research. Carrier learned of an intermediate gas produced in its manufacture. Midgely, who saw no use for it, sent his handwritten notes and a sample of the fluid to Carrier. The gas, Freon-11, CCl3F, was superior to Carrier's current refrigerants because it was easier to compress and did not cause leaks as frequently as ammonia. Dubbed "Carrene-2," it became the basis for Carrier's own refrigerants for centrifugal compression.

Lyle became president of the American Society of Heating and Ventilating Engineers. "Psychrometrics" (the study of moist air) advanced by leaps and bounds as Carrier and Lyle, armed with slide rules and logarithm tables, published papers, catalogs, charts, and textbooks that remain gold standards today. In 1911, thirty-five-year-old Carrier published "Rational Psychrometric Formulae"—known as the "Magna Carta" of psychrometrics—and presented it before the American Society of Mechanical Engineers (ASME). He methodically illustrated how to determine the precise correlation between temperature and humidity. Carrier eliminated the guesswork and imprecision that his peers had tolerated and worked around for decades. His seminal paper and charts published in ASME's scientific journal still stand today as the cornerstone of all fundamental calculations in the air-conditioning industry.

Carrier's relentless theoretical research affected not only air-conditioning, but also agriculture, aeronautics, food engineering, pharmaceuticals, meteorology, weather reporting, and more. As Carrier himself pointed out in his "Rational Psychrometric Formulae" paper:

The application of this new art to many varied industries has been demonstrated to be of greatest economic importance. When applied to the blast furnace, it has increased the net profit in the production of pig iron from $0.50 to $0.70 per ton, and in the textile mill it has increased the output from

5 to 15 per cent, at the same time greatly improving the quality and the hygienic conditions surrounding the operative. In
many other industries, such as lithographing, the manufacture of candy, bread, high explosives and photographic films,
and the drying and preparing of delicate hygroscopic materials, such as macaroni and tobacco, the question of humidity is
equally important.

Inspired by his Kentucky farm boy days, it was Irvine Lyle's idea to
reach out to tobacco farmers for business. He sold a $1,850 system
to a Henderson, Kentucky, tobacco exporter after demonstrating
how moisture control would improve the accuracy of his weighing
and pricing. Building on that success, Lyle and Carrier visited a cigar
plant in Newark, New Jersey, which led to nationwide contracts for
an air-conditioning system that enabled mass production of tobacco
products. Carrier paid a visit to one of their big-name clients in the
industry, the American Tobacco Company, in 1913. He described the
stifling contamination at the Richmond, Virginia, plant: "I could see
only a few feet in front of me . . . could not see the windows across the
room even when sunshine fell on them." Workers tied handkerchiefs
over their mouths. Dust was everywhere. Carrier installed a humidify-
ing system in the tobacco stemming room of the factory, and then
devised a set-up to blow large quantities of air into a room without
kicking up dust.

Workers flocked to the stemming room for relief from the humidity, heat, and dirt. "The results," Carrier reported succinctly, "were
wonderful."

The Carrier team sold its products to businesses, large and small,
that spanned the spectrum of human needs and wants. The American Chicle Company on Long Island, maker of the famous Chiclets
chewing gum that still sits on a shelf at your grocery checkout stand,
bought a Carrier refrigeration system to maintain constant temperature and humidity in its gum breaking, coating, polishing, and

packing rooms. Whitman's boxed chocolate-makers, still in business today, installed Carrier's first centrifugal chiller at their Philadelphia plant. Powder plants, chemical plants, cheese-makers, bakeries, pop-corn snack designers, glass manufacturers, precision tool makers, and pencil producers all bought Carrier parts and systems. During World War I, Carrier apparatus cooled the International Arms and Fuse company in New Jersey and the Winchester Repeating Arms Co. in New Haven, Connecticut. During World War II, the military took advantage of Carrier's top engineering talent and produced classified machinery and parts, including airplane engine mounts, sight hoods for guns, tank adapters, and antisubmarine bomb dis-chargers.

Two more companies that benefited directly from their work were William Painter's Crown Cork & Seal and King Gillette's razor empire. Carrier executive Edward T. Murphy explained his company's role in aiding their manufacturing processes. "Did you ever consider," Murphy asked, "that refrigeration had anything to do with a crowned seal as well as the contents itself?" William Painter's creations were lined with a cork substance, which was mixed with a binding agent before it was pressed. The binder had to remain on the surface of the cork without penetrating its pores. "To accomplish this, cold dry air is blown into the mixers, rapidly evaporating the moisture from the agglomerate before the binder could be melted into the pores of the cork. A very successful installation of this kind was made at the Crown Cork & Seal Co. at Baltimore."

Murphy reported that Carrier engineers had also solved a man-ufacturing headache at King Gillette's razor plant. "Mr. Gillette was very much troubled with the fact that he was rusting your razor blades before he could ship them to you." The rust was coming from high-pressure air used for operating pneumatic machinery. "To prevent this," Murphy said, Carrier men "installed a refrigerating system to remove the moisture from the compressed air before it was expanded in use." Gillette was sold to Procter & Gamble in 2005 for $57 billion.

Hollywood Blockbuster:
"Yes, the People Are Going to Like It"

Adolph Zukor was an ambitious and visionary Hungarian Jewish immigrant. He arrived in New York Harbor in 1888, a sixteen-year-old orphan, with forty dollars sewn into the lining of his coat. Zukor swept floors in an upholstery store for two dollars a week, then became an apprentice in a fur shop and learned to cut and sew pelts. Captivated by the 1893 Columbian Exposition, young Zukor traveled to Chicago along with millions of other attendees who soaked in the sights, sounds, and stimulation of the World's Fair and its celebration of the Age of Progress. The young entrepreneur stayed in the Midwest and established a fur manufacturing company. After the business prospered and he found a wife, he returned to New York in 1900, where he fell in love—with the movies.

Zukor invested in vaudeville, penny arcades, and nickelodeon theaters, where customers lined up individually to view minute-long films projected by Thomas Edison's Kinetoscopes. With the advent of the Vitascope celluloid motion picture projector, the idea of mass screenings in large-scale entertainment venues took hold. The theater impresario partnered with Marcus Loew, a fur merchant turned movie theater magnate, who converted retail and office buildings into movie complexes. Zukor served as treasurer for Loew's Inc., which later became the parent company of Metro-Goldwyn-Mayer Pictures. But he wanted more creative control. From his days in the fur business, Zukor had honed a sense of high style. The budding showman wanted to produce movies with glamorous celebrities and lasting artistic value beyond the short one-reel features then in vogue. In 1912, he established his own production company. Among his founding partners: feature-length film pioneer Jesse Lasky and director Cecil B. DeMille.

By the mid-1920s, studio-owned "picture palaces" and "wonder theaters" were all the rage. America boasted twenty thousand movie theaters with a combined seating capacity of 18 million, generating some $75 million in revenue and employing more than 350,000 people across the country. Among the most famously luxe entertainment edifices of the time: the Chicago Theater in Illinois, Loew's Penn in Pittsburgh, and impresario Sid Grauman's Chinese and Egyptian Theaters in Los Angeles. These buildings boasted grand staircases, majestic murals, sumptuous drapes, stately pipe organs, and lavish chandeliers. But in the summertime, all the posh accommodations and appointments in the world couldn't compensate for the stifling heat. The theaters closed during hot weather or operated at a loss while playing to scant audiences.

Enter the entrepreneurial engineers. Inventor Walter Fleisher attempted to cool the Folies-Bergère theater in New York City with a primitive air washer, but lack of mechanical refrigeration doomed it. At Chicago's Central Park and Riviera Theaters, impresarios Barney and Abe Balaban and Sam and Maurice Katz unveiled a new, carbon dioxide–based cooling system devised by Frederick Wittenmeier that blew chilled air out of "mushroom" vents at the feet of moviegoers. The mushroom ventilation worked fine for heated air, which rises, but since cold air is heavier, it would sink to the bottom of the auditorium and result in frozen toes and unhappy customers.

As an alternative, Logan Lewis of the Carrier Engineer Corporation offered a new system with outlets in the ceiling and return grills in the floor to create a gentle, even, barely perceptible air flow. In 1922, at Grauman's Metropolitan Theater in L.A., he installed the new setup, which cooled the air through downdraft air distribution and bypass circulation. Lewis recounted how movie patrons would resort to wrapping their feet "in newspapers to protect them from the cold" generated by the old mushroom ventilation system. Lewis's new method "made it possible not only to maintain low humidities with less refrigeration but also practical to control temperature and humidity independently of each other. The trick was to cool only one-third of the air about twice as much and then to mix it with warm bypass air coming back from the theater." Carrier engineers were initially mocked by theater snobs for their "upside down system." But they persisted and tested and perfected and adapted in a continuous feedback loop.

Two years later, the company installed air-conditioning systems in several Texas movie theaters, which combined the bypass/downdraft methods with Carrier's groundbreaking, multipatented centrifugal refrigerating apparatus ("the chiller"). This sophisticated machinery was the first practical means of cooling large spaces. As Willis Carrier had explained to his team in a 1920 memo on "Development Possibilities for Improvement in Refrigeration," the current technology of their time hadn't advanced much since the advent of David Boyle's ammonia compressor in 1872. Traditional "reciprocal compressor" devices were large units that operated like back-and-forth pistons on a locomotive. Carrier's insight was to apply the same rotary power breakthroughs in electricity transmission, pioneered by the likes of George Westinghouse and Nikola Tesla, to refrigeration. Carrier wrote:

> The entire system of electric transmission has been developed from nothing to an enormous industry with relatively simple motors that are high-speed rotative equipment.
>
> Industry has gone from low-speed reciprocating steam engines to high-speed rotative turbines. Pumping machinery is rapidly changing from reciprocating types to high-speed rotative pumps for both liquids and gases. Modern power plants have installed high-speed, direct-connected centrifugal, boiler-feed pumps almost exclusively in replacing the old type of steam-driven reciprocating machines.
>
> Refrigeration, though classed among the older mechanical arts, has shown no such material progress. The same improvements that have taken place in electrical transmission and in steam machines and pumps must come in refrigerating machines.

Carrier went to work assembling a centrifugal compressor, condenser, and cooler with a direct drive that made "the chiller" suitable for high operating speed. The system incorporated compact and cheap heat exchangers, along with a new, nontoxic refrigerant. Carrier's dynamic sales team approached leading movie studio Paramount Pictures to install its system at the New York Rivoli Theater in Times Square. The engineers also had to persuade city health regulators that their main refrigerant of choice—dielene (that is, dichloroethylene, or $C_2H_2Cl_2$)—was safer than the toxic ammonia everyone else was using as a coolant. At a meeting with a Big Apple bureaucrat, Carrier dramatically dropped a lit match into a jar of dielene to demonstrate its safety. The nontoxic substance burned down much more slowly—and safely—without ammonia's high level of volatility. The government relented.

The Rivoli contract called for a 133-ton machine to be in operation when the theater opened on Memorial Day 1925. Founder Willis Carrier himself (whom his loyal employees affectionately called "The Chief") stayed up all night with his team at the Rivoli, preparing for the high-stakes demonstration. His description of that historic day was as suspenseful and cinematic as anything onscreen. Of the thousands of moviegoers lining up long before the doors opened, Carrier recalled: "It was like a World Series crowd waiting for bleacher seats. They were not only curious, but skeptical—all the women and some of the men had fans—a standard accessory of the day."

A few logistical glitches heightened the Carrier team's anxiety:

Final adjustments delayed us in starting up the machine, so that the doors opened before the air conditioning system was turned on. The people poured in, filled all the seats, and stood seven deep in the back of the theater. We had more than we had bargained for and were plenty worried. From the wings we watched in dismay as two thousand fans fluttered.

The clock ticked and the Carrier men held their breath:

> It takes time to pull down the temperature in a quickly filled
> theater on a hot day, and a still longer time for a packed house.
> Gradually, almost imperceptibly, the fans dropped into laps
> as the effects of the air conditioning system became evident.
> Only a few chronic fanners persisted, but soon they, too,
> ceased fanning. We had stopped them "cold" and breathed a
> great sigh of relief.

The most important member of the audience that memorable Memorial Day was Adolph Zukor. Remember the production company I told
you he founded after he split with Loew's Inc.? That company was
none other than Paramount Pictures, the Tinseltown movie production giant and owner of the Rivoli Theater on Broadway. As Willis Carrier and his engineers sweated bullets waiting for the air-conditioning
to kick in, Zukor was watching stealthily from the theater balcony. Carrier eyed the cinema mogul nervously as he focused on moviegoers'
fluttering fans instead of watching the movie. The Chief related the
denouement:

> We then went into the lobby and waited for Mr. Zukor to come
> downstairs. When he saw us, he did not wait for us to ask his opin-
> ion. He said tersely, "Yes, the people are going to like it." That was
> a jubilant moment for us—we had passed the "acid test."

The innovative weather manipulators won raves from Rivoli customers
and were the "talk of Broadway" for weeks. The theater's managers
drew up newspaper ads describing their venue as "cool as a mountaintop." The Rivoli's main marquee blared "REFRIGERATING PLANT"
and the doorway entrance sign boasted "COOLED BY REFRIGERA-
TION." The theater was more than just a picture palace. It had become
an "ideal summer resort," generating year-round profits and patrons

thanks to the "marvelous equipment which absolutely assures a temperature that is just right."

The happy ending at the Rivoli was just the beginning of Carrier Engineering's success in the movie industry. In 1926, Zukor built his thirty-six-hundred-seat Paramount Theater and thirty-nine-story headquarters on Broadway, air-conditioned with Carrier's centrifugal chiller. The company also installed its system at the famed Roxy theater in New York, a fifty-nine-hundred-seat palace billed as "the cathedral of the motion picture." By 1930, Carrier had installed three hundred air-conditioning systems in movie theaters across the country. Theater owners weren't the only ones in show biz who embraced Carrier's technology, of course. Theater performers welcomed the relief from oppressively heavy costumes and sweltering klieg lights. Celluloid film companies relied on Carrier products to clean the air in their labs and control the temperature and humidity. Proper air-conditioning prevented cracks and curdling of film as it dried. The inventive genius and capitalist ambition of Carrier, Lyle, and their crew transformed summertime, once a box-office bomb, into Hollywood's most profitable season. Among the notable, modern summer blockbusters we would have missed out on: *Jaws, Star Wars, Jurassic Park*, and *Back to the Future*.

Today's entertainment industry, which so often demonizes industrialists as rapacious enemies of the arts, culture, and all that is good, might very well have gone under during the Depression without profit-maximizing capitalists Carrier and Lyle. But the fathers of air-conditioning didn't just save jobs in Tinseltown.

They also saved lives.

Babies, Germs, Pills, and Polio

At Luna Park on Coney Island, amid blaring lights and carnival sounds, a hand-painted sign advertised in 1906: "INFANT INCUBATORS WITH LIVING INFANTS." The incubator baby exhibits were run by German immigrant neonatologist Martin Couney. He ran a ten-cent sideshow for the public, allowing curious gawkers to watch and ogle as he and a full staff of trained nurses treated premature babies no other hospital would or could accept. Dr. Couney, who did not charge parents for his medical services, took the show on the road, treating babies at World's Fairs and European expositions, the Atlantic City Boardwalk, San Francisco, Omaha, Chicago, Denver, Rio de Janeiro, and Mexico City. Loud-mouthed barkers lured attendees away from the bearded ladies, sword swallowers, and cotton candy with crass enticements: "Don't pass the babies by!"

Dr. Couney certainly raised awareness of neonatal care and is credited with rescuing many children. But setting aside the unsettling spectacle of preemies as amusement park oddities, there were more fundamental problems with the circuslike clinics that put babies on display for decades: The incubators Couney used were made of iron and glass, heated by hot-water pipes connected to a central boiler.

As Carrier Air Conditioning Company of America engineer T. A. Weager explained in 1916, this "sort of oven" was "kept at a uniform temperature" with "moisture supplied by evaporation," but "with this arrangement the air became stagnant and dry." At the Allegheny General Hospital in Pittsburgh, Pennsylvania, the Carrier crew installed the nation's first baby incubation system. The conditioning apparatus, located on the hospital roof, used a centrifugal fan belted to an electric motor. The air passed through a set of heating coils, then through a Carrier Air Washer and Humidifier, where nozzles forced water into a spray chamber. Dirt, bacteria, and other contaminants in the air were removed as discharge through a set of vertical eliminators; the mechanism controlled moisture content in the air by adding hot water to the cold being sprayed through the nozzles. The purified air then traveled through a second set of heating coils, into a fan, through a duct, and into an incubator room encased in glass that had four baby beds. Carrier used the same downdraft distribution and bypass techniques it applied in theaters, so that air entered the incubation room at low velocity through the ceiling and exited through registers at the floor line.

Company engineers had gained experience a few years earlier installing an air washer at an Illinois hospital. They expanded on comfort-air principles first advanced by Dr. John Gorrie, who devised an air-conditioning system to treat yellow-fever-stricken American troops at the U.S. Marine Hospital in Apalachicola, Florida, by blowing air over buckets of imported ice into the sickrooms. He received a patent in 1851 for the "first machine ever to be used for mechanical refrigeration and air conditioning," but was unable to create a viable business out of the invention. Gorrie's ice maker "made enough ice to chill bottles of champagne for a party but could not get the financial support he needed to develop his idea commercially," *American Heritage* magazine observed. The Carrier company, by contrast, aggressively and successfully pursued every commercially viable lead in its tireless quest to do good by doing well. By the late 1950s virtually all new hospitals were installing air-conditioning.

Carrier also made life-saving inroads in the pharmaceutical industry, most notably in manufacturing improvements for Detroit-based Parke-Davis. Carrier engineers provided air-cooling and dehumidifying systems for the drug company's capsule-making division. The company also supplied its most sophisticated temperature and humidity equipment to Dr. Jonas Salk for the production and manufacture of his polio vaccine. Salk had worked with Parke-Davis on his previous research and development of commercial flu vaccines. Parke-Davis and fellow pharmaceutical company, Eli Lilly, led the commercial mass-manufacturing of the polio serum in America. Carrier executive William Bynum explained that Salk's lab required not only precision control of the air's temperature and humidity, but also stringent control over air purity to prevent contamination of thousands of test tubes and slides.

"Keeping the test tubes alone sealed tightly against contaminating bacteria, yeast, and mold found in ordinary air would have slowed

down their work considerably," Bynum noted. And as the polio epidemic raged, there was no time to waste.

Carrier Corp. designed a special system for Salk that pressurized
his lab against infiltration of outside air, purified the conditioned air
supply through five separate filtering processes, and held humidity to
low levels. Like the incubation ward Carrier had built for the Allegheny General Hospital, incubation rooms in Salk's facility used Carrier equipment to maintain constant temperatures in the vats where
polio virus strains grew. Carrier cold diffusers kept the virus strains at
forty degrees F. The rest is history. The Salk vaccine saved thousands
of lives and spearheaded the vaccine revolution.

Never ones to rest on their laurels, Carrier's weather-obsessed
engineers forged ahead into new areas. A year after assisting Salk's
life-saving endeavors, in 1944, Carrier installed its equipment at the
lab facilities and insectarium of Christ Hospital in Cincinnati, Ohio,
where researchers were experimenting with cures for malaria. Temperature and humidity controls were the most important factors in
rearing mosquitos successfully. A few years later, Carrier engineers
traveled to Rome, Italy, to install a centrifugal chiller at Laboratori
Palma, a subsidiary of American pharmaceutical company Squibb.
Carrier's equipment provided temperature control and sterile conditions for the production of the wonder drugs penicillin and streptomy-
cin (the antibiotic for treatment of tuberculosis).

These medical breakthroughs for the public good would not have
been possible without Carrier and Lyle's pursuit of private profit. They
begged, borrowed, and made stock sales to friends and neighbors.
Carrier even enlisted his dentist for cash to get Carrier Engineering
Corporation up and running in 1915. Carrier, Lyle, and five founding
engineers together pitched in $32,600 in start-up funds.

This magnificent seven of manufactured weather raised and
risked this capital in defiance of an economic depression and amid
the tumult of world war. They couldn't afford their own factory and
scrounged for made-to-order parts wherever they could find them.

And when needed, the leaders of these merry weather-makers dug into their own pockets to cover salary shortfalls. Carrier's inventive genius was necessary, but not sufficient, for commercial success. Lyle's aggressive and creative networking and promotional activities were vital in the company's nascent days. By 1927, they had turned their initial investment into a $1.35 million business. (Today, Carrier Engineering Corp. is a $13.5 *billion* company.) The wealth wasn't handed to them. Carrier and Lyle drove their men hard and themselves harder.

The company founders were farm boys turned industrial giants with big dreams, engineering know-how, and a diehard commitment to using their talents to create products and services that people wanted and needed—even if their customers didn't know it yet.

Remaking the American Landscape

Carrier's industrial successes were followed by widespread adoption of its air-conditioning systems in banks and hotels, department stores and malls, office complexes and skyscrapers, trains, planes, ships, and cars. Carrier and Lyle didn't just change *how* businesses manufactured their products or delivered their services. They also changed *where* Americans worked, which led to historic shifts in where Americans *lived* and how *much* they could work. The weather-makers of Carrier Corporation made it possible and desirable to settle in the otherwise stifling environs of Florida, Texas, and the Sun Belt. Company officials had already made inroads in southern movie theaters.

Unfortunately, the successful quest to control hot air unintentionally created *more* of it year-round in Washington, D.C. Carrier and Lyle secured important contracts to install air-conditioning on Capitol Hill (the House in 1928, the Senate in 1929). As a result, the business of government became a hopelessly permanent fixture. This was great news for sweaty Beltway blowhards, but not so great news for taxpayers. Washington bureaucrats and politicians who used to abandon the sweltering congressional swamp en masse in March now stay parked in their perfectly comfortable offices—devising new and endless ways to impede entrepreneurial progress all year long.

Through the 1930s, the company's windowsill-height Weathermaster units spread across the country, from the U.S. Supreme Court buildings to Louisiana State University's campus in Baton Rouge; multistory office buildings in Phoenix, Arizona; and the California Bank of Los Angeles. Like Irvine Lyle, Carrier engineer I. H. Hardeman recognized even more lucrative commercial opportunities for air-conditioning in the Deep South. In addition to tobacco, southern textile mills beckoned as a natural market for Carrier products.

Carrier and Lyle assembled an extraordinary industrial family of thinkers, makers, and doers who turned the seemingly ordinary—air, vapor, water—into a multibillion-dollar industry. They multitasked as scientific researchers, hands-on builders, and capitalist adventurers. They conducted workshops, opened up a training and testing facility (Carrier University), and established dealerships. Willis Carrier mastered the theory of weather control. Irvine Lyle mastered its standardization, manufacture, and practice. Their experiments and sales brought them into contact with an orbit of makers all committed to the highest quality goods and services.

Lyle died after a brief illness in 1942 while still serving as president and director of the Carrier Corporation. Carrier continued to work, invent, and improve upon his designs and products until a heart attack forced him to retire in 1948; he died two years later just short of his seventy-fourth birthday. Engineer Edward T. Murphy, one of Carrier Corporation's magnificent seven who gave his savings and dedicated his life to getting the company off the ground, identified what bound Willis Carrier, Irvine Lyle, and the founding fathers of cool together through good times and bad:

> We had faith and enthusiasm in our enterprise, with loyalty to each other and to a common cause.

We had courage and vision to seize opportunity when it appeared.

We supplemented each other in all phases of an intricate business.

We had a superior product, applied with sound engineering. . . .

We held steadfastly to a high standard of integrity in our products, in our engineering methods, and in our financial dealings with others.

It would seem also that we had fate on our team. Perhaps it was because we had selected a business that contributes to better health and living for people by which a real service is rendered to mankind.

Call it the *esprit de tinkerpreneur* that infuses the air we breathe, the clothes we wear, the food we eat, the medicines that prolong and improve our lives, and the spaces in which we live, travel, work, and play.

Carrier's founding corporate motto was not only a pledge to customers. It was also a reflection of the engineers' culture of optimism— the culture of American capitalism—in which innovative risk-takers do everything in their power to make:

"Every Day a *Good* Day."

3.

ROEBLING:

The Family That Built America's Most Famous Bridges

Lector, si monumentum requiris, circumspice.
(Reader, if you are seeking his monument, look around you.)
—LATIN INSCRIPTION CARVED ON FAMED ARCHITECT CHRISTOPHER WREN'S
TOMB BENEATH THE DOME OF ST. PAUL'S CATHEDRAL

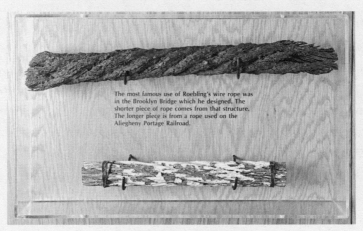

The most famous use of Roebling's wire rope was in the Brooklyn Bridge which he designed. The shorter piece of rope comes from that structure. The longer piece is from a rope used on the Aliegheny Portage Railroad.

Courtesy of National Park Service

Have you ever tried building a popsicle stick truss bridge? With just one hundred or so of the skinny craft sticks, a bottle of glue, and the right design, you can create a twenty-inch span that holds up to two hundred pounds! Alas, my own grade-school attempt didn't turn out so well. I readily admit that my woeful lack of precision and patience produced a sticky jumble of broken wood splinters.

Still, my childhood obsession with bridge-building has never ceased. And America's skylines have an incredible tale of courage and capitalism to tell, if you open your eyes and ears. San Francisco's majestic Golden Gate Bridge celebrated its seventy-fifth anniversary in 2012, New York City's George Washington Bridge marked its eightieth anniversary in 2011, the famed Brooklyn Bridge reached its 130th birthday in 2013, and the Covington-Cincinnati Suspension Bridge over the Ohio River turned 148 years old in 2014.

Who built all that? The answer lies not with bureaucrats, unions, and public works collectivists, but with three individual love stories intertwined in one unforgettable family.

The central story is the life story of patriotic Johann (John) Augustus Roebling, his love affair with American freedom and free enterprise, and his unrelenting quest for engineering greatness.

The second is the story of faithful Washington Augustus Roebling, his love for his father, and his loyalty to the family business.

The third is the story of passionate Emily Warren Roebling, her love for her husband, and her dedication to lifelong learning and civic duty.

At the heart of the family's enduring legacy are the revolutionary wire ropes patented by John Roebling and used not only for suspension bridges but also for elevators, telegraphs, telephones, cable cars, airplanes, electricity, mining, and oil drilling. Before the Roeblings helped usher in the industrial age of iron and steel cables, rope-making was a tedious and time-consuming craft that required walking backward for miles.

What inspired the patriarch to leave his German homeland, seek opportunity in America, and fulfill his entrepreneurial ambition? The same ineluctable, forward-moving drive that fueled the Founding Fathers:

To make something new in a new land, ever better, and monumentally built to last.

A Short History of Rope-Making

The makers of the tomb of Prince Khaemwaset, a son of Pharaoh Ramesses II, left a vivid hieroglyphic scene at the mausoleum that might be best titled "Twist Like an Egyptian." The drawing depicts two rope-makers spread apart, facing each other while twisting stretched yarns, with a third in the middle regulating the tension of the final twist. Other ancient Egyptian tombs showed rope-makers with cord wrapped around their waists, enlisting stones, swivels, and crude spindles as hand tools.

The Bible contains more than a score of references to rope and cord. Ecclesiastes 4:12, touting the figurative and literal strength of a triple-braided cable, counsels: "Though one may be overpowered, two can defend themselves. A cord of three strands is not quickly broken." In China, ingenious workers made cable out of bamboo, which they used to tow boats up the Yangtze River and construct the world's first suspension bridges. Peruvians used a reed called *totora*; Polynesians used coconut husk fibers. By the Middle Ages, secret guilds protected the art of rope-making and trained members on the use of flax and hemp as their primary textile materials.

From the fledgling nation's first days, America's founders stressed the importance of native hemp and flax production. Before you conjure up images of the Founding Fathers rolling doobies with parchment paper, though, please note: Industrial hemp is a distant member of the marijuana (*cannabis sativa*) plant family with negligible levels of THC (the psychoactive ingredient in medicinal and recreational pot). Virginia's colonial leaders required each family to grow one hundred plants for cordage; the governor himself grew five thousand plants.

Rope walks flourished in Boston and other port cities along with other maritime trades. There was even a rope walk on Broadway in New York City, between Barclay Street and Park Place. Benjamin Franklin showed how integral the industry was to everyday colonial life when he invoked a cordage simile in his 1747 call to arms, *Plain Truth*: "At present we are like separate filaments of flax before the thread is formed, without strength because without connection. But union would make us strong."

The Plymouth Cordage Company reported that rope-making dated back to 1641 or 1642 in Beantown, when city leaders invited Brit roper John Harrison to set up his trade and guaranteed him a monopoly to lure him here. Competitors thrived after Harrison's death.

"Rope walks" were built on the outskirts of towns, near shipyards, to get the job done. They consisted of narrow brick buildings or dirt lanes, sometimes close to fifteen hundred feet long. The extreme length was necessary because the spinning of fiber into yarn, and then the twisting of yarns into strands and strands into rope, had to be done in a straight line. It took a 1,000-foot-long path to produce a 100-fathom (600-foot) rope. By the end of the eighteenth century, there were 14 major rope walks in Boston; by 1810, 173 rope walks were in operation from Maine to Kentucky.

Finished ropes were plunged in large vats of boiling tar, derived from pine trees, to prevent decay and provide water resistance. For centuries, Europeans continued to make rope in the same basic manner as generations of hand-twisters and hand-braiders before them. When domestic supplies of hemp ran low, they imported Manila hemp from the Philippines, derived from the abaca plant, and sisal from Africa and Brazil.

Like the ancient Egyptians, early American ropers worked in pairs and trios to twist, wrap, and finish. Henry Wadsworth Longfellow famously described the dreary work through the eyes of a daydreaming spinner in his poem "The Ropewalk." It was mundane, but vital, work that touched the ordinary lives of "fair maidens in a swing," the woman on the homestead "drawing water from a well," bell ringers, sailors, and more:

Then a school-boy, with his kite
Gleaming in a sky of light,

And an eager, upward look;
Steeds pursued through lane and field;
Fowlers with their snares concealed;
And an angler by a brook . . .
. . . All these scenes do I behold,
These, and many left untold,
In that building long and low;
While the wheel goes round and round,
With a drowsy, dreamy sound,
And the spinners backward go.

The division of labor at a typical rope walk worked like this:

In the long building, a roper spun hemp, backing slowly away from a revolving hook turned by an apprentice manning a crank. The roper wrapped a bundle of hackled hemp around his waist and fed fibers from it to the twisting, lengthening yarn. Next to him, two men twisted two yarns into a strand of marline. One of them turned a crank that rotated two whirl hooks in a direction opposite to the twist of the yarn so that the strand would not unwind. The second man formed his strand by guiding the yarns through two spiral grooves cut into a bullet-shaped wooden block called a "top."

Another team operated a grooved top and laid and twisted three ropes reaching from the hooks to a swivel at the far end of the rope-walk. To make a yard for each yarn in a one-inch-diameter rope the length of a football field, spinners would have to walk several miles backward. Some of the manual work was supplemented by horse or water power. But guild workers "resented the employment of any hands who had not served a regular apprenticeship at the trade, and there was bitter opposition to the introduction of machinery." In the end, innovation trumped antitechnology forces. By the mid-1790s, George Parkinson and John Pittman had filed the first U.S. patents for flax- and hemp-spinning machines to manufacture cordage.

These were literally historic steps forward, because the new machinery replaced backward-walking spinners with upright, rotating devices that could spin several thousand feet of rope in just a few square feet of space. As the Industrial Age dawned, hemp remained America's primary rope-making material of choice. Kentucky led domestic production of hemp by the 1850s, with a peak of forty thousand tons produced annually, but hemp rope was relatively expensive and short-lived. Despite being tarred for water-resistance, hemp rope would rot in damp climates. More frequently, it would break from its own weight while hoisting modern machinery used in the booming railroad, maritime, mining, drilling, and construction industries.

Dissatisfaction with the status quo—the eternal catalyst for human progress—sparked the imagination and ingenuity of a German immigrant yearning for the golden opportunity to be better and do better.

"A New Fatherland Free from Tyranny"

Dominated by medieval, half-timbered houses and almost a dozen towering Gothic churches, Mühlhausen is an imposing walled city in central Germany, formerly the kingdom of Prussia. Johann Sebastian Bach served there briefly as an organist at age twenty-three, composing his first cantata for a city council musical celebration. In 1806, with the country under the thumb of Napoleon, Christoph ("Polycarp") and Friederike Röbling welcomed son Johann August into their world. He was the youngest and brightest of four children. Perhaps inspired by the city's proud connection to Bach, Röbling learned to play piano and flute. He spent his childhood constructing toy towers and filling sketch pads with intricate drawings of his hometown.

Life in the "town of spires" was comfortable enough in the Röbling family's middle-class home. Father Polycarp made a living running a small tobacco shop. He was a go-along, get-along merchant who never worked harder than he had to; the family called him a "crank." But mother Friederike, a natural go-getter and domestic CEO—who "made everybody work, managed her household, family, the business, and her quarter of town besides"—wanted much more for her mechanically inclined, mathematically and artistically gifted son. She scrimped and saved to send him off to study at the age of fifteen with eminent scholars in Erfurt and Berlin. There, professors nurtured his passions for algebra and geometry, architecture, bridge and building construction, and hydraulics. In Bamburg, on a student trip, he saw a chain suspension bridge that captured his imagination and provided lifelong inspiration. On the bank of the Regnitz River, young Röbling squatted with notebook and drafting pencil in hand as he sketched the iron bar chains, stone towers, and majestic arc of this "miracle bridge."

Röbling earned a surveyor's certification, and then worked on a military road-building project in Westphalia in 1825. He was well on his way to becoming a government engineer, a cog in the Prussian building machine, but the talented visionary chafed under autocratic rule. No decisions could be made, no actions taken, Röbling noted, "without first having an army of government councilors, ministers, and other functionaries deliberate about it for ten years, make numerous expensive journeys by post, and write so many long reports about it, that for the amount expended for all this, reckoning compound interest for ten years, the work could have been completed."

Bureaucrats rejected two of his proposals for radically new suspension bridges; they favored conformity over creativity. As his son Washington would later recount, Röbling faced a monumental choice:

> Should he remain in the fatherland, tied down to the strict rules of semi official life—a perpetual subordinate with no opportunity to gratify a laudable ambition or to follow the bent

of his genius[?] Or should he in the prime of his youth seek his fortune in new fields, untrammeled by official supervision[?]

America was the goal which all young men aimed to reach then as well as now. After contentious village meetings and much planning, twenty-five-year-old Röbling, along with his twenty-seven-year-old brother, Karl, and ninety other voyagers, set sail for the U.S. in May 1831 aboard the American-built ship *August Edward*. The ship manifest shows that the passengers ranged in age from one to sixty-five, including a total of twenty-five children under eighteen. All of the German immigrants survived the seventy-eight-day journey except a one-year-old girl, who died after contracting a cold and diarrhea and was buried at sea in a box weighted with iron. When the waters were rough, the crew served spirits, wine soup, or seltzer water mixed with sugar and alcohol to alleviate seasickness. When the waters were calm, Röbling passed the time playing his flute, singing folk songs, reading poetry and science books, and writing in his diary about his hopes and dreams "to found a new home in the western continent beyond the ocean, a new fatherland free from tyranny . . . guided by firm convictions and upright motives, not by the whim of the moment."

Though Röbling was able to afford a more spacious cabin, he showed great concern for the steerage passengers who roomed four abreast in double berths below deck. He protested when the first mate cruelly insisted on tightening all the hatches one night when the weather was fair. When it rained, he helped construct a "wooden pentroof" in steerage to provide protection and ventilation. Röbling also helped build safer and more humane restroom facilities on board the ship so those in steerage didn't have to risk being tossed into the sea while relieving themselves on the "sailor's seat" that extended out on the bowsprit. And when the captain unfairly tried to limit the amount of space on deck that the steerage passengers could occupy, Roebling fought successfully against the usurpation. In his diary, the business-minded Röbling frequently noted that such disputes could have been minimized by a clearly defined, thorough contract that included "the smallest particulars and the most insignificant points," so that nothing was left unsettled beforehand.

He immersed himself in nautical engineering, weather, and day-to-day operations. When the ocean travel grew monotonous, he turned his thoughts to his destination. Röbling had yearned to arrive in the new world on America's birthday, but the ship was still more than a month away from seeing land. In the first week of June 1831, he wrote:

> I believe we can reasonably allow ourselves the hope of arriving in America in good time to celebrate the anniversary of the Declaration of Independence (the Fourth of July) with the free citizens of the United States. This day must be of the greatest interest to every free-minded man, a day which fourteen million free citizens of a state can thank for their present condition of freedom and well-being, and on which their brave ancestors, with the splendid and high-minded WASHINGTON at the head, cast off the servile fetters of the proud and overbearing motherland. We are all desirous of arriving in time to join the celebration.

A month later, he lamented:

> The Fourth of July, as the day of the fifty-fifth anniversary of the Declaration of Independence, was hailed by us with sympathy and celebrated in our thoughts. In vain had we cherished the hope of celebrating this holiday in company with the free-minded citizens of the Union.

But Röbling celebrated his own personal Independence Day soon enough, on August 8, 1831, when the *August Edward* pulled into Delaware Bay:

How long have we not been without the sight of land and vegetation! Already it has been over ten weeks since we have seen
nothing but sky and water. Everyone is rejoicing and longs to
tread the solid earth, which will be a good mother to us also
in this new part of the world.

After undergoing mandatory health inspections at the Lazaretto
quarantine station, where immigrants with infectious diseases were
detained, the passengers sailed the final eight miles up to the port
of Philadelphia. Röbling and his party made the city their base camp
for two weeks. He marveled at the "public spirit" he immediately observed and the swiftness with which Americans had built up the City of
Brotherly Love. That public spirit, he was keen to point out to friends
back in Germany, was the result of a political system that allowed its
citizens to pursue their own best, private self-interest. Admiring the
contrast to the government-centered, top-down autocracy of his Prussian homeland, Röbling immediately embraced American autonomy,
capitalism, and self-governance:

> The numerous hindrances, restrictions, and obstacles, which
> are set up by timid governments and countless hosts of func-
> tionaries against every endeavor in Germany, are not to be
> found here. The foreigner must be astounded at what the
> public spirit of these republicans has accomplished up to now
> and what it still accomplishes every day.
>
> All undertakings take place through the association of
> private persons. In these the principal aim is naturally the
> making of money; nevertheless a noble and beneficent public
> spirit also exhibits itself in the public institutions. . . .
>
> Someone now may ask how trade and communication are
> provided for. Whence has the multitude of splendid steam-
> boats, mail-boats, highways, railways, steam-cars, canals, and
> stages sprung up in so short a time, where previously only

wildernesses and wild Indians were to be found? In part, of course, this is the result of the natural and fortunate situation of the land and its manifold resources; *but it is principally a result of unrestricted intercourse in a concerted action of an enlight-ened, self-governing people.* [Emphasis added.]

Only much later did Röbling and his brother learn that their mother, whose spirit guided them here, had died in a cholera epidemic shortly after they departed. But there was no going back or looking back. Johann Röbling was exactly where his mother had sacrificed every-thing for him to be—in the land of the free, home of the brave, eager to work, and ready to make something from nothing.

"God Is Good": From Failed Farmer to Famed Civil Engineer

Though classically educated, experienced as a surveyor, and passion-ate about bridge-building, Johann Röbling first embarked on his American life as a farmer. He, his brother, and another Mühlhausen family traveled by wagon over the Appalachian Mountains to western Pennsylvania, hoping to establish an "earthly paradise" for fellow and prospective German immigrants. His geographic choice was no ac-cident, but the result of careful study and forward-looking anticipa-tion of industrial progress and development. Wood, iron, wool, and cotton were plentiful in the region. Maximum freedom was also key. Adamantly opposed to slavery, Röbling wrote in his journal that he re-fused to consider the South because of its unjust treatment of blacks. He and his fellow immigrants were "frightened away from the South by the universally prevailing system of slavery," he noted, "which has too great an influence on all human relationships and militates against civilization and industry with an ever-hindering effect." He expressed hope for slavery's eventual abolition and moved forward on settling "in a *slave-free* state in a locality, which has, where possible, good communication with the Eastern coast, with the principal centres of the American civilization, and at the same time communication with the principal markets of the West." As the hopeful pilgrim wrote a good friend back home in December 1831:

> We now live as *free* men . . . we live in a section of the country where nature is beautiful and where every diligent person can easily earn a livelihood; and also, we are in one of the most advantageous sections of America, in the vicinity of a good market, which is improving from year to year, where we can dispose of all products for *cash*, with little trouble—what more do we want just now?

The answer was more company. Roebling lobbied hard for his family and old village neighbors to join his American colony. He updated German friends the following spring with a lengthy and prophetic progress report, in which he felt vindicated and still impressed with his fellow adopted countrymen:

> So much remains correct and always true: the Americans now are the most enterprising people on earth and in time will become the most powerful and the most wealthy.

The idealistic Roebling brothers dubbed their new community "Saxonburg." In 1836, Johan married Johanna Herting, daughter of the village tailor. Despite their complete inexperience in agriculture, the brothers set about buying sheep, cows, and plows, building log houses, and planting crops. Unfortunately, Johann proved more adept at building things than growing them. When he failed to make a profit, he turned to raising canaries. Then he tried silkworm-farming, fabric-dyeing, and rape seed oil farming. And when those failed, after six years of valiant toil, tinkering, and manual labor on the farm, he decided to risk everything he had to pursue his lifelong calling: engineering.

Failure didn't crush the stubborn pioneer's ambition. It motivated him. "If one plan won't do, then another must," he preached adamantly and practiced relentlessly.

The year 1837 was a game-changing one for Röbling: His wife gave birth to their firstborn of nine children, son Washington Augustus. His brother Karl died of heatstroke while farming. It was also the year Johann Röbling proudly became a naturalized American citizen and changed his name to John Roebling. He knew that assimilation, which he embraced from the moment he started studying American history and the English language to prepare for his New World voyage, was key to success. Despite a nationwide banking crisis, economic depression, and doubts about starting another career, Roebling pushed forward again. He devoured scientific and technical journals, brought out his sketchbooks, and revved up his inventive engines. Drawn back to Philadelphia and the waters around it, Roebling patented an improved boiler for steamships and a safety gauge for a steam-boiler flue. A boom in canal and railroad construction in Pennsylvania, spurred by the earlier completion of the Erie Canal in 1825, offered crucial employment opportunities. He traveled wherever he could use his skills—constructing dams on the Beaver River, consulting on hydraulics on the Croton River Aqueduct, knocking on doors and making introductions in Pittsburgh and Harrisburg.

When he couldn't find work, he furthered his studies and sketched more patented designs—including a steam-powered motorcycle. As word of his intellect and initiative spread, the consummate networker widened his circle of professional contacts and friends, perfecting his English and burnishing his reputation. He penned a treatise on reservoir locks for the *American Railroad Journal* and also wrote on hydraulics for the *Journal of the Franklin Institute*. The latter journal was edited by Dr. Thomas Jones, a physician, engineer, and patent solicitor for the U.S. Patent Office, who later served as Roebling's patent agent.

After reading engineer Charles Ellet's article on wire suspension bridges in the *American Railroad Journal* in 1840, Roebling reached out to him. The German-trained engineer offered his services and bridge-building suggestions to the French-trained Ellet, but was snubbed. Two years later, when Roebling aligned himself with another engineer who had won a contract to build the country's first cable suspension bridge across the Schuylkill River at Fairmont, Pennsylvania, Ellet lobbied government officials hard and wrested away the contract. Ellet was a showboat and glory hound whose arrogance would come back to bite him in the derriere soon enough.

Disappointed but undaunted, Roebling landed a gig on the Pennsylvania canal, which led to a surveying position for a railroad route across the Allegheny Mountains. What he saw changed his life, industrial history, and America's horizons forever.

While on the job, Roebling witnessed several accidents involving workers trying to hoist portage cars on inclined planes over the mountains.

Workers used nine-inch hemp rope hawsers (towing lines) for hoisting in a system resembling modern ski lifts. When the too-weak hemp cables frayed and snapped, the cars came crashing down. In one catastrophe, two men at the foot of the slope were killed when a runaway car and canal barge crushed them. The incidents triggered Roebling's memory of having read a German scientific journal referencing wire rope. In the Harz Mountains of northern Germany, which teemed with silver, tin, lead, and copper, mining engineer William Albert had experimented in the 1830s with hand-twisted iron cables to replace weak chains and hemp ropes. He tried for years to make them a commercially viable product, but failed. English inventors Andrew Smith and Robert Newall were separately testing their own wire-rope designs and machinery in London.

Drawing on his academic studies and his practical experience gained in both his native and adopted homelands, Roebling became the first engineer to attempt wire-rope manufacturing in the U.S. He first made the cables by hand, employing the rope-walks of old and enlisting his sons, neighbors, and friends in Saxonburg to stretch and twist just like the Egyptians of yore.

Son Washington recounted how rope men were "collected from around the neighborhood" and cared for by the Roebling family through the grueling workday:

> My mother fed them; they commenced work in summer at 5 a.m., came to breakfast at 6:30; at 10 a.m. I carried down a basketful of rye bread and whiskey, at 12 I blew the horn and they came to dinner, at 4 p.m. I carried down a basketful of rye bread with butter and more whiskey, and at 7 p.m. they came up for supper.

The workers were farmers, shopkeepers, weavers, shoemakers, and jacks-of-all-trades—ready, willing, and able to help achieve Roebling's American Dream by achieving their own through hard work. Washington came to know all the ropers and spinners intimately and recalled his childhood role fondly:

> One cause which led to my intimate relations with many of the people arose from a simple circumstance. In the process of rope making, seven strands are first manufactured, by a regular force working daily. But when the strands were laid up into the large rope, a force of twenty men was required for one or two days; this force had to be summoned from all the neighborhood and I was a little messenger who did the running.

Roebling purchased his wire from industrial pioneer Robert Townsend, who had founded the first iron wire mill west of the Allegheny Mountains in 1816. Townsend's Quaker ancestors sailed to America from England with William Penn on the good ship *Welcome* in 1682. At sixteen, Townsend learned the wire-making trade from Baltimore wire weaver Hugh Balderson. He moved to Pittsburgh and opened up a plant on the Beaver River, operated partially by water power. The Townsend company manufactured rivets, nails, fasteners, and telegraph wire, in addition to supplying Roebling with wire for his early experiments and projects. Samuel Wickersham's Pittsburgh Wire Works also supplied wire as Roebling gained more project work. And the Sligo Iron Works made charcoal "blooms" for Roebling wire— large blocks cast from molten iron and later steel, which were then "hot rolled" at high temperatures between two rotating cylinders into wire rods.

The men of Saxonburg laid the wires out across a large, twenty-five-hundred-foot meadow behind the family farm. Roebling devised an iron top with grooves, carried on a crossbar by two strong men, to form a nineteen-wire strand. At the meadow's end, two more men operated a simple twisting machine, spurwheel, pinion, and crank. At the opposite side, another weighted mechanism let the twist out of the wires and workers finished off the cables by cutting and looping the end. It took a day or more to make a thousand feet of strand, and then seven strands were laid up into rope. Ropers signaled across the meadow by a flag system to indicate when they needed rest breaks. Finished ropes were loaded into a large, four-horse wagon by a winch attached to a tall gallows frame. Ten miles away in Freeport, Pennsylvania, the ropes were transferred to a canal boat and sent east.

Roebling quickly realized the commercial potential of his wire-rope innovations and the promise of a viable family business for all four of his sons (Washington, Ferdinand, Charles, and Edmund). He secured U.S. Patent 2,720A in July 1842 for "A Method of and Machine for Manufacturing Wire Ropes," which described his plan for spinning wire rope while maintaining uniform tension on all of its strands. He outlined another improvement for preventing the twisting of fibers during laying, using annealed wire or swivels. He also described his wrapping machine to give the rope a rodlike rigidity by binding the cable with greased insulating wire. Roebling submitted a patent model of the wrapping device, made of brass and wood, as part of his application. (It's housed today at the Smithsonian's Museum of American History.) Frugal and financially savvy, Roebling operated on saved capital and refused to borrow. Several of his new clients paid him in stock, and he soon had a lucrative investment portfolio. Coal-mining companies in the anthracite region snapped up the sturdy cables. Roebling continued to improve his wire-rope process and designed a vertical-spinning machine in 1855 that eliminated the long rope-walk and automated the process for twisting six nineteen-wire strands around a core strand.

A forceful and combative personality who thrived on competition and strove for perfection, Roebling promoted his work aggressively and shared his engineering insights in public letters and journals. The hemp rope industry opposed him vigorously. But Roebling put his money and reputation where his mouth was and persuaded the Pennsylvania Canal Board to allow a test installation of his six-hundred-foot wire rope—at his own expense. James Potts, a toll collector on the Pennsylvania Canal and Allegheny Portage Railroad and a friend of Roebling's, later recounted the brazen sabotage that caused the rope to fail and nearly doomed the man who would go on to design some of the world's most famous bridges still standing today:

> The manufacturer of the hempen ropes in Pittsburgh, backed by a powerful and interested influence, endeavored to prevent the introduction of the wire cable. The superintendent and employees on the road partook in the opposition. If the wire cable was a success it would supersede the profitable hempen-rope enterprise. The cable, however, was put on the [inclined plane].

But the test did not go smoothly. Roebling's sneaky rivals made sure of that. He discovered that someone had purposely cut the cables, which bore telltale file marks. Potts recalled Roebling's despair after viewing the wreckage:

> Mr. Roebling found his cable stretched on the plane— condemned. He came to the Collector's office and asked an interview with me in the parlor. He stated with the tears of grief, if not of agony, that he was a ruined man. The labor of his life, the hope of his fame and fortune, were lost forever.

Potts realized what Roebling realized about the protectionist conspiracy against him:

> His cable was condemned by the great Commonwealth of Pennsylvania. It was condemned, not because it was worthless, but because it would supersede the hempen rope.

Roebling begged Potts and canal commission president John Butler for another chance.

"Roebling, have you confidence in your cable?" Butler demanded.

"I have, sir," Roebling answered unequivocally.

Butler gave him the opportunity to reconstruct the plane and told him that if the ropes held up, he would install them "on all the planes on the road, and this is all I can do for you."

Potts recalled Roebling's reaction:

> . . . with tears of joy rolling down his cheeks, his only reply was *"God is good!"*
>
> I shall never forget the reply. He gave thanks to that Source from whom all blessings flow. He left with a joyful heart and greatly encouraged. The plane was reconstructed, ready for the spring business. The cable worked like a charm.

At the urging of another friend, his wire supplier Robert Townsend, Roebling bid on a project to replace the deteriorating Pittsburgh aqueduct. He won a contract to build an eleven-hundred-foot-long wire-rope suspension aqueduct to extend the Mainline Canal across the Allegheny River and into Pittsburgh. Roebling's vision and productivity were extraordinary. The Pittsburgh aqueduct, opened in the spring of 1845, featured seven spans of 163 feet each with a wooden trunk to hold the water, all supported by a continuous, seven-inch-diameter wire cable on each side of the structure.

Roebling never took for granted the entrepreneurial opportunities available to him in America. Son Washington noted:

> My father often told me when referring to the [Pittsburgh] Suspension aquaduct [*sic*] that he never would have been allowed to build such a structure in Prussia.
>
> The dignity and pride of the supervising engineer would have ground down the ambitious attempt of the young engineer in even proposing such a structure which had no precedent.

The *Pittsburgh Daily Gazette* praised the "noble structure" and effused that Roebling had "erected a work which will secure him a high reputation, and eventually an ample return in a pecuniary sense." It also gave him priceless experience in suspension bridge projects to come—from manufacturing the wire-ropes to designing and constructing the suspension systems and tower supports, to anchoring the cables. The next year, he designed and built Pittsburgh's stout and sturdy Monongahela River Suspension Bridge. Its eight spans measured 188 feet each. The spans were supported by two four-and-one-half-inch cables made on land separately for each span; they were hoisted in place from flatboats.

Rebounding from sabotage, Roebling had used the Pennsylvania lifeline to pull himself up, out, and forward once more.

"Trenton Makes, the World Takes"

With multiple new contracts for aqueduct and bridge construction in the works and transportation costs rising, Roebling took another bold, strategic step: In 1849, he moved his family and business from Saxonburg to Trenton, New Jersey.

Another leading tinkerpreneur, Peter Cooper, encouraged Roebling to relocate. Cooper was an extraordinary manufacturer and inventor in his own right who developed the famous "Tom Thumb" locomotive, operated a glue factory, patented the gelatin-manufacturing process that led to the development of Jell-O, and owned an iron foundry in the growing Quaker town of Trenton. The city was halfway between New York and Philadelphia on the Delaware River; shipping facilities abounded. Cooper took advantage of the river as a water power source. He used the canal system to ship iron ore from his Maryland mines up to New Jersey, and he shipped coal from Pennsylvania to fuel his forge. Roebling bought property adjacent to Cooper's Trenton campus, giving the engineer a steady and convenient wire-rope production source and the eclectic industrialist a prestigious customer.

Later, Roebling's sons Charles and Ferdinand built a two-hundred-acre, state-of-the-art manufacturing campus, steel plant, and village ten miles from the Trenton headquarters. Employing eight thousand workers, the Kinkora Works would produce everything from chicken wire and telegraph wire to tramway and elevator cables. The suspension cables on the Golden Gate and George Washington Bridges were manufactured by the Roeblings. So were the control cables in the *Spirit of St. Louis*, the first airplane to cross the Atlantic Ocean nonstop, and the tramway and construction cables used to build the Panama Canal. Even the wires used to stabilize the wings of the Wright Brothers' aircraft used Roebling trusses.

The Roeblings' ethos and ubiquity inspired their newly adopted hometown's motto: "Trenton makes, the world takes."

A "Cry of Agony" and a Call to Arms

Roebling was achieving his dream, but it was never, ever easy. After the political jockeying he experienced in his encounter with rival bridge engineer Charles Ellet and the sabotage episode during the Allegheny Mountains portage test, the now-famous tinkerpreneur had to protect his business with even fiercer vigilance. As a hands-on executive, he personally built and designed his Trenton works from scratch. He continued to travel nonstop to provide direct project supervision. Aqueduct construction took place amid brutal Pittsburgh winters, mudslides, howling wolves, and utter desolation.

And then, barely three months after moving to Trenton, as the family's wire-rope factory bustled with new business, forty-three-year-old John Roebling suffered a horrific workplace accident.

Washington Roebling was twelve years old at the time. It was just before Christmas at the plant. Roebling was on the factory floor, standing near the countertwist machine, along with loyal company manager and friend Charles Swan. In a rare moment of absentmindedness, Roebling unconsciously grabbed hold of the wire-rope that pulled up the weight box of the machine. His left hand was drawn into the groove of the rope sheave. Washington captured the scene in his memoirs: "His cry of agony was fortunately heard by Swan who happened to stand near the engine—he instantly reversed the machine, and the mangled arm was slowly liberated, then he fell backwards into the pit apparently lifeless." The tendons in his left hand were lacerated; his fingers permanently disfigured. Roebling would never play the flute or fiddle again. Young Washington became his nurse and secretary as his father recuperated. Irascible and stubborn, the elder Roebling scolded his son for poor penmanship and lectured him on the benefits of strange forms of hydrotherapy—Old World quackery using water to cure wounds that the brilliant engineer curiously clung to despite his doctor's protestations.

When Roebling was well enough to travel again, Washington accompanied him to monitor progress on four suspension aqueducts underway along the Delaware and Hudson Canal, which connected the anthracite coal regions of Pennsylvania with the tidewater of the Hudson River: the Lackawaxen and Delaware in Pennsylvania, and the High Falls and Neversink in New York. The specs:

- Lackawaxen Aqueduct, 2 spans of 115 feet each, and two 7-inch cables;
- Delaware Aqueduct, 4 spans of 134 feet each, and two 8-inch cables;
- High Falls Aqueduct, 1 span of 145 feet, and two 8½-inch cables;
- Neversink Aqueduct, 1 span of 170 feet, and two 8½-inch cables.

Roebling and his workers finished them all in two years' time by 1850. His design, construction, and manufacturing experience prepared him for the next big milestone in his career: spanning Niagara Falls with the world's first railway suspension bridge.

The roaring waters at Niagara attracted some one hundred thousand visitors a year at the time. Currier & Ives, the famed nineteenth-century "printmakers to the American people," celebrated the scenic wonder in a series of lithographs depicting the falls from various vantage points. Railroad moguls on both sides of the New York–Canada border wanted to double their profits and join their lines across the eight-hundred-foot-wide, two-hundred-foot-deep gorge. The bridge would sit at the narrowest point of the Niagara chasm above the Whirlpool Rapids, offering passengers panoramic views of the American and Horseshoe Falls. Roebling's old nemesis, Charles Ellet, boasted he could build a wire-cable suspension bridge "safe for the passage of locomotives and freight trains, and adapted for any purpose for which it is likely to be applied." He won the initial contract on a $190,000 bid for an eight-hundred-foot-span bridge featuring two carriageways, two footways, and a central railroad track with a due date of May 1, 1849, right before the summer tourist season kicked off.

The publicity hound Ellet held a kite-flying contest to get the first cable across the gorge. A fifteen-year-old boy from Nebraska, Homan J. Walsh, won the competition with a homemade kite he dubbed "the Union." With great fanfare, Ellet two months later opened a temporary service bridge with a gangway to limited construction and human foot traffic. He charged twenty-five-cent tolls and steered all the revenue away from the railroad owners to . . . himself. The hot-headed Ellet commandeered control of the American side of the bridge and fired off a cannon loaded with buckshot. It backfired. Ellet lost his job when the thievery was discovered. He then lost a bid to sue the bridge sponsors, who paid him a five-figure sum to go take a long hike off a short bridge. He scurried off to Wheeling, Virginia, to finish another bridge project.

The American and Canadian railroad execs reached out to Roebling. Though he had been initially snubbed yet again in favor of Ellet, he didn't let pride interfere with progress. He eagerly drew up plans to improve on Ellet's flawed design using two platforms, four of his wire-rope cables, and the unique concept of a box truss, constructed of wooden members and a lattice of iron rods further stiffened by inclined cable stays. The engineer plunged into the project with such intensity that he only learned of the birth of one of his children during bridge construction via business letter. In fact, he appeared to have forgotten that his wife was pregnant at all. "You say in your last" communication, he wrote to his close friend and factory manager Charles Swan, that "*Mrs. Roebling and the child* are pretty well. This takes me by *surprise*, not having been informed at all . . . what do you mean?"

A description of the multiple tasks at hand might explain Roebling's rather extraordinary lapse of memory. Lives, money, and reputation were at stake. He was undergoing the ultimate stress test of his life. Failure was not an option:

When his Niagara Bridge opened in 1855, Roebling attained international fame. He was called to Kentucky where he designed two suspension bridges with the longest main spans in the world. Shortly after construction began, both projects were interrupted by the financial crisis of 1857. Although each of the bridges he conceived was slightly different from all the others, he devised and adhered to a scheme whereby the load of a long span was shared between main cables and a system of overfloor, incline cable stays. This system resulted in an exceptional degree of stiffness and it became his signature.

The Covington-Cincinnati Bridge connecting Ohio and Kentucky opened to traffic in January 1867. Roebling had battled the vested interests of steamboat and ferry operators who lobbied the Ohio legislature to block the project. He had persevered over the nationwide financial downturn of 1857 and through the Civil War. Some southern opponents feared the bridge would facilitate the escape of slaves to the North, which undoubtedly fueled Roebling's drive to get it done.

Roebling passionately opposed slavery from the moment he set foot on American soil. He called it "the greatest cancerous affliction from which the United States are suffering." And remember: He refused to settle in the South because of his abhorrence of the practice. In both his diary and his letters, Roebling protested the mistreatment of blacks, and he imparted his views to his eldest son, Washington. A staunch Republican and supporter of Abraham Lincoln, Roebling told his son at the dawn of the Civil War that "had he been a little younger he would have entered the army and become its commander in chief in a year."

In February 1861, President Lincoln came to Trenton to ask for support. He addressed twenty thousand citizens, including John and Washington Roebling, at the statehouse. The *New York Times* the next day reported on his speech and its rousing reception:

I shall do all that may be in my power to promote a peaceful settlement of all our difficulties. The man does not live who is more devoted to peace than I am. [*Cheers.*] None who would do more to preserve it, but it may be necessary to put the foot down firmly. [*Here the audience broke out into cheers so loud and long, that for some moments it was impossible to hear Mr. LINCOLN's voice. He continued.*]

And if I do my duty and do right, you will sustain me, will you not? [*Loud cheers, and cries of "Yes yes, we will."*]

The freedom-loving, slavery-abhorring Roeblings most certainly were among those who raised their voices.

Courage, Catastrophe, and Caissons

Washington Roebling, John's firstborn son, would fulfill many of his father's dreams. The first: heeding their president's call to fight. After enlisting in the Union army, Washington served in the artillery, protected Union shipping on the Potomac River, built suspension bridges in Virginia and Harpers Ferry, wrote military engineering manuals, and conducted reconnaissance from a hot-air balloon. In Fredericksburg, Maryland, Washington rebuilt a strategic bridge destroyed by a flood in two weeks' time. His father helped supply maps to Union generals and donated $100,000 to support the cause. Washington participated in the Second Battle of Bull Run, Antietam, and Little Round Top at Gettysburg. He attained the rank of colonel and received several brevets for gallant conduct. After meeting and marrying Emily Warren, the charismatic sister of his commanding officer, he returned to civilian life to oversee the completion of the Covington-Cincinnati bridge.

From the spinning of the first cable to the laying of the last piece of the Covington-Cincinnati, Washington led every step of the way on behalf of the family. The bridge still stands today, a registered national historic landmark and the busiest of Cincinnati's four nonfreeway automobile or pedestrian bridges. The span, which Washington called "a striking example of what can be accomplished by one man overcoming great difficulties," was renamed in his father's honor in 1983.

Roebling's bridges and cables were rigid, like the man himself. Roebling's left-hand fingers were stiff by tragic accident. But his spine, principles, personality, and concentration were ramrod by design and will. Like everything else he did, his son Washington observed, John did things to "the extreme limit of an iron constitution." The price of his greatness was paid in health. Washington reflected:

> He worked hard all day out in the winter weather, losing a meal now and then. At night fall, in place of resting he had to work at his plans until midnight or later, attend to his books, lay out work for the morrow, make bargains, and purchase supplies. When tired nature would succumb, stimulants were resorted to, smoking and strong coffee, thus laying the foundation for his lifelong ailment—constipation.

Roebling's prolonged absences were excruciating for his wife and children. But his presence could be just as difficult. In his candid and unvarnished memoirs, son Washington made frequent mention of his father's short fuse and "quarrelsome" temperament. With his own children, John Roebling was a brutal perfectionist and disciplinarian. Youngest son Edmund ran away over their violent confrontations and led a troubled life that caused his other brothers much angst. John was an unapologetic micromanager, yet he took his long-suffering and oft-abandoned wife Johanna for granted. She died of a protracted illness in Trenton while he was working in Cincinnati in 1864. Only then did he finally express appreciation of her "unselfish love and devotion," her "forbearance, patience and kindness," and her love for their children.

John was a voracious workaholic, but also vigorously engaged in the world of ideas. Though he eschewed most recreational activities (he forbade his family from playing cards or reading newspapers), he enjoyed opera and dabbled in philosophy, ranging from Hegel (with whom he had studied in Germany) to Ralph Waldo Emerson. He rarely spent "quality time" with his children, sending them away to live with tutors or at boarding schools at young ages. But he made sure their futures were secure. Education had been critical to his own success, so John Roebling arranged for his first three sons to be thoroughly schooled in both technical and business pursuits. First- and second-born sons Washington and Ferdinand attended prestigious Trenton Academy. Charles was sent to Methfessel Institute, a Staten Island school founded by Anton Methfessel, the husband of Roebling's oldest daughter, Laura Roebling Methfessel. The brilliant Charles would go on to invent the eighty-ton wire-rope machine, modeled after his father's, which spun 1.5-inch cable railway and surface mining wire-ropes. The massive device was designated a national historic mechanical engineering landmark in 1981. Washington and Charles both studied engineering at Rensselaer Polytechnic Institute. Ferdinand studied at Columbian College (now George Washington University) and Polytechnic College of Philadelphia.

At the height of his fame and creative glory, the forward-looking patriarch was grooming his sons to take over his booming business. But none of them could have ever foreseen the shocking circumstances of when and how the torch would be passed—on the water's edge, at the base of the beginnings of the Brooklyn Bridge, which John Roebling conceived but never lived to see.

In 1866, the state of New York had approved a bill to build a bridge across the East River. Roebling won the appointment to serve as chief engineer. He drew up plans for a magnificent, sixteen-hundred-foot suspension bridge of steel wire, anchored by two 250-foot high neo-Gothic towers, which would be longer, stronger, safer, and more beautiful than any other in the world. It would loom over one of the world's busiest ports in the fastest-growing city in the country. This Eighth Wonder of the World would support two roadways, 135 feet above the water, accommodating traffic by train, carriage and horse, foot, and trolley. More than science, more than art, Roebling proclaimed, the bridge would stand as a patriotic symbol and structural tribute "to the energy, enterprise and wealth of that community which shall secure its erection."

Once again, Roebling battled technophobes, jealous naysayers, big business special interests, and inertia-plagued political power brokers. But the deal was sealed not long after a group of Brooklyn elites toured John Roebling's greatest suspension cable hits: his bridges on the Monongahela River, the Allegheny, the Cincinnati-Covington, and Niagara Falls.

With salt in the air and the electricity of anticipation in his veins, Roebling stood atop a cluster of pilings at Brooklyn's Fulton Ferry dock in June 1869. He was surveying the site and taking final compass readings and calculations. Perhaps he was imagining the Brooklyn tower soaring above. But in a fateful moment, the sixty-three-year-old visionary didn't see a ferry pulling into the slip. It knocked him down and pinned his foot against the pilings. His foot was completely crushed and doctors rushed to amputate all of his damaged toes. John Roebling, the invincible ironmaster, had survived the ocean voyage to America, early failure at farming, rivals' sabotage, economic depression and panic, the horrific Trenton accident that mangled his left hand, and civil war. Could he survive this, too?

As he had been when he was a child, faithful eldest son Washington was at his father's side when disaster struck. Washington stiffened his resolve and became the family's iron truss.

According to family lore, when Washington was fifteen years old, he and his father were traveling together on a ferry in the East River. They got stuck in an ice jam, and the seminal experience inspired

John Roebling to start thinking about spanning the waters. One of his sketches dated March 1857 depicts a hulking Egyptian pylon with a winged lion's head looming over the roadway entrance to his Manhattan and Brooklyn Bridge. The incident must have inspired Washington, too. He studied hard in school, producing a thesis on suspension bridges at Rensselaer and earning a degree in civil engineering. Washington accompanied his father on construction trips whenever he could and assumed more responsibility for project oversight after graduation. When the senior Roebling summoned his firstborn son to assume operations at the Trenton wire-rope factory while plant supervisor Charles Swan recuperated from his own workplace accident, Washington came immediately and without complaint.

Now, facing "the crowning catastrophe of all," Washington whisked his father from the Fulton Ferry dock to his home and called in a doctor. Incapacitated but stubborn as ever, John refused anesthesia during the toe amputation, banished the medical professional from his room, and resorted to his beloved hydrotherapy treatments. He soaked his foot in a tin dish and contracted tetanus. As the dread lockjaw set in, gradually muting and paralyzing the outspoken man who had always been on the move, Roebling scribbled furious deathbed notes. He issued illegible orders about his treatments until violent spasms consumed him.

After sixteen agonizing days, German immigrant Johann Augustus Röbling turned American engineering and entrepreneurial giant John A. Roebling died at sixty-three on July 22, 1869. The *New York Times* obituary reported that up until three o'clock in the morning before the day he died, Roebling had "continued to direct his attendants. . . . In these last wandering moments his mind dwelt upon the East River Bridge plans. . . . About an hour previous to his death he failed to recognize his friends, and was soon attacked by three spasms which operated upon his heart and lungs."

Roebling's deathbed condition was a horrifying seizure known as "opisthotonos," in which the patient leaps from the mattress, shoulder blades drawn back with the body contorted, and "the face stuck in the sardonic grimace of spasm just before consciousness is lost and respiration ends." Washington confessed in his memoirs how shell-shocked he had been during his father's last throes:

> Daily and hourly, I was the miserable witness of the most horrible titanic convulsions, when the body is drawn into a half circle, the back of the head meeting the heels, with a face drawn into hideous distortions—each attack sapping the rapidly waning vital forces—hardened as I was by the scenes of carnage on many a bloody battlefield, these horrors often overcame me.

After a wrenching funeral and family meetings with his brothers to reorganize John A. Roebling's Sons Company, there was no more time for Washington to mourn or dwell. The young civil engineer needed to build the most ambitious bridge in the world, sustain and grow the wire-rope enterprise, carry on his father's legacy, and support his whip-smart wife pregnant with their first child. "Here I was at the age of 32," Washington later recounted, "suddenly put in charge of the most stupendous engineering structure of the age! The prop on which I had hitherto leaned had fallen."

Washington and Emily's extended honeymoon, paid for by his approving father, had taken them across Europe two years before the patriarch died. John had needed his son to study pneumatic *caissons* (French for "box") in preparation for the Brooklyn Bridge project. A trio of engineers accompanied the couple on their one-year trip abroad.

The caissons were an engineering wonder all on their own. Crowds gathered at the nearby Webb & Bell shipyard to watch their construction. The giant yellow pinewood and iron structures, filled with compressed air, were used to begin the bridge-building process underwater. The wood came from North Carolina; the steam engines that pressurized the caissons were manufactured in Massachusetts. The sides of the boxes, known as "shoes," were reinforced with cast-iron. Roebling planned to sink a pair of the sixteen-thousand-square-foot chambers, equipped with telephones and gas-powered limelights, on either side of the East River. Several shafts in the roofs of the caissons, equipped with iron hatches, would allow passage of workers and materials. A false floor would be torn apart to allow the crews to dig up the river bottom. The entire success of the bridge rested on successful submersion of these water-tight workspaces. The newlyweds' "vacation" also included trips to steel mills and other wire-rope manufacturers. Little did the young couple know as they toured Germany, England, and France that wife Emily would soon be drawn into the family business—like cable pulled into the groove of a rope sheave—to take a leading management role unheard of for a woman in the late nineteenth century.

Washington had survived military, economic, and political battlefields. But what happened in the East River caissons would test his will, marriage, the very foundations of the Brooklyn Bridge project, and the Roeblings' creative enterprise.

"A Strong Tower to Lean On"

For Washington, it was love at first sight when he spotted the sister of his commanding Union general, Gouverneur Warren, at a military camp. "She has very much captured your brother Washy's heart at last," he confessed in a giddy letter to his sister, also named Emily. "It was a real attack in force." After an intense, eleven-month courtship by correspondence, the soul mates married in January 1865. Emily came from a prominent *Mayflower*-descended family that was socially connected, though not wealthy. She was polished, patriotic, and educated in rhetoric and grammar, algebra, French, and piano. She joined her husband in Trenton when John Roebling summoned him for help, then moved with her spouse to Kentucky for his first bridge management assignment. While on their work-study honeymoon in Europe, Emily gave birth to their first and only child. In a poignant homecoming, the Roeblings had stopped at the family's ancestral hometown of Mühlhausen in November 1867. They were greeted and treated like rock stars, and it was there in the land of John Roebling's birth that Washington A. Roebling II entered the world.

Barely two years later, Washington and Emily endured their first family tragedy with the patriarch's death. With her toddler son in tow, Emily took care of matters on the home front while her husband worked grueling hours to finish what her father-in-law had started. Of some eleven thousand engineering drawings documenting step by step the construction of the bridge, Washington personally sketched and signed five hundred of them. The already Herculean task of building and sinking the caissons was made more difficult by the uneven terrain of the river floor. Master mechanic E. F. Farrington explained that since pilings could not be driven, his crew traveled more than forty-four feet below in the caisson to reach a sturdy bedding of clay, sand, and boulder. It was so hard, he said, that only iron tools could pick it apart. Explosive charges were used to break up the bedrock. Washington altered his father's plan to adapt to the terrain by leaving a cushion of sand between the caisson and the bedrock to distribute bridge pressures. Tons of masonry were piled atop the caisson to sink it; once it reached position, the massive box was filled with concrete. Twenty-three-ton anchor plates, embedded deep in massive artificial anchorages, were then hooked to the bridge cables "in a never-relinquishing embrace." Again, Washington had to tweak his father's plans by enlarging them.

In March 1870, with three thousand spectators in attendance, the finished Brooklyn caisson was launched. But it took two months of dredging and basin work before the vessel could be floated down the East River and guided into place near the same Fulton Ferry slip where John Roebling suffered his deadly accident. The Manhattan-side caisson was sunk a few years later. Inside, the temperature of each muggy caisson rose to a stifling eighty degrees. It was Dante's *Inferno* in a pressurized box, master mechanic E. F. Farrington recounted, "with half-naked bodies, seen in dim, uncertain light."

One of those bare-chested laborers was Frank Harris, who described the hellish caisson conditions in his 1922 memoir. He relayed the warnings that greeted him on his first day about the dreaded decompression disease known as the "bends":

> In the bare shed where we got ready, the men told me no one could do the work for long without getting the "bends"; the "bends" were a sort of convulsive fit that twisted one's body like a knot and often made you an invalid for life.
>
> They soon explained the whole procedure to me. We worked, it appeared, in a huge bell-shaped caisson of iron that went to the bottom of the river and was pumped full of compressed air to keep the water from entering it from below: the top of the caisson is a room called the "material chamber," into which the stuff dug out of the river passes up and is carted

away. On the side of the caisson is another room, called the "air-lock," into which we were to go to be "compressed." As the compressed air is admitted, the blood keeps absorbing the gasses of the air till the tension of the gasses in the blood becomes equal to that in the air. . . .

After two hours' work down below we went up into the air-lock room to get gradually "decompressed," the pressure of air in our veins having to be brought down gradually to the usual air pressure. . . .

One day, just as the "decompression" of an hour and a half was ending, an Italian named Manfredi fell down and writhed about, knocking his face on the floor till the blood spurted from his nose and mouth. When we got him into the shed, his legs were twisted like plaited hair. The surgeon had him taken to the hospital. I made up my mind that a month would be enough for me.

Washington Roebling didn't have the option to quit working. During the sinking of the caissons, "he never left Brooklyn, not even for an hour," the *American Engineer* reported, "and at all hours of the day and night, he visited the work going on under the water." Like his father, he pushed forward while critics caviled and naysayers neighed and scheming politicians attempted to enrich themselves. The unavoidable and infamous Boss Tweed, a trustee of the New York City board overseeing the bridge who had opposed Washington's appointment as chief engineer, was convicted of filching public funds and sent to jail. Several fires and explosions erupted during construction. Experts attacked Washington's use of steel over iron. Chin-pullers at the *New York Times* stirred public fear that the extra weight of steel trusses would overload the bridge. The know-nothings in the media had the chutzpah to accuse Roebling of "stupidity." They derided him for being an inferior engineer because he was simply copying his father's instructions, even as he was innovating unprecedented design and manufacture of steel wire, splicing, and an elevated footbridge atop the towers. Running and wrapping the bridge's mighty cable ropes "was so tedious," recalled master mechanic E. F. Farrington, "that frequently not more than 15 feet was wrapped in a day."

In December 1870, a careless workman held a candle too close to the oakum caulking of a wooden seam inside the Brooklyn caisson. Washington was on scene to help with the valiant effort to extinguish the fire. He labored with the crew for twelve hours straight through the night, then came down with a painful case of the bends as he ascended. He passed out, was rushed to his home, and then returned to work after a short respite. Three other bridge workers died of the awful disease and more than one hundred others suffered nonfatal occurrences of the decompression syndrome as caisson work continued. Two years later, Washington suffered a second, more debilitating bout of the bends. He was carried out of the Manhattan caisson and into bed. Wife Emily took him to the famed spas at Wiesbaden, Germany, to recuperate for six months. Upon return, the illness and pain persisted. But as a writer for *American History Illustrated* later noted, the "the emotional pain caused by ignorant criticism, fraudulent contractors, the virulent opposition of the press, and interference by trustees with neither ability nor vision, hurt him far more."

Working from home, he willed himself to draw up detailed plans for finishing the bridge. Though he had a team of able assistant engineers, he leaned on his life partner and most trusted confidante, wife Emily, to implement his wishes. He taught her the nuts and bolts of bridge specs, the "complexities of cable construction," physics, and structural engineering. Emily acted not just as secretary, nurse, and caretaker, but as a public relations specialist, office supervisor, diplomat, lobbyist, financial adviser, and, in essence, America's most prominent field project manager.

"I thought I would succumb to disease," Washington later wrote in his memoirs, "but I had a strong tower to lean upon, my wife, a woman of infinite tact and wisest counsel." Emily was masterful at conveying her husband's instructions, fielding questions, responding forcefully to public attacks, and representing the Roebling enterprise at social functions. So much so, Brooklyn bridge historian David McCullough observed in his epic work *The Great Bridge*, that "it was common gossip that hers was the great mind behind the great work and that this, the most monumental engineering triumph of the age, was actually the doing of a woman, which as a general proposition was taken in some quarters to be both preposterous and calamitous. In truth, she had by then a thorough grasp of the engineering involved." To illustrate her proficiency, the *New York Times* reported:

> When bids for the steel and iron work for the structure were advertised for three or four years ago, it was found that entirely new shapes would be required, such as no mill was then making. This necessitated new patterns, and representatives of the mills desiring to bid went to New York to consult with Mr. Roebling. Their surprise was great when Mrs. Roebling sat down with them, and by her knowledge of engineering helped them out with their patterns, and cleared away difficulties that had for weeks been puzzling their brains.

Schemers spread false rumors that Washington was paralyzed or "really as one dead." Emily delivered a rousing speech in defense of her husband before the American Society of Civil Engineers in 1882, employing the same gifts of persuasive communication that had captured "Washy's heart." That same year, Rossiter Raymond, the president of Rensselaer Polytechnic Institute (Washington and Charles Roebling's alma mater) paid tribute to Emily's role, exposing the wider public to the hidden engineer behind the scenes:

> I think it can be said of us in this time, our time, whatever may have been the subjection and insignificance of women in other days, or whatever it may be today in other lands, that no good man here and now, does any good thing but does it under the inspiration, or with the help, or for the sake of a woman, or the memory of a woman.

A year later, on May 24, 1883, bridge directors recognized Emily's critical role by giving her the honor of being the first to cross the finished span. Iron manufacturer and New York mayor Abram Hewitt hailed the bridge as "an everlasting monument to the self-sacrificing devotion of woman, and of her capacity for that higher education from which she has been too long barred."

After a fourteen-year battle against inertia, political wrangling, bureaucracy, disease, death, and disbelief, Washington watched from his bedroom window as his extraordinary wife carried a red rooster symbolizing "Victory."

The Brooklyn Bridge was not merely a landmark architectural and engineering achievement. It became a towering iconic symbol and literary inspiration that permeated America's culture—and the world's. Pulitzer Prize–winning poet and consummate Big Apple lover Marianne Moore published "Granite and Steel" in *The New Yorker*. She extolled the "enfranching cable, silvered by the sea, of woven wire, grayed by the mist," with a view of the Statue of Liberty dominating the bay, "her feet as one on shattered chains, once whole links wrought by Tyranny." Moore paid homage to "John Roebling's monument/ German tenacity's also;/composite span—an actuality."

Poet Walt Whitman "returned to his beloved city and saw the nearly complete bridge," the Academy of American Poets noted, declaring that the visit provided "the best, most effective medicine my soul has yet partaken—the grandest physical habitat and surrounds of land and water the globe affords." His poem "Crossing Brooklyn Ferry" commemorated the East River passage from the Fulton Ferry Landing where the Brooklyn Bridge is anchored—and where John Roebling suffered his fateful accident:

> *Crowds of men and women attired in the usual costumes, how*
> *curious you are to me!*
> *On the ferry-boats the hundreds and hundreds that cross, returning*
> *home, are more curious to me than you suppose,*
> *And you that shall cross from shore to shore years hence are more to*
> *me, and more in my meditations, than you might suppose.*

Poet Hart Crane moved into a Brooklyn Heights apartment in 1928 with a view of the majestic span. He spent the next two years laboring on his ambitious, modernist epic tribute of fifteen lyric poems, "The Bridge." Complex, sweeping, and controversial, it was Crane's attempt to connect the Roeblings' monument to his own metaphysical "'bridgeship' as a figure of the American experience" encompassing Columbus's discovery and the days of Pocahantas to the advent of skyscrapers and subways. The opening ode, "To Brooklyn Bridge," marvels:

> *O harp and altar, of the fury fused,*
> *(How could mere toil align thy choiring strings!)*

Upon publication of his book-length series, Crane discovered that he had been living in the same apartment building at 100 Columbia Heights where Washington Roebling supervised the span's construction from his bed.

Afterward, the resilient Washington, blind in one eye and bent over permanently, continued engineering pursuits and took up mineralogy. He built a fine mansion with his wife, traveled with her when his health permitted, and amassed a fortune estimated at $29 million. After his younger brothers Ferdinand and Charles died, the eighty-four-year-old became president of the Trenton wire-rope company, overseeing the booming business for telegraph wire, electrical wire, wire cloth, mining wire, copper wire, and cable car and elevator cables.

Emily pursued her loves of technology, learning, and civics. She served on the ladies' board for the breathtaking 1893 Columbian Exposition in Chicago, where she planned the state of New Jersey's exhibit. The "bridge builder in petticoats" served as national vice president of the Daughters of the American Revolution, where she worked on a memorial to honor the Founding Fathers. She was one of forty-eight women pioneers who earned a law degree from New York University in 1899. She penned a biography of her husband, historical essays on the Brooklyn Bridge construction, legal papers on giving money to charity and the "value of being your own executor." And though the years aiding her husband had taken a physical toll, Emily traveled to Russia, shared tea with Queen Victoria, and organized relief efforts for U.S. troops returning from the Spanish-American War at Montauk, New York, where she worked as a nurse and construction foreman. Emily died after fighting muscular and stomach complications at age fifty-nine in 1903.

The gossamer steel-webbed Brooklyn Bridge, sturdy as ever, turns 132 in 2015. It's the most glorious and visible legacy of the Roeblings' risk-taking, wealth-creating leap of faith from Mühlhausen, Germany, to Saxonburg, Pennsylvania, and the Delaware Valley, down to Kentucky and Ohio, up to Niagara Falls and Trenton, New Jersey, through Europe, and across the East River. These three heroes of industrial progress, John, Washington, and Emily, were unique strands of an unyielding family cable. The pilgrim, the soldier, and the female trailblazer bound themselves to greatness by their shared steel will, endless thirst for self-improvement, and veneration of American ideals.

On the Manhattan side of the span, in the shadow of its galvanized steel cords and high neo-Gothic granite towers, the Brooklyn Engineers Club erected a plaque that joins the three Roeblings together at the base of their most famous labor of love.

The dedication reads:

THE BUILDERS OF THE BRIDGE

DEDICATED TO THE MEMORY OF

EMILY WARREN ROEBLING

1843–1905

WITH FAITH AND COURAGE SHE HELPED HER STRICKEN HUSBAND

COL. WASHINGTON A. ROEBLING, C.E.

1837–1926

TO COMPLETE THE CONSTRUCTION OF THIS BRIDGE

FROM THE PLANS OF HIS FATHER

JOHN A. ROEBLING, C.E.

1806–1869

WHO GAVE HIS LIFE TO THE BRIDGE

PART II

THE MIRACLE OF THE MUNDANE

But what most strikes me in the United States is not the extraordinary
size of a few projects; it is the countless numbers of small ones.
—ALEXIS DE TOCQUEVILLE

4.

I, TOILET PAPER

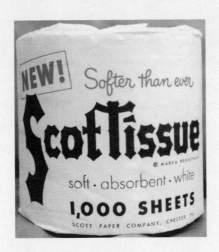

One of my all-time favorite essays is a classic by the late philosopher Leonard E. Read called "I, Pencil." His brilliant little piece turned a mundane writing instrument into an elementary lesson about free-market capitalism by tracing the pencil's rich, deep genealogy—from the loggers who harvest its cedar wood grown in Oregon, to the millworkers in San Leandro, California, who cut the wood into thin slats, to the railroad employees who transport the wood across the country, to the graphite miners in Ceylon and refinery workers in Mississippi, to the farmers in the Dutch East Indies who produce an oil used to make erasers.

"I, Pencil" illustrated what left-wing fossils on college campuses and central planners in Washington, D.C., stubbornly refuse to admit: Governments *and bureaucrats don't make what people want and need. It is individuals, cooperating peacefully and voluntarily, working together without mandate or top-down design, who produce the world's goods and services.*

What is true of the lowly pencil is true of another humble, but essential, product we take for granted—one you reach for every day, countless times a day, without a moment's thought (until you run out of it, that is).

I am a roll of toilet paper.

I am utterly disposable, yet completely indispensable in modern life. The average consumer uses 8.6 sheets of me per restroom visit, which amounts to nearly 60 sheets per day and nearly 21,000 sheets per year. I am soft, cheap, convenient, and reliable. Americans alone spend $8 billion per year on bathroom tissue.

Before I came along, people used everything from scratchy leaves, saltwater-soaked sponges, and stones, to wool, lace, mussel shells, corncobs, and paper bags to get the dirty deed done. Resourceful families used the rough catalog pages of Sears & Roebuck's (which parodists dubbed "Rears & Sorebutts"). Dependence on bathroom reading for bathroom wiping was once so common that *The Old Farmer's Almanac* came pierced with a hole for easy hanging in outhouses and water closets.

Lowly and simple and mundane though I may be, my life story is truly a grand and magical and extraordinary American story— starting with the first manufacturers of paper. It is a story of innovation, persistence, and entrepreneurial savvy. It's not just a genealogy of one company or one inventor, but of myriad private businesses and individual creators, all pursuing their own separate goals in the marketplace.

Did you know that in ancient China, rulers would order the creation of ridiculously large sheets of paper, two feet by three feet, and made of mashed-up mulberries, old rags, and hemp fibers, to meet their sanitary needs? As you can imagine, these imperial megawipes were not exactly ready to be stacked in family-sized economy packs on the shelves at a big-box store. It took centuries for papermaking to evolve from craft to commerce for the masses. This transformation took tireless trial and error, failure and retinkering, risk, capital, patriotism, and passion.

I, toilet paper, owe my existence to early colonial American artisan-entrepreneurs who saw the importance of domestic paper manufacturing in our new land. Their primary goal had nothing to do with the health of our bottoms, but with the wealth of their bottom lines. They and their business partners wanted to maximize profits and pass down family businesses to their children and grandchildren.

The papermakers' top customers in the printing business had their own self-interest that served the national interest: to establish a free press *and make a good living doing it.*

Among my unsung forefathers is William Rittenhouse, an ambitious Dutch-German Mennonite businessman, who built the very first paper mill in America in 1690 along Monoshone Creek (also known as Paper Mill Run) near Philadelphia. The creek's rushing waters turned the Rittenhouse wooden water wheel, which powered the mill machines. Rittenhouse acquired his manufacturing know-how from working at a paper mill in Holland, making this one of early America's technology-transfer milestones. He skillfully lined up prominent investors who put their capital on the line for a daring and untried venture.

Neighboring Germantown, where weavers and flax producers abounded, provided the linen rags and cotton cloth essential for pulp. Rittenhouse employed an entire village of workers who sliced up the rags, stirred the pulp-filled vats, oversaw the "stamper" machines that pounded the pulp, molded the paper into sheets, squeezed water out of tall piles of paper sheets using a gigantic screw press, and laid the paper between sheets of wool felt for drying. Overcoming floods and fire, the Rittenhouse mill dominated colonial papermaking in the

Delaware Valley for the next forty years. Inventive great-grandson David Rittenhouse constructed a model watermill as a young boy while living in the crowded family compound. He later became a clock-maker, surveyor, mathematician, astronomer, and maker of scientific instruments and laboratory glassware. A total of eight generations of the Rittenhouse family would continue to make paper products in the thriving community known as RittenhouseTown.

William Rittenhouse's most noteworthy business partner, another member of my extended family, was William Bradford, a Quaker printer who owned a shop nearby and needed a reliable, steady, high-quality supply of paper. At the time, he was the only active printer south of Boston. Together, Rittenhouse and Bradford oversaw the manufacture of white paper for writing and printing at twenty shillings per ream, and brown paper for wrapping at two shillings per ream. The financial symbiosis benefited all involved. Bradford became a pioneer printer of the colonies. He went on to publish the Charter of Pennsylvania, New York's first law book, the first printed proceedings of an American legislature, the first New York paper currency, the first American Book of Common Prayer, the first history of New York, and New York's first newspaper, the *New York Gazette*.

Bradford's New York print shop was "a veritable seed farm for future printers," where his apprentices included John Peter Zenger (crusading journalist and champion of the free press), Henry De Forest (founder of the *New York Evening Post*), and James Parker (colonial New Jersey's famed printer and journalist who partnered with Benjamin Franklin to publish books). The Rittenhouse clan eventually bought out Bradford's share of the mill on the Monoshone; Bradford built a new one of his own in Elizabeth, New Jersey. Rittenhouse's son, Claus, helped ensure the paper mill's prosperity and longevity by immersing family members in the business. He trained his son, William, who in-herited the factory in 1734, and he shared the secrets of the trade with his brother-in-law William DeWees, who set up his own mill outside

Chestnut Hill, Pennsylvania. Historian John Bidwell wrote that the Rittenhouse family's strategic location took advantage of "a promising market, a rapidly developing transportation network, excellent commercial facilities, and optimum manufacturing conditions."

The Rittenhouse dynasty's financial success fueled the growth of paper mill start-ups, first across the Pennsylvania countryside and then nationwide. Ben Franklin was not only a prolific printer and publisher, but also invested in eighteen of these early American paper mills. With his wife, Franklin supplied rags, felt, molds, and skilled workers for the start-up mills. The enterprising Franklins also ran their own lucrative wholesale paper business. Papermaking, of course, catalyzed the American Revolution not only through the dissemination of information and dissent, but also by galvanizing the colonists against Britain's oppressive Stamp Act taxes and Townshend Act duties on paper.

Another patriotic paper mill owner, Stephen Crane, founded the Liberty Paper Mill in Boston in 1770. The factory furnished cotton paper for revolutionary newspapers and for Paul Revere's engraved colonial Massachusetts banknotes, which helped finance the American war for independence. The currency was printed with the defiant slogan: "Issued in defence of American liberty." Revere even stabled his horses at the Crane mill. Crane's sons and grandsons established Crane & Company, innovating paper wrapping for the Winchester Arms Company's repeater rifle bullets and special thin paper for Bibles, along with their internationally renowned fine stationery. Still in business after two centuries and eight generations, the privately owned, family-held Crane & Company in Dalton, Massachusetts, remains the top supplier of paper for U.S. currency and is now a leading pioneer in currency security technology.

By 1810, the U.S. Census reported that 179 paper mills had been established in seventeen states, producing an annual output of three thousand tons. This domestic manufacturing foundation was vital to the growth of America's fledgling newspaper, magazine, and book

publishing companies—which, in turn, paved the road for the eventual introduction of then-unimaginable and wholly unanticipated
paper commodities. Like me!

Thousands upon thousands of business transactions and interactions
took place between colonial mill owners, pulp and paper workers, linen
and flaxseed merchants, printers, press operators, newspaper editors,
writers, and their customers. All of these individuals, and many more
at the periphery of the papermaking process, exercised their skills at
their separate farms, homesteads, mills, and shops. Then they profited
and traded on their specialized knowledge and know-how. They coop-
erated with each other to manufacture and deliver their goods and
services as a result of enlightened self-interest, multiplied thousands
and millions of times over.

That's the miracle of the free market. It's the spontaneous order of
capitalism, a voluntary and organic configuration of creative human
energies. The pursuit of profits empowers and enriches both producers and consumers far beyond the bounds of imagination.

Chemists, engineers, and tinkerpreneurs toiled away on all cor-
ners of the planet through the eighteenth and nineteenth centuries
to improve the painstaking papermaking process. In 1799, French inventor Louis-Nicolas Robert devised a papermaking machine using
a continuous wire-cloth belt stretched around two rolls. A pulp and
water mixture formed paper on the wire, with excess water draining
off while the wire web picked up the paper. Brothers Henry and Sealey
Fourdrinier, two British investors who owned a stationery business,
brought Robert's invention to market. The Fourdrinier machine could
now produce rolls of newsprint fast and cheaply.

The Industrial Revolution yielded related breakthroughs—the
spinning jenny, the cotton gin, and the steam engine—that helped
boost the supply of rags for paper manufacturing. But with the
demand for printed products skyrocketing, the world needed new raw
material for paper. Inventors took out patents for making paper with

straw, cornstalk, sugar cane, hemp, and jute. The search continued for something more efficient, renewable, and low-cost. French scientist Rene de Réaumur had found inspiration in nature in the 1700s after observing wasps building their nests out of a paste made of dry wood mixed with saliva. The idea of wood pulp bounced around Europe for more than a century and a half, however, before it gained commercial success.

Among my countless creative ancestors, I salute American Civil War soldier, chemist, and inventor Benjamin Tilghman and his entrepreneur brother Richard, who figured out how to liquefy wood fibers with a sulfite chemical solution. In 1867, they secured one patent for making paper pulp out of vegetable material by boiling wood pulp in a high-temperature pressure cooker and another patent for preventing the paper pulp from becoming burned or discolored by adding calcium to the mixture. (The Tilghmans went on to make a fortune after inventing the sandblasting process.) Wood pulp mills sprouted up in poplar-abundant Maine, then flourished across New England and the Midwest.

My family tree also includes another Civil War veteran, Charles B. Clark, who recruited capitalists John Kimberly, Havilah Babcock, and Frank Shattuck to invest a total of $30,000 to establish a paper mill in Neenah, Wisconsin, in 1872. Strategically located on the banks of the Fox River, the company started out selling linen- and cotton-based newsprint, then took over the neighboring Atlas paper mill. Atlas was the first mill in Wisconsin to use wood pulp, which it transformed into manila wrapping paper. The Kimberly & Clark company encouraged vigorous experimentation and product development among employees. Its researchers created the paper used for rotogravure, the photochemical process for printing photographs using a rotary press. A few decades later, Kimberly & Clark lead scientist Ernest Mahler invented creped cellulose wadding from sugar cane pulp. The tissue, used as a substitute for scarce surgical cotton dressing to treat soldiers' wounds, saved countless lives during World War I. Thanks to

Kimberly & Clark's brilliant marketing and product development teams, cellucotton became the foundation of its Kotex and Kleenex personal hygiene lines, which today are just two of the Fortune 500 company's billion-dollar brands.

One of Kimberly & Clark's workers, German immigrant John Hoberg, left the company to incorporate his own paper mill in Green Bay, Wisconsin, along the East River in 1895. The Hoberg Paper Mill introduced the world to a disposable tissue that employees dubbed "Charmin" for its charming, baby-soft quality. According to family lore, Hoberg died in a tragic machinery accident at the factory. But capable family members kept the business going. Consumer goods giant Proctor & Gamble bought out Charmin in 1957. Hoberg's neighboring competitor, Green Bay's Northern Paper Mills, rolled out "Northern Tissue" (later renamed "Quilted Northern") in bundles of one thousand sheets strung together with a wire loop. Both brands are still bestsellers today.

Here's what you undoubtedly take for granted, though: The acceptance of me, toilet paper, didn't happen overnight. It took shrewd marketing and persistent innovation to persuade embarrassed consumers to forgo their corncobs and catalog pages and buy me instead at their local drug stores. Joseph Gayetty had started selling factory-produced bundles of flat, aloe-treated "Medicated Sheets for the Water Closet" in 1857 at a cost of fifty cents for five hundred, watermarked with his name on every sheet. Gayetty trumpeted his manila hemp paper as "the greatest necessity of the age" and a soothing pharmaceutical alternative to the coarse pages of Rears & Sorebutts catalogs. But Gayetty's business venture flopped, even as indoor plumbing and the modern toilet were becoming staples of everyday American life.

Another New York businessman, Seth Wheeler, patented an "improvement in wrapping-papers" that transformed Gayetty's flat-sheet bundles into perforated rolls. In U.S. Patent 465,588, issued in December 1891, Wheeler described his invention, consisting of "a roll of connected sheets of paper for toilet use, said roll having incisions at intervals extending from the side of the web toward the center, but not meeting, and terminating in an angular cut, whereby the slight connection left may be separated without injury to the connected sheets."

It seems so simple now when you reach and rip me off the roll, but someone had to build that. Wheeler's Albany Perforated Wrapping Paper company had figured out how to solve manufacturing problems involved in winding and bonding the sheets, so that each sheet could be "separated from the next without liability of the incisions turning in a direction parallel with the web and tearing off a considerable part of the contiguous sheet." In other words: No more wasteful mess. As Wheeler's ads for his "perforated paper" touted: "Clogged pipes with consequent impure air and disease prevented."

Still, the consumers' blush factor persisted. In Victorian America, potty prudishness was a social disease in need of a cure. Enter my ingenious progenitors, the Scott brothers.

Thomas Seymour Scott started his work life as a lawyer in New York. Bitten by the entrepreneurial bug, he quit his job and launched a wholesale paper business that lasted two years. He next enlisted his younger brothers, Irvin and Clarence, in a new venture selling straw paper, wrapping paper, and paper bags. The siblings embraced the business with a passion. Clarence was a "born salesman;" Irvin took orders in his office clothes by morning and morphed into cart-pushing delivery boy by afternoon. Thomas moved into the publishing niche as an executive at the Curtis Publishing Company (publisher of the *Ladies' Home Journal*). Irvin and Clarence incorporated as the Scott Paper Company in 1879 in Philadelphia. They turned to manufacturing toilet paper rolls after Irvin's father-in-law, James Hoyt, inspired them with his patented, enclosed bathroom tissue container in 1885.

The process for making toilet paper rolls is basically the same now as it was when the Scott brothers perfected it and supplied their private-brand bathroom products to paper distributors nationwide:

First, two long strips of wood pulp material (cardboard) about three inches wide are manufactured and cut on a series of rollers. Next, the top cardboard strip's underside is coated with glue. The two strips are then diagonally wound around a hollow metal cylinder to create a continuous cardboard tube that is extremely long. It's cut up into 65-inch tubes and transported by an "elevator" to a winding machine. There, two strips of newly-formed toilet paper are wound around the core. It's sliced into 4 inch [rolls] by a circular saw and then packaged. And there you have it—a roll of toilet paper!

As for the bathroom tissue paper itself, the manufacturing process starts with the debarking and chipping of trees at the mill. Fifty-ton batches of chips are mixed into a chemical stew in a "digester," eventually reduced to about fifteen tons of usable pulp. The pulp is washed and separated from lignin (wood's natural binding agent) and the cooking chemicals. After the pulp is bleached, it's mixed with water to produce a paper stock that is sprayed on mesh screens and drained. The process results in large, eighteen-foot sheets of matted fiber, which get transferred to a huge drying cylinder known as the "Yankee Dryer." The dried paper, produced at a mile a minute, is sprayed with adhesives so it can stick to the cylinder while being "creped" for softness. A creping tool called a "doctor blade" crinkles, scrapes, and stretches the paper, adding microfolds without cutting through it.

The paper can be scented, embossed, or dyed. Jumbo reels of the creped paper are then loaded onto converting machines, unwound, rewound onto the cardboard tubing, and sealed at the ends with adhesive. A gigantic circular saw slices the paper logs into sixteen standard, four-inch-wide rolls. Finally, the rolls are packaged for either commercial or residential sale.

As company historians tell it, the Scott brothers faced an uphill battle: "The market was limited and the subject was considered unmentionable . . . consumers wouldn't mention it, merchants

wouldn't display it and publications wouldn't advertise it." To circum-
vent the cultural barriers, the Scotts offered "private-label" customized
toilet paper products to hotels, department stores, and other merchants.
Thousands of clients signed up. Capitalizing on the opulent reputation of its hotels, Scott Paper bought out the brand-name rights to the
WALDORF® trademark and turned it into the company's first branded
product. The *Atlantic Monthly* broke the bathroom tissue advertising
barrier when it agreed to run "a small, single picture" of a WALDORF®
package, but "with no advertising copy allowed" in accordance with a
prudish editor's wishes. The company later developed family-friendly
ads featuring moms and babies touting the brand's "luxury texture."

Irvin's son, Arthur Hoyt Scott, revolutionized the business by
openly associating the family name with its marquee product ("Scot-
Tissue"); promoting the health benefits of toilet paper in women's
magazines such as *Good Housekeeping* and uncle Thomas's *Ladies'
Home Journal*; and marketing specialized, company brands boasting
high quality and low cost. By 1910, *Time* magazine reported in a special "Tissue Issue" that it was apparent that Arthur's "idea of special-
ization was correct; his six brands provided 80% of the total sales of
$726,264.09." A tireless tinkerpreneur, Arthur Hoyt Scott patented a
machine for tightening rolls of paper, a supporting device for toilet
paper packages, and several toilet paper cabinets that improved upon
the one his father's father-in-law had invented.

I am proud to point out that this inventive ancestor of mine also
created and patented my sibling, the paper towel, in 1915. "The object
of my invention," Arthur Hoyt Scott announced, "is to provide a
cheap towel formed from paper and adapted for all general uses of
the lavatory, factories, hospitals, laboratories, and for general use." In
his patent application, he described the special absorbent nature of
the two-ply crinkled paper, its low cost, disposability, and its unique
manufacture on a roll. Scott paper towels were actually an accidental
invention—born of an experimental batch of creped paper rolls that
were too heavy and thick to cut into toilet paper. ScotTowels arrived

on the market just in time. Cold and flu epidemics had raised public awareness of the need for better hand-washing and germ prevention. The flu pandemic of 1918 alone killed an estimated 50 million worldwide. According to company lore, Scott told his daughter that he was inspired in part by the story of a vigilant Philadelphia teacher, who reportedly replaced cloth-roll towels in the school bathrooms with individually cut pieces of heavy copy paper to prevent students from infecting each other.

By the late 1930s, Scott Paper sales had reached $13 million. From the Scott brothers' humble beginnings delivering butcher paper in pushcarts, the company had grown into the world's largest manufacturer and exporter of a product whose name had once been unspeakable. In 1995, Kimberly-Clark bought Scott Paper for $9.4 billion. In 2012, Kimberly-Clark reported sales of $21.1 billion worldwide. Today, the conglomerate employs a whopping fifty-eight thousand people at manufacturing facilities in thirty-seven countries. Its billion-dollar brands include Scott, Kleenex, Kotex, and Huggies diapers and Pull-Ups.

I owe my existence to valiant, relentless, and inspired American patriots, scientists, soldiers, salesmen, engineers, mechanics, laborers, loggers, printers, writers, editors, and ambitious immigrant entrepreneurs and their heirs to enduring family businesses. As Leonard Read, free-market-championing author of the famous "I, Pencil" essay, put it, I symbolize—just as the ordinary pencil does—the miraculous "configuration of creative human energies—millions of tiny know-hows configurating naturally and spontaneously in response to human necessity and desire and *in the absence of any human master-minding!*"

I, lowly toilet paper, am the lofty result of faith in freedom, not the product of a bureaucrat's mandate. Innovation can't be manufactured by force or decree. It's the outcome of constant self-improvement and entrepreneurial synergies. What I want you to remember the next time we're alone together is this:

Government bureaucrats didn't make me possible. Capitalists did.

5.

CROWNING GLORY:
How William Painter's Bottle Caps
Became a $9 Billion Business

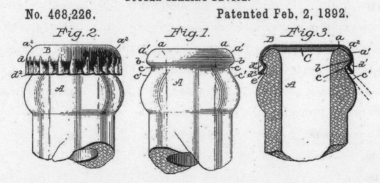

Fun fact: I am a sucker for old-fashioned cream soda. Frosty-blue, orange, raspberry, pink—you name it, I'll drink it. There's something about the old-timey, medicinal sweetness of the beverage that has had me hooked since childhood.

While cracking open a bottle of the bubbly goodness for one of my own kids, I was struck by the humble miracle of the cream soda's bottle top. It's the size of a quarter and lighter than a penny, flimsy and forgettable. Its inventor *meant* for his creation to be tossed in the trash without a nanosecond's thought. Yet after 122 years in existence, the disposable bottle cap still endures. The invention of this mundane metal top has revolutionized, rescued, and inspired multiple industries in America and around the world—from beverages, bottle-making, and bottle openers, to the Gillette razor, pharmaceuticals, aerosols (including the containers for Pledge furniture spray and Lysol disinfectant), and processed foods spanning Cadbury chocolates to Spam.

"Crown caps"—the same ones you flip off your Coca-Cola and Coors Light bottles today—were the brainchild of William Painter. Born in 1838, he was the son of a Quaker preacher and the eldest of seven children. This irrepressible tinkerpreneur, who loved chess and practical jokes, grew up poor on a Maryland homestead farm. He told friends and colleagues that his boyhood aspiration always and ever had been to "make something." Once he started, he never gave up. And once he succeeded, he never let up. The genius of Painter's success could be summarized in a single directive: Invent something "which everybody needs, better and more cheaply provided than ever before." Competition in the manufacture of the best and cheapest necessities was fierce in the Age of Progress. The quest for the perfect bottle closure was crowded. Winning the war of the bottle tops would be Painter's crowning glory. But not without a lifetime of hard work and a significant amount of heartburn first.

Planted Early: Seeds of Entrepreneurship and Invention

The story of how William Painter's bottle caps became a multi-billion-dollar business begins in, of all places, an asparagus patch. Pastor Edward Painter issued an early work challenge to one of his daughters and his resourceful young son William: *"My son, if thee and thy sister will thresh that asparagus and get the seeds all ready to sell, I'll give thee what it amounts to."*

To retrieve and prepare the seeds, the Painter children cut off the ferny tops of the asparagus plants after their berries turned bright red in the fall. Hung upside down for perhaps a week, the foliage and the berries dried out. Pulled from the stems, the berries were then soaked in water for a few hours. After soaking them, the children broke open the berries and painstakingly separated ripe seeds from the plant pulp. The seeds were then dried thoroughly for another week and occasionally stirred to prevent sticking. Finally, the siblings packed the seeds in envelopes or sealed glass containers for sale.

William made an honest dollar for his labor. He learned the values of long-term planning, patience, and follow-through. With the earnings he reaped, he invested not in childhood trifles, but in basic carpentry tools. Instead of pining for toys that his parents could not afford, he made them himself. In his memoir, Painter's son Orrin described playing with one of the amusing contrivances that highlighted his father's mischievous side. It was "a little windmill which contained flour, and which, when blown, instead of operating the windmill, would throw flour upon the one blowing it." Another was a pinky finger ring "attached to a cylinder containing water, held unseen, in the hand, which was discharged by a piston operated by the thumb, upon unsuspecting observers." Painter would have loved the Whoopee Cushion (invented about twenty years after he died).

Young William's formal education ended at high school graduation. Painter's father, a pastor-turned-physician who served on an Indian reservation in Omaha, Nebraska, "had not the means to send him to college." Instead, he read voraciously, constantly exercised his God-given tinkering faculties to the fullest, and honed both his mechanical and business sense on the job. Son Orrin joked that Painter earned his degree from the "University of Hard Knocks." He was, in modern parlance, a lifelong learner.

In 1855, at the age of seventeen, Painter began an apprenticeship in the Wilmington, Delaware–based patent leather manufacturing shop of Pyle, Wilson & Pyle (later the C. and J. Pyle Company). The Pyles were relatives from his father's side. During his five-year stint, Painter invented a machine for softening leather. It caught the eye of the shop foreman, who reportedly appropriated the device (along with the financial rewards) as his own.

Other inventors might have allowed themselves to be permanently embittered and crippled by such intellectual thievery and indignity. Painter was undeterred. He learned the value of intellectual property rights the hard way, but the earlier the better. Among his most trusted colleagues after striking out on his own was patent lawyer William C. Wood, "a staunch and devoted friend" who worked with Painter to protect his myriad inventions from 1874 until his death in 1906. "When his leather-softening machine was literally filched from him," another business colleague recalled, Painter "didn't become discouraged; he simply profited by that experience. Nobody should ever get the best of him again by putting clothes on the children of his brain and endowing them with his or her name." That fertile brain was just warming up.

Painter patented many useful and profitable things before turning his attention to soda bottles and caps. He invented a fare box (for collecting bus or train tickets), several pumps and valves for emptying cesspools, lamp burners, a counterfeit coin detector, a sheet roofing machine, transit tanks, a fountain pitcher, a safety ejection seat for passenger trains, and an electric railway. That last innovation "came to him in a dream," his son Orrin recounted, probably after dozing off late into the night while catching up on the latest issue of one of his favorite publications: *Scientific American* or the *Patent Office Gazette*.

When family members cleaned up after their workaholic patriarch, they'd find his latest inventive schemes doodled in the margins of the magazines. To the irritation of the household washwoman, Painter also had a peculiar habit of scribbling memos to himself on his own shirt cuffs. (Painter would surely have been an enthusiastic user of Post-it notes, invented by 3M engineers in the 1970s.) Sometimes, when epiphanies struck, Painter would grab a piece of chalk, drop to his hands and knees, and draw designs on his shop floor. Then he would rise, dust off his pants, and walk on, oblivious of everything and everyone around him. Absorbed in inventive thought, even after a long day's work, he'd walk several blocks past his downtown Baltimore mansion on Calvert Street before realizing he had missed it.

But the man with eighty-five patents to his name was no flaky mad scientist with his head stuck in the clouds. Practicality, profit potential, and persistence were the keys to his success. It's no surprise the down-to-earth inventor would find his greatest entrepreneurial triumph in little bits of crimped metal used to solve a most prosaic problem: how to keep popular bubbly beverages fresh, clean, and sealed airtight.

The Loop Seal: Topping "America's National Beverage"

Got indigestion? Americans looking to cure their stomach ailments or quench their thirst have mixed homemade drinks made of sassa-fras, elderberry, vanilla, and other roots and herbs since the country's founding. *Miss Beecher's Domestic Receipt Book* of 1846 shared several folksy recipes for her popular "effervescing fruit drinks" and soda pow-ders. In case you had a hankering for sarsaparilla mead (and a spare pound of Spanish sarsaparilla lying around), Miss Beecher prescribed:

One pound of Spanish sarsaparilla.
 Boil it in four gallons of water five hours, and add enough water to have two gallons.
 Add sixteen pounds of sugar, and ten ounces of tartaric acid.

The Martha Stewart of her time, Miss Beecher quoted the advice of a presumably reputable doctor vouching for these good things: "Water charged with carbonic acid forms a cool and refreshing beverage. It acts as a diaphoretic and a diuretic (i.e., to promote perspiration and the healthful action of the kidneys), and is a most valuable agent for checking nausea and vomiting."

Several inventors, including John Mathews and his namesake son, quickly went to work manufacturing commercial soda fountain equip-ment. By the late 1880s, the market for carbonated drinks in the U.S.

was bubbling frothily. Most of the familiar soda brands we still buy now got their start as patent medicine cure-alls. Pharmacist Charles Hires sold a woodsy medicinal syrup he marketed as "root beer" at the 1876 Philadelphia Exposition. Around 1885, pharmacist Charles Alderton created an energy tonic called the "Waco" in Waco, Texas, which was later dubbed "Dr Pepper." Pharmacist John Pemberton famously introduced Coca-Cola to customers at an Atlanta, Georgia, drugstore in 1886.

The origins of these bubbly beverages actually can be traced back much further. Mother Nature, of course, manufactured the original soft drink: mineral water from natural springs. The Paris-based Compagnie de Limonadiers served up a lemonade-flavored syrupy beverage in the seventeenth century. A British pharmacology professor had traced the first documented mention of "soda water" across the pond to 1798. This reference described an "aciduous soda water . . . prepared and sold in London by a Mr Schweppe." Yep, that's the same Schweppe whose name you still see on your ginger ale can. Investigators in the U.K. discovered a glass soda water bottle at the site of the wreck of the *Royal George*, a British ship that sank near Portsmouth, Massachusetts, in 1782. And nearly two decades before that, British scientist Joseph Priestley had announced his method of "impregnating water with fixed air" to help cure or prevent scurvy on long voyages.

Illustrating just how thoroughly soft drinks had already saturated American culture, Thomas Jefferson's nineteenth-century biographer, Jason Parton, paid tribute to Jefferson's good friend Priestley this way: "His invention of soda water is why Americans should join in the scheme to honor his memory. He not only did all he could to assist the birth of the nation, but he invented the national beverage." But how best to cap and preserve America's favorite drinks? Priestley advised that the containers for carbonated concoctions should be stored upside down, "well corked, and cemented." Others advised laying the bottles, made with rounded bottoms, on their sides. One problem: Corks dry up and shrink, leading to leakage and defizzing. Moreover, storing bottles sideways and upside-down was impractical for grocers and merchants. Rubber and metal stoppers, for their part, affected the taste of their bottles' contents and raised hygiene concerns. Wire rusted after prolonged contact with the beverage; dirt accumulated around bottle mouths in the spaces and grooves left by rubber stoppers that did not completely seal a bottle top.

"Triumph" vs. "Loop Seal"

Enter American thinkers and tinkerers thirsting for success. Throughout the nineteenth century, thousands of problem-solvers flooded the U.S. Patent Office with bottle closure contraptions made of cork, glass, wire, ceramic, loops, gaskets, thread finishes, levers, and bails, or some clunky combination thereof. All were designed to be reusable, and it was the custom to plug the stoppers into the bore of the bottle neck. Among the most notable: the "Lightning" stopper for beer bottles (also used on wide-mouth fruit jars); the Codd's Ball stopper, which featured an internal marble stuffed into the bottle bore; the Matthews gravitating stopper; and the Hutchinson spring stopper, made of a rubber gasket held between two metal plates attached to a wire spring loop. Before William Painter came along, the U.S. Patent Office had approved an estimated fifteen hundred bottle stopper patents.

Painter became preoccupied with building a better, cheaper bottle stopper while working as a mechanical engineer for Baltimore's Murrill & Keizer machine shop. He immersed himself in every aspect of bottle-sealing, with a focus on sodas, beers, and malted beverages. After much experimentation, he unveiled his first attempt: a wire-retaining stopper known as the "Triumph." Ever the tinkerer, Painter received a patent for his next improvement, dubbed the "bottle seal" or "Baltimore loop seal," in September 1885.

In introducing the new innovation, Painter identified the fundamental deficiencies of bottle closures then on the market:

"Stoppers have heretofore been made secure against internal pressure in one of two ways—by mechanical means exterior to the bottle, as by using a tie-wire, also by special stopper-fasteners, which have been made in large variety; or by placing the stopper inside the bottle and so arranging it that the stopper is forced against a seat or packing by the pressure within.

The first of these methods is objectionable because of the expense, and in some cases the inconvenience of its use and liability of accidental opening. The second is so for the same reasons, and for the additional one that the presence of the stopper inside of the bottle is an obstruction to ready and effectual cleansing both of the bottle and stopper. Stoppers secured by external fastenings are retained solely by the power of the device to overcome the internal pressure. Those within the bottle are retained because they present a solid mass too large to pass through the bottle-neck. In neither case referred to does the lateral expansion of the stopper itself against the interior of the bottle-mouth enter as an element of its action in resisting internal pressure, as it does with stoppers made according to my method."

Painter's loop seal consisted of a flat rubber disk with a convex-shaped bottom. This stopper, fitted into a grooved bottle-mouth ("reverse taper"), formed an "inverted arch" that resisted the internal pressure of carbonation. The seal was tight and leak-proof; the liquid was protected from contamination or obstructions. The "loop" on the device was formed with small wire at the top of the rubber disk; a simple hook or other pointed implement could be used to remove the stopper from the bottle. Most important, the closures (for either carbonated or fermented, "still" drinks) could be manufactured cheaply and economically. In a novel advancement, the loop seals could be thrown away after one use. Painter's Triumph stoppers sold at $3.50 per gross (twelve dozen); the Bottle Seal sold at twenty-five cents per gross.

With business partner Samuel Cook, Painter formed the Bottle Seal Company to manufacture the disposable disks. The firm acquired the U.S. and Canadian rights to the bottle seal patent and established a factory adjoining the Brush Electric Light Company's plant on East Monument Street in Baltimore. Cook contracted with Painter and Lewis Keizer in 1889 to buy the foreign rights to the bottle seal. He went on to helm the company's European offices, manufacturing facilities, and sales in Germany, England, and France.

Among the early and enthusiastic adopters of the single-use loop seal: the makers of a New England soft drink called "Moxie." Its creator, homeopathic physician Augustin Thompson, originally marketed Moxie as "nerve food." He described the bitter-tasting elixir as a cure for "paralysis, softening of the brain, and mental imbecility." Essentially the godfather of today's energy drinks, this health-and-vigor beverage gave rise to the familiar expression, "You've got a lot of Moxie." Thompson trademarked his product the same year the loop seal was patented. It remains the official beverage of the state of Maine today.

Painter's company provided bottle manufacturers with the tools they needed to modify their containers for the loop seal disks. An ad for the breakthrough stopper published in an 1886 edition of the

National Bottlers' Gazette summed up the selling points in five words: "Pure, clean, neat, tight, cheap." The loop seal was true to the Painter imperative: Invent something "which everybody needs, better and more cheaply provided than ever before." The indefatigable inventor could have quit while he was ahead. But the all-consuming challenge of the tinkerpreneur beckoned:

Could it be made even better and cheaper?

Never in his wildest dreams or sleepless nights could William Painter have imagined how spectacularly the results of his constant fiddling and retooling would turn out.

Restless Energy and Indomitable Perseverance

Business was booming for the Bottle Seal Company at the turn of the nineteenth century. Barely out of his teens, William's son Orrin was dispatched by his father to buy barrels to hold the seals and to deliver groove-making devices to glass manufacturers around Baltimore. "We first sold them by weight and then by measure, knowing their weight and bulk by the gross," Orrin recalled. Painter's managers reported that it was a large and profitable venture, paying satisfactory dividends to shareholders. The firm's innovations would spell profits and success for countless other businesses, too—and at just the right time for the glass industry.

In 1888, artisan/industrialist Edward Libbey moved his family's New England Glass Works to Toledo, Ohio, where new sources of cheap natural gas beckoned. He was joined by West Virginia–born glassblower-turned-prolific inventor Michael Owens, who would soon invent the revolutionary automatic glass bottle-making machine; found or cofound nine companies with Libbey's support; and successfully file a total of forty-nine patents. By 1900, Painter's company would be supplying stoppers for Owens bottles. The two enterprises dominated their respective markets and forever changed the beverage industry. I couldn't find any records showing that these three remarkable dynamos—Painter, Owens, and Libbey—had ever met. But their separate pursuits of self-interest and mechanical superiority brought them together in the marketplace. These men of progress were bound by the same wide-ranging creativity, commitment to intellectual property rights, and relentless drive of their era's successful tinkerpreneurs.

Naturally, Painter was not satisfied with the loop seal. While on a rare family vacation in Narragansett, Rhode Island, he conceived the idea for a metal, corrugated cap lined with a cork disk that "crowned" a bottle's mouth. Made of pressed tinplate, the original closures featured twenty-one crimpings (later increased to twenty-four). The single-use cap created a gas-tight seal through exterior contact only; the cork kept the liquid separated from the metal. Painter confided in his oldest son that the improvement "would revolutionize all then existing methods of bottling" and swore him to secrecy. In February 1892, after much experimentation, Painter obtained three historic patents for his new bottle-sealing system. The first application disclosed and claimed the novel, throwaway bottle-sealing device; the second added more in-depth information about the sealing disk's composition and locking mechanisms; and the third further detailed the use of cork and other composite disk materials with various protected coatings.

In a culture where everything from diapers to utensils to contact lenses to cameras is disposable, the idea of throwaway bottle caps seems wholly unremarkable. But in the late 1800s, it was as exotic as 3-D printed food or mind-controlled robotic limbs. Painter spelled out the radical notion of intentional disposability: "I have devised metallic sealing-caps embodying certain novel characteristics which render them highly effective and so inexpensive as to warrant throwing them away after a single use thereof, even when forcible displacement, as in opening bottles, has resulted in no material injury to the caps."

The hard-working Painter gave notice that he would soon be filing a new patent for an accompanying bottle opener as part of his system. He also painstakingly explained the evolution of his precedent-setting

manufacturing principles, while outlining the obstacles and chal-
lenges he faced every step of the way:

> So far as my knowledge extends, I am the first to seal bottles
> by means of sealing-disks each compressed into close solid
> contact with the lip of the bottle and maintained in that con-
> dition by means of a flanged metallic sealing-cap, the flange
> of which is bent or crimped into locking contact (while the
> disk is under pressure) with an appropriate annular locking-
> shoulder on the head of the bottle.

Through trial and error, the cap evolved:

> Considerable manual force must be applied for detaching the
> caps from the bottles, and therefore in the early stages of my
> invention the use of loops of some kind or of equivalent holes
> in the tops of the caps was deemed essential, and the caps
> had wide or deep pendent flanges and they contained sealing-
> disks of considerable bulk or thickness. . . . Contingencies led,
> after much devising and experimenting, to the production of
> a cap without a loop or hole in its top, a thinner disk, and con-
> sequently narrower flanges, thus substantially reducing the
> cost of the sealing device.

The transformed cap required a transformed bottle lip and edge, to
which a bottle opener or other sharp tool or utensil could be applied:

> These improved caps having in themselves no special
> provision—such as loops or openings in their tops—for de-
> taching them from bottles led to my further devising a novel
> method of their combination with the bottle, in accordance
> with which the pendent edge of the flange below the bent
> portion is so far projected from the adjacent surface of the

bottle-head as to afford an engaging-shoulder, to which a bottle-opener could be readily applied.

Son Orrin, who served and signed as a witness for his father's groundbreaking patents, drew up a crown logo. The family dubbed Painter's new brainchild the "crown cap." Joseph O'Brien, editor of *Invention* magazine, marveled at the deceptively mundane device. The name was fitting, he noted, as the "metal cap crowns the bottle neck to hold the sealing disk compressed against the bottle mouth; its crimped flange presents an appearance resembling that of a crown; and the invention crowned one of the most troublesome inventive problems with a success which is simply dazzling."

Later in 1892, the inventor and his business associates formed the Crown Cork & Seal Company in Baltimore. The new firm acquired all the domestic manufacturing rights for both the loop seal and crown cap. Business partner Samuel Cook organized the Crown Cork Company Limited to acquire syndicate rights for all countries outside the United States and Canada. European water, soda, and beer bottlers including Apollinaris Company in Germany and Schweppes in London quickly signed up; interest and factories spread to France, Japan, and Brazil.

As promised, Painter delivered his "capped bottle opener" two years after the introduction of the crown cap. Resembling a church key, the handy metal lifter engaged the side of the cap and popped it off with fulcrum power. Here's how Painter described it to the Patent Office:

> My bottle opener essentially embodies a handle, having at one end thereof, a cap centering gage, and also a cap engaging lip, and however these three elements may be formed and combined, the centering gage should also afford a fulcrum . . . so that when the opener is applied to a capped bottle, the gage will . . . enable the handle to serve as a lever for removing the cap from the bottle.

Phew. That's a mouthful for a simple function that seems almost re-
flexive now. But many had tried and failed before Painter showed the
way. On New Year's Eve 1894, Painter and Cook's colleagues in Britain
toasted the firm's founders in verse:

> *Let us hope in the year Ninety-five*
> *Ev'ry country, city, and town*
> *Will abolish both wire and cork*
> *And use the American "Crown."*

By 1897, the company employed some two hundred people directly
and fueled another one thousand jobs in the related production of
rubber, cork, tin, and other materials. At the end of that fiscal year,
Crown Cork & Seal had sold more than a whopping 280 million combined crown caps and loop seals. That's close to a million pieces for
every actual working day in the year. The next year, Painter introduced
a foot-powered machine for filling bottles with syrup and sealing them
with the crown cap. The cast-iron contraption replaced the old, time-
consuming method that involved separate processes for adding syrup
to the bottom of a bottle, then moving the bottle to another station for
adding carbonated water, and then shifting the bottle to yet another
machine for capping.

An appreciative John T. Hawkins, who worked for Painter as a
leading machinist, wrote in the *Baltimore Journal of Commerce* that his
boss was the "epitome of restless energy and indomitable perseverance" whose genius "largely consists in taking infinite pains." His
mind was never at rest. Discouragement, to Painter, was an "unknown
sensation." While some accounts describe the crown cap as an imme-
diate success, it took considerable outreach, education, skill, and re-
inforcement to bring about Painter's revolution. Some bottlers clung
to old methods and equipment. Bottles needed to be redesigned with
a new recessed neck tip on which the crown cap gripped. As "proof
of concept," to borrow modern start-up language, Painter convinced

a Baltimore brewer to send a cargo of crown-capped beer to South America and bring it back. After forty days, the ship and the cargo returned. Crown Cork & Seal threw a welcome back party and invited Charm City reporters to witness the taste tests. It was a frothy success.

To spread the word, Crown Cork & Seal needed a dedicated sales force and marketing team that shared the inventor's tireless spirit. He wisely surrounded himself with both mechanical movers and entrepreneurial shakers. One of the charismatic men he recruited would go on to establish his own multibillion-dollar empire. His name is known the world over: Gillette.

Just as King Gillette's disposable razor business was taking off, William Painter fell deathly ill. He passed away in July 1906 at Johns Hopkins University in his beloved Baltimore. Painter's last words came from John 14:6: "I am the way, I am the truth, I am the life." He was a godly, humble man who gave it his all. Though none of his own children followed in his entrepreneurial footsteps, son Orrin assisted Crown Cork & Seal in its nascent days as an illustrator and marketer. He also paid lasting tribute to his father in vivid family memoirs. Painter's spirit lived on in a generation of countless employees, most prominently King Gillette, who benefited from his wise counsel and warm mentorship.

Most important for the future of Painter's company, his success attracted another boundary-pushing tinkerpreneur with the vision and drive to bring Crown Cork & Seal into modernity.

An Effervescent Legacy

The singular obsession of early-twentieth-century businessman Charles McManus was also a decades-long obsession of one of America's most entrepreneurial founding fathers, Thomas Jefferson. Their shared passion? Cork! For Jefferson, it was a matter of both intense personal interest and national pride. He was a fanatical wine connoisseur who had toured European vineyards and evangelized his countrymen about the superiority of fine wines. He practiced what he preached: At Monticello, Jefferson built two of his own vineyards. The nation's "first viticulturalist" not only conducted numerous grape-cultivating experiments, he also planted several cork oak trees and tried to produce his own corks.

Jefferson didn't have much luck at cork cultivation at Monticello. But nearly a century later, cork trees took root in Virginia, Maryland, and South Carolina.

The bulk of the nation's cork supply, however, continued to be imported from abroad. In addition to wine and beverage bottle closures, American manufacturers used cork for insulation, gaskets, automotive parts, shoes, and flotation devices. Demand was plentiful. William Painter's first generation of crown caps alone used thin, compressed layers of natural cork to produce millions of bottle toppers. His patents proposed the use of other composite materials. Could his crown-cap liners be made even *more* efficiently?

Painter may not have lived to find out the answer, but Crown Cork & Seal did.

In a small New York factory, husband and wife Charles and Eva McManus worked together to devise a new method for processing cork. They manufactured an apparatus for making composition cork sheets. The McManus family formed the New Process Cork Company and patented a synthetic cork product dubbed "Nepro." These particle cork liners could be made even thinner than current natural cork ones. Nepro saved money by allowing crown caps to be made shallower and with less tin metal. In good times and bad, every penny counted.

After William Painter's death in 1906, one of his sons-in-law took over the business and almost ran it into the ground. Painter's original crown cap patents expired in 1911; Prohibition nearly destroyed the bottling industry. Crown Cork & Seal wisely shifted its manufacturing focus away from beer to soft drinks, but the company needed a leader. McManus, a Baltimore native with a mission, moved back home from

New York. He bought shares in Crown Cork, merged it with New Process Cork Company, and injected new energy into the fizzy biz.

After the New Process/Crown Cork merger, McManus continued to invent and patent dozens of improvements in cork and bottle-cap manufacturing. He bought up cork companies on both coasts and built export facilities in Europe and North Africa. To weather the Great Depression, Crown Cork diversified to include cork for car mats; tin cans for coffee, tea, biscuits, and pharmaceuticals; Mason jar caps; and post-Prohibition beer cans. By 1937, the company was producing more than 103 million bottle tops a day. The firm also manufactured metal parts for ammunition, antiaircraft guns, fighter plane fairings, and an award-winning gas mask canister.

During World War II, America's dependency on foreign cork became a national security issue. Thomas Jefferson's zeal for planting cork oak trees domestically looked all the more prescient. The nation's military used cork—60 percent of it imported from abroad—to make washers, oil seals, insulation for planes and rockets, and other critical components. Several suspicious fires in Baltimore and New York just before and then during the war raised the ominous specter of sabotage. Spurred by current events and commercial concerns, Crown Cork & Seal spearheaded the patriotic McManus Cork Oak Project to plant cork seedlings across America and "to add to the natural resources of our country and to provide in the United States a source for at least a part of the nation's cork requirement." About a dozen states joined the effort, but McManus died of a heart attack in the summer of 1946, before the project bore any real fruit. Or rather, cork.

McManus successfully consolidated Crown's operations and boosted sales to $11 million. His able and dedicated sons, Charles Jr. and Walter, took over the company after his death. Another practical-minded Crown Cork executive, blacksmith's son John Connelly, helmed the company from the transformative 1960s through the 1980s. He slashed unprofitable lines of business, kept overhead low, and kept the company out of debt. Meanwhile, Crown Cork pioneered the aerosol can, adopted pull-tab pop tops, and expanded into household markets. Composite cork gave way to polyvinyl chloride. Foreign markets for the company's packaging solutions boomed.

In 1992, Crown Cork & Seal celebrated its centennial anniversary. Two years later, the American Society of Mechanical Engineers designated William Painter's crown cap and crown soda machine "international historic mechanical engineering landmarks." The two inventions were "the foundation of today's vast bottling industry," the professional group declared. A few of the original crown soda machines still exist today and can be found at the company's Baltimore machinery division offices. There, Painter's successors now manufacture high-speed stainless-steel bottle- and can-filling machines that can fill two thousand cans or twelve hundred bottles per minute. The company is now an astonishing $9 billion global packaging empire. Crown manufactures one out of every five beverage containers in the world, and one out of every three food cans across North America and Europe.

Patient. Resourceful. Nurturing. Meticulous. William Painter absorbed his first entrepreneurial lessons as a boy harvesting asparagus seeds. By nature, he tinkered tirelessly and bequeathed a legacy of constant innovation to his company's successors. And from his early encounter with the intellectual property thief who stole his leather-softening device, he learned to vigilantly protect his patent rights. His life was a "great lesson in rational achievement," Crown Cork's London manager William A. Lewis wrote in tribute in 1901. "Mr. Painter never began any invention that he didn't finish, never devised anything that wasn't of practical use, and never created any appliance but has been of benefit to his race and has reflected pecuniary advantages to himself."

Painter's contemporaries in business, engineering, and the law fully appreciated what so many take for granted today. As a 1901 court decision upholding Painter's patent rights concluded: "The protection and hope of profit held out by our patent laws inspires that stimulating energy which leads to experiment, invention, and all the resulting benefits. A refusal of that protection in a proper case will deaden and destroy it." The ruling recognized the vital contributions not just of William Painter, but of all humble engineers and mechanics toiling away quietly in their garages and workshops in pursuit of the faster, cheaper, and ever better:

> Painter's invention is not one of those great epoch-marking discoveries like that of printing or the steam-engine or the electric telegraph, which opened to their inventors the portals of the Pantheon of the immortals. For such as these the love of fame and the glory of being benefactors of human kind served alike as motive and reward; but to the patient laborer in the workshop and factory the incentive of fame and glory is absent.
>
> For the stimulus of the rewards offered by our patent laws is needed to encourage by the hope of profit that zealous eagerness to improve processes, to remedy defects in machinery, to invent new methods and appliances for saving labor and cheapening production in the numberless articles that are in daily use. It is this stimulus that has made the American mechanic the most alert, observant, and studious of any in the world, and it is the indefinite multiplication of these small inventions and improvements that has wrought an industrial revolution and brought his country to the forefront of the world's commerce.

Spectacular feats of invention such as the telegraph or airplane may garner the greatest fame and biggest headlines. But it's the innumerable and cumulative multitude of modest, profit-driven undertakings that drive an Age of Progress. One man's successful innovation begets more successful innovation. The pioneer tinkerpreneur's economical and effective design inspired and unleashed an entire new industry of bottle opener manufacturers, who added everything from corkscrews and folding knives to can openers and "Prest-O-Lite" valve openers to ornate handles and wall mounts. One hundred twenty years later, in 2012, a group of young men named their company—which manufactures titanium sunglasses with bottle openers built into the sides—after William Painter. They explained that Painter inspired them to be "passionate about living life with a creative twist and creating products that challenge conventional thought."

The life and legacy of William Painter show:

From tiny bottle caps, mighty economies and myriad other businesses grow.

6.

"KEEP LOOKING":

How Painter's Razor-Sharp Genius Inspired King Gillette

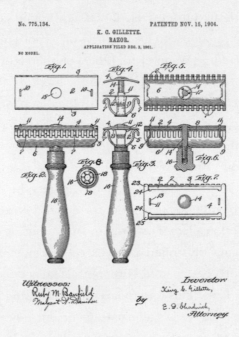

Long before King Camp Gillette met bottle cap titan William Painter, inventing was in his blood.

He came from a family of creative dynamos. Mother Fanny Lemira Gillette authored and published the famous *White House Cookbook* in 1887, which sold millions of copies and remains in print today. Father George Wolcott Gillette was a writer, small newspaper editor, consummate tinkerer, and patent agent in Chicago. He manufactured "japanned tinware" and promoted a shingle-making machine. In 1873, the elder Gillette copatented a tool for drilling openings into the staves or heads of barrels to retrieve their liquid contents. King's brothers, George H. and Mott, also inherited the inventing bug.

Like William Painter, the Gillette boys worked with their hands from an early age. "My impulse to think and invent was a natural one," Gillette wrote in his memoirs. His parents inculcated self-sufficiency and persistence in all of their children. After the devastating Chicago fire of 1871, George W. and Fanny moved with their younger children to New York to start anew. King remained in the Windy City to take work in the hardware business. He found a calling in sales, but continued to tinker on the side with his brothers on various improvements to barrels. While George W. never hit it big commercially with his tools, he urged King to keep at it: "Just invent something that the people need, and you'll make yourself wealthy for life. Keep looking. You'll hit upon something that a lot of people want."

In his twenties and thirties, Gillette wandered—both physically and intellectually. He rode the rails peddling tools. He sailed to London to sell soap. He patented a few gadgets, he confessed, that "made money for others, but seldom for myself." Next, he published a bizarre manifesto called "The Human Drift" touting utopian socialism. The tome came illustrated with a creepy drawing of giant communal towers for workers who would live in his idealized metropolis, to be built at Niagara Falls. This was apparently in tribute to George Westinghouse and Nikola Tesla's alternating-current power plant, under construction at the time. Fortunately for Gillette, not to mention the fate of hairy men everywhere, the oddball book flopped. Marriage and a child on the way kept the would-be philosopher grounded. His career as a traveling salesman put food on the table. He was good at it and his reputation grew.

In 1891, William Painter invited King Gillette to join the Baltimore Bottle Seal Company and soon after, Crown Cork & Seal, as a traveling sales rep in New York and New England. "It was at [Painter's] solicitation that I joined the company," Gillette recalled fondly. Given their mutual passion for invention, a deep friendship was inevitable. Painter welcomed Gillette into his home for "intimate talks on inventions." He freely dispensed business advice to Gillette as he had done with countless other aspiring tinkerpreneurs pursuing the American Dream. Gillette soaked up Painter's wisdom and fully understood the business significance of his bottle cap innovations. He appreciated the miracle of the mundane.

"Mr. Painter was a very interesting talker when interested in his subject and thoroughly conversant with all the details and possibilities of his own inventions," Gillette reflected, "which though little in themselves seemed without boundary to their possibilities when one realizes their unlimited fields of applications."

As Gillette told it in his own company's history, Painter steered him toward the practical and the disposable. The razor-sharp businessman gave Gillette the consumer-driven focus he had been lacking. "[Y]ou are always thinking and inventing something," Painter told Gillette. But he had never sustained a viable business. Painter advised Gillette: "Why don't you try to think of something like a crown cork, which, once used, is thrown away, and the customer keeps coming back for more—and with every additional customer you get, you are building a foundation for profit?"

Those words, Gillette said, "stuck to me like a burr." When Gillette doubted that he could come up with anything beyond the "corks, pins, and needles" that had already been conceived, Painter persisted: "You don't know. It is not probable that you ever will find anything that is like the Crown Cork, but it won't do any harm to think about it."

Gillette's famed epiphany that led to the creation of the ubiquitous safety razor struck in 1895 as he stood in front of his bathroom mirror: "[W]hen I started to shave, I found my razor dull, and it was not only dull, it was beyond the point of stropping and it needed honing, for which it must be taken to a barber or a cutler."

At age forty, his long-sought "Aha!" moment had arrived.

"As I stood there with the razor in my hand," Gillette recalled, "my eyes resting on it lightly as a bird settling down on its nest—the Gillette razor was born." He "knew practically nothing about steel." His idea "was looked upon as a joke by all my friends." Experts told him that putting an edge on sheet steel for shaving couldn't be done. His own father and brothers, preoccupied with their own new endeavor manufacturing horse clippers, blew him off.

But as William Painter had counseled family, friends, and colleagues: "The only way to do a thing is to do it." Grappling with the mental weight of his own business and the physical ravages of overwork, Painter was not in a position to become invested or involved in Gillette's enterprise. But in addition to providing inspiration and intellectual fuel to Gillette, he supplied as much moral support as he could. After viewing a model razor Gillette showed him, Painter urged: "[I]t looks like a real invention with great possibilities. I am sorry I cannot join you in its development, but my health will not permit it. But whatever you do, don't let it get away from you."

Gillette continued to work for Crown Cork & Seal while he conducted experiments, sought financial support, and solicited technical help in perfecting his blades. He ignored the mockers and detractors. During his crown-cap business trips, he met clients who referred him to MIT-trained chemist and mechanical genius William Nickerson.

Nickerson had more than one hundred patents to his name. "He is an inventor by nature," a scientific journal wrote, and "his genius consistently running in the direction of producing something new and better in the industrial arts." Unfortunately, he had suffered several business setbacks in leather tanning, gold-mining, elevator safety device manufacturing, lightbulb manufacturing, and food-weighing machinery. At first, he turned Gillette down. But innate stubbornness served them both well. "I was a dreamer who believed in the 'gold at the foot of the rainbow' promise, and continued in the path where wise ones fear to tread, and that is the reason, the only reason, why there is a Gillette razor today," Gillette reflected.

Once Nickerson became convinced the idea was viable, he toiled obsessively on the hardening and sharpening machines that would turn ribbon-thin steel into disposable blades. In September 1901, the engineer reported to company representatives that after giving the idea much thought, "I am confident that I have grasped the situation and can guarantee, as far as such a thing can be guaranteed, a successful outcome." The first blades he produced were "so crooked and crumpled as to be wholly useless." While he perfected the blade-making process, his machinists worked on the blade holder and handle. Nickerson's employees went for weeks without pay as they figured out how to automate the machinery for putting edges on the hardened blades.

Nickerson also grappled with how to prevent the blades from buckling under the heat-intensive steel-making process. The Carrier Corporation helped solve a related, nettlesome manufacturing problem: rusting. The company provided a refrigeration system to remove moisture from compressed air used in its pneumatic machinery.

Meanwhile, Gillette scrounged up investors and incorporated the safety razor company bearing his name. He and his representatives recruited twenty investors to pitch in $250 each for five hundred shares of the company per investor. Their lawyer ensured that the patent application would be an "airtight instrument against infringers." Just as the business was coming together, Gillette was sent by his employer, his mentor William Painter's Crown Cork & Seal, to work in London. He went reluctantly, but was able to parlay the stint into overseas outreach and market research for his safety razor.

In 1904, Gillette received his breakthrough patent. Five years later, thanks to an aggressive marketing and promotional campaign that put his face on every package, the once-struggling bottle cap salesman was a worldwide, household name. Nickerson continued to innovate, inventing an automatic blade-honing machine a decade later that dramatically improved the company's manufacturing efficiency and productivity.

The next year, Gillette rolled out the first-ever razor designed and marketed specifically for women. It was called the "Milady Decolette Gillette." Just as the Scott brothers of toilet paper fame had to tiptoe around issues of hygiene at the tail end of the Victorian era, Gillette salesmen also bowed to cultural norms of the time. "Do not use the term 'shaving' as applied to this operation," managers instructed. "Smoothing" was the euphemism of choice. A 1915 newspaper advertisement proclaimed that the "sleeveless evening gown" had made "insistent demand for a smooth skin." The fourteen-karat gold-plated razor came encased in a "velvet and satin-lined French ivory case" of "dainty size." The famous Gillette Blue Blade—double-edged, rust-proof, oxidized, and dipped in a signature blue lacquer—entered the market in 1932.

Sadly, Gillette didn't live to see the Blue Blade reach the market. After a long battle with intestinal disease, he died in his sleep at a ranch he had built for himself and his family in Southern California in 1932. Though plagued by Depression-era financial troubles at the end of his life, his Fortune 500 company, which was acquired by Procter & Gamble in 2005, now employs nearly thirty thousand, with sales topping $10 billion.

Despite his strange dabbling in utopian literature, Gillette was in practice a fierce capitalist who eloquently embraced the intellectual property rights of inventors. In a memo to his patent lawyers on one of countless patent infringement cases they pursued in defense of Gillette's work, he wrote:

> It is often true that invention involves underlying principles, purposes and questions of utility which are lost sight on in mere technical descriptions. To say that the Gillette blade only differs from other razors or blades in degree does not in any way describe the invention involved, or the principles or purposes that are inherent within it. . . . It is manifestly true that no one—previous to the Gillette invention—had conceived the idea of producing a blade . . . that would be so cheap to manufacture that its cost to the consumer would permit of its being discarded when dull.

Gillette further pointed out that before he came along, untold numbers of men did not shave themselves because they lacked the mechanical skill and had no alternative but to go to the barber, which cost precious time and money.

> [T]he question of invention does not alone rest upon the fact that hundreds of thousands are now able to shave themselves who could not before, and do so without involving the question of skill in keeping their razor in condition, but it rests on its use by millions of men who have discarded other old style razors because the Gillette has reduced the art of shaving to such a cheap and simple process.

Patent rights are as important for the inventors of Big Things, such as electricity or the airplane, as they are for the inventors of small things, such as bottle caps or razors.

The serendipitous introductions of Painter to Gillette and Gillette to Nickerson—all lifelong tinkerers who turned their dreams into practical realities—underscore the importance of expanding your creative orbit. You never know who might be of help unless you expose as many people as possible to your ideas, failures, and aspirations for success. Self-sufficiency never means self-containment.

Successful tinkerpreneurs surround themselves with passionate investors, talented engineers, legal eagles, tireless marketers, and gifted salespeople. These concentric circles of creativity not only help secure success, but also ensure its expansion.

7.

SEEING DOLLARS IN THE DIRT:
The Wisdom of Charles E. Hires

Courtesy of the Lower Merion Historical Society

If you grew up in or around Philadelphia, as I did, "Hires" is as familiar a soft drink name brand as Coca-Cola or 7-Up. Nothing hit the spot better on a steamy summer's day by the Jersey shore than an overflowing mug of chilled Hires root beer and vanilla bean ice cream. Ahhhhh!

Charles Elmer Hires, a southern New Jersey farmer's son, got his start at age twelve as a "drugstore boy." His family was fairly well-off, but Hires insisted on independence: "I was not interested in farming and wanted to make my own way." Training in a quaint country pharmacy, he earned his twelve-dollar-a-week pay by sweeping floors, cleaning out spittoons, polishing mirrors, cleaning mortars, and delivering medicines. He absorbed practical knowledge of chemicals and compounds while fulfilling his duties. After serving as a ten-dollar-a-week apprentice for four years, he became a clerk at a Philadelphia city drug store. Though he never went to college, he attended open lectures and night classes at the Philadelphia College of Pharmacy, learned the ropes of operating a small business, and saved up his earnings.

When Hires had amassed $400, he struck out on his own. He established an independent retail pharmacy, sleeping in a room above the storefront and taking his meals at a boarding home next door. He stretched every dollar to cover both fixtures and stock. Local historians differ on what exactly inspired Hires to pursue the woodsy, licorice-sarsaparilla-vanilla concoction. One legend has it that Hires borrowed his root tea recipe from a hostess he met at a farm while on his honeymoon with his new wife. Another version claims he teamed up with Reverend Dr. Russell Conwell, the founder of Temple University, to market a temperance-friendly drink that would appeal to blue-collar workers (thus the marketing name change from "root tea" to "root beer").

Before Charles Hires hit it big in the beverage business, though, he first had to get his hands dirty.

Really dirty.

Hires shared the story of his earthy beginnings in business in an October 1913 essay, "Seeing Opportunities," for the *American Druggist and Pharmaceutical Record*. His entrepreneurial wisdom is timeless and his work ethic is at the foundation of every successful American Dream. As the pharmacy journal's editor wrote in his preface to Hires's reflections, the beverage creator's philosophy of success was rooted in a firm belief "that business life is full of opportunities for those who are shrewd enough to see them and energetic enough to grasp them." He wanted to inspire the next generation of young American capitalists to open their eyes to the limitless, profit-making possibilities all around them.

For Hires, the road to prosperity began with a mundane hole in the ground.

"I Longed for Greater Things to Do"

With the savings he earned as a teenager, Hires bought a small lot of land in what is now Center City Philadelphia. With the help of a carpenter, he built with his own hands an eighteen-by-sixty-foot store at Sixth and Spruce Streets. "The interior of the store was fitted up in plain wood," Hires recalled, "enameled white with a gold stripe around the border and paneling of the closets, cases, and shelving." He built his counters and soda fountain out of Tennessee marble—a popular, pinkish gray limestone from the quarries of Knoxville. The soda fountain was topped with a Lippincott gas light fixture, which Hires later called "pretentious" for its time, "but which I imagine would not find room in a second or third class store of today."

When business was slow at the pharmacy, Hires would grow restless. "I have always been active and energetic," he confessed, "and the time spent behind the prescription counter, especially in the dull part of the day, often became irksome and I longed for greater things to do." Outside, the neighborhood was bustling with construction. It was 1869 and Philadelphia boomed with immigrants, railroads, and streetcars. Laundries, dry goods, and other retail shops rose near churches, hospitals, medical publishing firms, tanneries, libraries, and homes.

"One day while walking out on Spruce Street, I noticed a cellar being dug," Hires reminisced. Workers used hand picks, horse-drawn scrapers, graders, and steam-powered shovels. "From this excavation," he said, "I noticed a lead colored claylike substance which attracted my attention, as it seemed almost of the consistence of putty. I picked

some of it up and took it back to the store and after drying it and examining it I found it was fuller's earth or potter's clay."

Fuller's Earth

Many thousands of passers-by had walked past the chaotic construction site, three blocks from Hires's store, in apathy or aggravation. It
was loud, grimy, dusty, and dangerous. But Charles Hires paused when
a shovelful of the dirt sullied his shoes. He saw what others did not or
could not see.

And then he seized the moment.

"I returned to the place the next day and saw the contractor and
asked him if I could have some of this clay." The builder was glad to be
rid of the nuisance and to off-load the dirt on someone much closer
to the construction site than the company's usual dumping grounds.
"I had him bring it to my place, and after boarding up a passage way
along the side of my cellar, I filled the entire balance of the cellar, up
to the ceiling, with this clay."

Fuller's earth is a naturally occurring clay found across the United
States. In Philadelphia, the brick clay was deposited in the region
at the end of the last glacial period. It is highly absorbent and has
been used since ancient times for cloth laundering or "fulling" (to
soak up heavy oil and grease spots from soiled wool, flannel, or other
textiles). The clay was also handy as a component in pharmaceuticals
(to remedy food poisoning and stop hemorrhaging) and in various
household cleaning chores. Manufacturers also used the clay to bleach
edible oils and decolorize petroleum used in medicinal products (such
as Vaseline oils).

Now that Hires had a cellar overflowing with the absorbent dirt,
what was he going to do with it? "It occurred to me that I might put
up potter's clay in convenient-sized cakes that would be handy to retail
and more convenient for people to use," he explained, "as at that time

potter's clay was sold in a loose way in broken lumps and powder which caused a great deal of dirt and dust in handling."

Once again, Hires turned to ordinary objects in his daily life taken for granted by others. He recalled seeing his female neighbors at the boarding home next door using "an iron ring on which to stand their irons on ironing day." He repurposed the cast-iron rings to cut out and mold his clay disks—only after obtaining the ladies' consent, of course, and only after "being charged very particularly to take care of them and return them in good order."

Hires wet the clay, turned it into a paste, and transformed the piles of dirt into round cakes "about one inch thick and about three inches in diameter." He set them out on a board to dry in the sun. "I was very much elated over my project and the possibilities of selling quantities of it," he recounted with pride. He enlisted a metal-working friend to construct a crude stencil with die-cut lead letters spelling out "HIRES' REFINED FULLER'S EARTH." The imprints didn't hold on the cakes, so he crafted a new stencil block out of cast iron.

Hires, an assistant, and a drugstore boy (serving the role Hires had played himself a decade ago) made the little clay cakes in their spare time at the pharmacy. They soon had several gross units (a dozen dozen or 144), and Hires filled up a commercial barrel, which held about ten gross. He was ready to put the dirt pies out for sale.

Now came the marketing campaign.

The promotion-savvy entrepreneur wrapped a few of the cakes in tissue paper. He approached a friend in the wholesale drug market, who embraced the product heartily "because it saved a great deal of weighing out and dirty work that the old method of dispensing Fuller's earth necessitated." He arranged to sell the dirt pies at $3.50 per gross to wholesalers, who turned around and sold them for thirty-five or forty cents a dozen. Multiple orders of between three and twenty-five barrels per call came in as word spread. Every wholesale druggist in town wanted in. One of his biggest clients, Smith, Kline & Co., founded in Philadelphia in 1830 as an apothecary and later to become one of the world's dominant pharmaceutical conglomerates (now GlaxoSmithKline).

Hires arranged to be paid in trade by his wholesale drug clients. "From these sales I was better able to stock my store, and after selling this supply of clay, I renewed it several times from cellar excavations, because I found that nearly all Philadelphia is underlaid with a strata of three or four feet of potter's clay." Hires took his product to New York and met similar success. Eventually, competitors caught on and contractors "stopped giving away fuller's earth to every Tom, Dick or Harry who came along." But Hires reaped the benefits of being first and happily turned to his next venture. The side business made $5,000, which provided the starting capital for the root beer project that would bring him worldwide fame and fortune.

"Merit Will Win"

"It is one thing to design and conceive a good article," Hires counseled, "and another to successfully introduce it to humanity." He famously quipped that "doing business without advertising is like winking at a girl in the dark: you know what you are doing, but nobody else does." Just as he had aggressively branded and marketed his clay cakes, Hires set about perfecting and publicizing the root beer concoction he had been blending at his pharmacy since 1870. He used his fuller's earth profits to fund his research and development over the next five years.

A childhood friend, rags-to-riches publisher George W. Childs, loved Hires's root beer so much he carried free promotional ads for the product in his newspaper, the *Philadelphia Public Ledger*. Like Hires, Childs had started out as a young clerk in his industry at the age of twelve and worked his way up through unrelenting ambition and infectious character. They were kindred spirits.

"Mr. Hires, why don't you advertise that root beer extract of yours? It is good stuff," Childs challenged him.

When Hires told his pal he had no budget for advertising, Childs cooked up a "sweet" deal.

"I'll tell you what to do," he offered. "You advertise in the *Ledger*, beginning right away, and I'll tell the bookkeeper not to send you any bills unless you ask for them."

The campaign caught fire. Hires quickly paid off his debt to Childs. He pioneered aggressive advertising on streetcars, benches, and barn signs, and in color advertising cards, lithographic postcards, magazines, and full-page, large-circulation city daily newspapers.

The legendary American soda debuted at the 1876 Centennial Exhibition in Philly, along with the Westinghouse air brake, Libbey cut glass, a Roebling cable prototype to be used in the Brooklyn Bridge, the Otis steam elevator, Alexander Graham Bell's telephone, Heinz ketchup, the Statue of Liberty's arm and torch, and the massive Corliss steam engine. Nine million people attended the world's fair, including future Crown Cork & Seal founder William Painter and his young son. Hires gave away free samples of his root beer to thirsty attendees. Once he reeled them in, he offered twenty-five-cent packets of his dry herb mix or tiny bottles of condensed extract. The beloved root-and-berry-derived drink is still sold today online and at select retail stores by Dr Pepper Snapple Group.

Thirteen years after he launched his soda company, the drugstore entrepreneur itemized not only the blood, sweat, advertising dollars, and promotional sense that went into selling his products, but also the wider benefits reaped to other private businesses and to Uncle Sam's coffers:

> *Over fifty thousand pounds* of barks, roots, berries, and flowers went into the composition of Hires Root Beer Extract made last year.
>
> *Two hundred thousand* pretty little looking glasses advertising the Extract were given away last year.
>
> *Four million* beautiful picture cards, printed in ten colors,

gladdened as many persons, brightening their homes and lives, and carrying messages of the Extract, last year. . . .

Twenty five thousand dollars were paid out to printing-houses last year. . . .

A good many thousand daily and weekly newspapers, periodicals, and journals each year contain the advertisements of Hires' Root Beer[; and]

Uncle Sam derive[d] a yearly revenue of *over six thousand dollars* paid by the Charles E. Hires Company as postage on mailing circulars and similar matter.

Even as Hires turned his $5,000 dirt-born investment into $5 million in root beer revenue, he relentlessly pursued myriad "sideline businesses." These inspired endeavors boosted his financial security, employed more workers, generated more tax revenue, and provided goods and services that consumers wanted. In addition to the glass works and clay cakes, Hires founded a Cuban sugar plantation, a condensed milk business (which he later sold to the Nestlé Company), a flavoring extract enterprise, and corporate partnerships with both U.S. and foreign potteries to produce stoneware mugs and bottles. He expanded beverage sales to London, Copenhagen, Canada, and Australia.

Everywhere he looked, starting with that shovelful of clay at his feet on Spruce Street, Charles Hires saw an opening for enterprise. Fortune didn't find him. *He* created a fortune from chance encounter after chance encounter. He believed firmly in the free market and in the ability of consumers to discern quality and integrity. His personal and business motto was simply: "Merit will win."

Reflecting on his own career road of risks, failures, and ultimate triumphs, Hires rejected tired excuses and lamentations from naysayers and capitalism-bashers:

I have often thought when I have heard of the difficulties of a young man in getting along, that surely the reason for their not getting along is because of their lack of initiative or the lack of making or seizing opportunities when they come, because *I think a business life is continually full of opportunities if one can grasp and utilize them.* [Emphasis added.]

To grasp opportunities, one must see them first. And therein lies the lesson Charles Hires wanted so passionately to get across in his proud retelling of how he came to make clay cakes:

Sometimes, seekers of success, the pay dirt is right in front of you.

This anonymous and thoroughly fitting poem ran alongside the 1913 *American Druggist* profile of Charles Hires.

SERVE

Strike while the iron is heated
Pause and the iron's cold.
If you strike too late on a hardened plate,
The weld will never hold.
Seek, and success will follow;
Wait, and it passes by.
Be quick to grasp, then hold it fast
And trust for a better try.
Serve, and the world serves with you;
Loaf, and you loaf alone.
This strenuous world is a continuous whirl—
It offers no room for the drone.
Life is an undertaking;
Death is a silent thought.
So let life's light illumine the night
With the service you have wrought.

PART III

BFFs: DYNAMIC DUOS
OF AMERICAN BUSINESS

But just buckle in with a bit of a grin,
Just take off your coat and go to it;
Just start in to sing as you tackle the thing
That "cannot be done," and you'll do it.
—FROM MICHAEL OWENS'S FAVORITE POEM, "IT COULDN'T BE DONE"

8.

DEATH-DEFYING MAVERICKS OF GLASS:

Edward Libbey and Michael Owens

Courtesy of Owens-Illinois Glass Company Collection, Ward M. Canaday Center, University of Toledo

Look out your window. Take a sip of cool water out of a clear tumbler. Open up a jar of fresh pickles. Scrape the ice off your car windshield. Swipe your finger across an iPhone screen. Put on your bifocals. Check yourself in the mirror. You're surrounded by glass, but do you know what it took to bring this ubiquitous resource into our daily lives?

The three-thousand-year-old story of glass-making is an epic tale of intrigue, sabotage, espionage, murder, poison, prison, bankruptcy, tyranny, and revolution. For centuries, glassblowers were sworn to secrecy. The masters of fire and sand guarded their recipe books like highly classified nuclear codes. In the thirteenth century, zealous Venetian rulers went so far as to imprison glassblowers and their families on the island of Murano. Those who attempted escape risked criminal prosecution and state execution. At the turn of the twentieth century, artisan guilds and glass workers' unions used their muscle to stifle competition.

Regressive vigilantes jealously destroyed innovative technology to protect their jobs and halt manufacturing advances. They were a real pain in the . . . glass.

So, how did the champions of progress defeat the defeatists? West Virginia coal miner's son Michael Owens and New England industrialist's son Edward Libbey played a critical role in modernizing glass manufacturing that is little known and rarely celebrated by anyone outside of their industry peers, hometown elders, and collectors. Owens and Libbey transformed the glass-making process from ancient hand-blown craft to full-blown machine automation. Together, they created or fueled more than two hundred companies, many of which continue to thrive and innovate today.

Owens the inveterate tinkerer and Libbey the consummate entrepreneur defied the monkeywrenchers, risking their fortunes and their lives. They endured economic crises, strikes, protracted patent battles, and myriad technical obstacles. Their extraordinary partnership yielded breakthroughs in lightbulb and kerosene lamp production, bottle-making, standardization of pharmaceutical packaging, mass-manufacture of flat glass and auto glass, and the invention of fiberglass. Once a luxury item for elites only, elegant glass tableware was brought to the masses by Owens and Libbey. They helped make the manufacturing process safer and eliminated the industry's reliance on child labor. Owens's mechanical genius paved the way for

lower production costs, higher output, and unprecedented uniformity
of product quality and size.

To fully appreciate this pair's enduring industrial successes forged
in America's heartland, we begin this journey of glass in the wild and
treacherous empire of ancient Rome.

The Legend of *Vitrum Flexile*

Take the Kardashians, add the Sopranos, dress them all up in togas
and sandals, and behold: You've entered the wacky world of Roman
emperor Tiberius Caesar. His mother, Livia, was an insatiable social
climber. His aristocrat father, Tiberius Claudius Nero, fled Rome with
Mark Antony after the assassination of Julius Caesar. After returning
home from exile, lascivious Livia caught the attention of ambitious
Octavian. Pregnant with her second child, she dumped her hapless
hubby and shacked up with Octavian (later Augustus, the first emperor of Rome).

During the reign of Tiberius Caesar, unsurprisingly, the troubled
emperor descended into depression, sexual debauchery, and vengeance. Tiberius was a total sleazebag. He dragged more than fifty of
his enemies into court for phony treason trials and executed dozens.
Ever-scheming Livia, the Roman Mom from Hell, is rumored to have
poisoned several of Tiberius's rivals, including Germanicus, two of Augustus's grandsons, and perhaps even Augustus himself.

In short: Tiberius Caesar and his insane family seized power, held
it, and abused it by any means necessary. Which brings us to the legend
of *vitrum flexile*.

The very first glass-makers came from ancient Egypt, Syria, and
Palestine, but Roman conquerors and traders get the credit for adopt-
ing, adapting, and spreading early glass technology across Western
Europe and the Mediterranean. "Glass was present in nearly every

aspect of daily life," a Roman art history specialist noted, "from a lady's morning toilette to a merchant's afternoon business dealings to the evening *cena*, or dinner."

Under corrupt Tiberius Caesar's reign, according to separate accounts by ancient historians Pliny, Petronius, and Dio Cassius, a guileless glassmaker happened to visit the emperor's palace. The craftsman brought with him a brilliant transparent vessel used for pouring libations to the gods. It may have looked like the same ritual offering vases found in typical Roman households. But this was no ordinary tableware. The gift was made of flexible glass (*vitrum flexile*), which the inventor proudly demonstrated by hurling the unbreakable object to the floor. The impact left nothing more than a small dent, which the emperor's guest miraculously repaired with a hammer (*matriolum*) he had brought along for the sales pitch.

As legend has it, Tiberius asked the glassmaker if anyone else had been informed of his breakthrough technology. He excitedly told the truth: Tiberius had been the first to learn of it. But instead of greeting the revelation with glee and offering a reward, the tyrant swiftly ordered his guards to drag the flexible glass creator away and chop off his head. If the invention were known, Tiberius feared, "gold would become as cheap as mud."

Then, as now, disruptive innovation posed a fundamental threat to the economic status quo of the ruling class. Tiberius feared that the advent of *vitrum flexile* would undermine the value of Rome's precious metals. This murderous dictator and his central planners cared more about protecting workers in the existing copper, silver, and gold industries than in pioneering anything new. They simply could not imagine how many more jobs, industries, and riches might result from pursuing the untried and untested. Competition and creativity were public menaces. Violent suppression, stasis, and government coercion were the cures.

The Captive Glass Masters of Murano

Lush, tranquil, and unearthly, the sparkling island chain of Murano in northern Italy hardly seems like jail. But in the thirteenth century, the Great Council of Venice (*Maggior Consiglio*) turned the marshy lagoon outpost into a de facto detention facility—a veritable Gitmo on the Mediterranean. The powerful Venetian council had been clamping down for decades on lucrative, luxury-glass artisans in order to create a tightly run government monopoly. In 1275, the rule-making body issued an edict banning exportation of sand or any other glass-making ingredient. Next, the politicians ordered the destruction of all high-temperature furnaces in Venice. Using fire hazards as a pretext, the city expelled all of its glassmakers from the mainland in 1291. Along with their apprentices, foremen, and furnace stokers, the maestros of glass were forced aboard ships and gondolas for a three-mile, one-way trip to Murano.

As long as they did what they were told, the artisans were treated relatively well. Their overlords gave them all the resources they needed for their art. But the velvet-handcuffed craftsmen risked life and limbs if they divulged their secrets or tried to escape. Venice's secret police would be dispatched to hunt them down to the ends of the earth.

For three centuries, the isolation plan worked. The trapped Murano artists brought bountiful glory and riches to Venice. But as Tiberius and the Roman Empire went, so went the Venetian monopoly on glass. Knowledge of glass-blowing spread despite the watery boundaries and oppressive rules enforced by the Venetian government. Many of the workers successfully escaped to Vienna, Belgium, France, and England. Others were targeted and lured away from the island by covetous foreign potentates.

In the mid-1600s, vain King Louis XIV was an insatiable customer of Murano glass. He had purchased thousands of pounds' worth of renowned Venetian mirrors and wanted more, more, more. The Sun King's top minister of industry and arts Jean-Baptiste Colbert hatched a plot to bring Murano glass-makers to France. A nefarious junk-shop merchant working for the French embassy in Venice infiltrated the island and scraped together three shady Murano glass workers (one a murderer of a priest). They all accepted large bribes and tax exemption promises to set up shop in Paris. The French ferreted away nearly two dozen of Murano's senior master mirror-makers, their journeymen, foremen, tool-makers, and metal polishers "aboard moonlit gondolas by secret agents" to work for Colbert's Royal Company of Glass and Mirrors—and they took all of their country's trade secrets along with them.

In 1684, after Colbert and his operatives gathered enough intelligence from the Murano glass-makers to continue mirror production on their own, King Louis XIV introduced the world to the resplendent Hall of Mirrors (*Le Galerie des Glaces*) at the Palace of Versailles. The dawn of Louis XIV's age of opulence signaled the end of Venice's stranglehold on luxury glass. However, a new cycle of government command and control would soon commence and grip the European continent.

This tumultuous and tyrannical backdrop set the stage for a radical technological revolution that would forever change the way the world made and used glass. To the ancient batch recipe of silica, alkali, and lime, the American mavericks of glass would add the freedom-enhancing ingredients of capitalism, enforceable and salable patents, automation, and mass production.

But first they had to get rapacious King George III and the Redcoats off their backs.

Colonial Patriots of American Manufacturing

THE LIBERTY SONG
COME, join Hand in Hand, brave AMERICANS all,
And rouse your bold Hearts at fair LIBERTY'S Call;

No tyrannous Acts shall suppress your just Claim,
Or stain with Dishonor AMERICA'S Name.
In FREEDOM we're BORN, and in FREEDOM we'll LIVE
Our Purses are ready,
Steady, Friends, Steady,
Not as SLAVES, but as FREEMEN our Money we'll give.
—"The Liberty Song," John Dickinson, 1768

A century after French and Italian potentates battled for control over glass blowers and manufacturers, British rulers faced rising dissent from their own subjects who yearned to produce their own goods and services without the yoke of government oppression. American poet, pamphleteer, lawyer, and champion of liberty John Dickinson galvanized his countrymen against tyranny. He played a critical role in leading citizen protests against Mother England's odious Stamp Act in 1766, which the panicked Brits repealed after a disastrous four months. The colonists' victory, however, was short-lived and bittersweet. Savvy Parliamentarians and then–prime minister Lord Rockingham tied passage of the Stamp Act repeal to passage of the Declaratory Act, which reasserted that Parliament "had, hath, and of right ought to have, full power and authority to make laws and statutes of sufficient force and vitality to bind the colonies and people of America . . . in all cases whatsoever."

Translation: We rule, suckers!

Money-grubbing British bureaucrats needed to milk their subjects for revenue and reassert control over their unruly domain across the pond. They didn't set up colonies to make their own stuff and compete with the merchants and manufacturers of Mother England. They demanded that the audacious colonists send back to them their best natural resources in bulk. Then, they demanded that the colonists buy the finished goods from the Brits. America's rulers forbade their subjects from making their own goods. Instead, Chancellor of the Exchequer Charles Townshend (Britain's Chief Bagman) crusaded for a new set of onerous import duties and the creation of a tax compliance police squad headquartered in Boston—where resistance to the Stamp Act had been most virulent. Parliament enacted a package of four laws in Townshend's name in 1767. The revenue would be used to pay the salaries of the colonial governors and magistrates. By commandeering the power of the purse and nullifying the colonists' ability to withhold salaries from corrupt or incompetent executives and officers, Townshend plotted to seize control over their local assemblies and legislatures.

Now, everyone remembers the infamous tax on tea that would soon serve as the last straw for the Sons of Liberty. But the very first commodity targeted by the Townshend Acts was precious glass, upon which would be levied:

> For every hundred weight avoirdupois of crown, plate, flint, and white glass, four shillings and eight pence.
> For every hundred weight avoirdupois of green glass, one shilling and two pence.

The Brits and their loyalists argued that since the Townshend duties were "external" (as opposed to the "internal" confiscatory penalties of the Stamp Act), they weren't reaaaaally taxes. But Dickinson, author of "The Liberty Song" and the influential "Letters from a Farmer in Pennsylvania to the Inhabitants of the British Colonies," spelled out the ruse. The Townshend Acts were:

> . . . expressly laid FOR THE SOLE PURPOSE OF TAKING MONEY. This is the true definition of "taxes." They are therefore taxes. This money is to be taken from us. We are therefore taxed. Those who are taxed without their own consent, expressed by themselves or their representatives, are slaves. We are taxed without our own consent, expressed by ourselves, or our representatives. We are therefore—S L A V E S.

Nineteen of twenty-three colonial newspapers printed Dickinson's "Letter from a Farmer" between 1767 and 1768. The Boston selectmen, including John Hancock and Samuel Adams, added their clarion voices after a historic town hall meeting in October 1767 at Faneuil Hall. The patriots drew up a target list of British goods and organized America's second major round of political boycotts (which were modeled after the successful nonimportation agreements pioneered by the Sons of Liberty in response to the Stamp, Sugar, and Currency Acts). The Boston leaders also agreed "to promote Industry, Economy, and Manufactures" domestically to avoid "the unnecessary Importation of European Commodities which threaten the Country with Poverty and Ruin."

At the top of the list of local industries to nurture and support: glass and paper.

The unruly dissenters put their money where their mouths were: British exports plunged from 2,378,000 pounds in 1768 to 1,634,000 in 1769. Defiant Americans, men and women alike, tarred and feathered the British tax collection squad. A furious King George sent the Redcoats, whom colonists were forced to quarter, to occupy Boston. Resistance and riots over the Townshend Acts precipitated the Boston Massacre on March 5, 1770. The next month, Parliament partially rescinded the Townshend Acts (retaining the tax on tea). But it was too late and too little. The Revolutionary War die had been cast.

As they brought British merchants to their knees through mass boycotts, colonial leaders worked hard to catalyze commercial self-sufficiency. The Founding Fathers took a deep and abiding interest in encouraging new manufacturers. Benjamin Franklin, who needed glass for his groundbreaking inventive activities (electricity, the glass armonica, pulse glass, and later, bifocals), befriended German immigrant Caspar Wistar and his family. The industrious soap merchant turned forge owner had founded America's first profitable glass factory in the 1730s in Salem County, New Jersey. Wistar's glassworks made glass electric globes for Franklin's electricity experiments and produced glass for the lab instruments of colonial Philadelphia mathematician, astronomer, and inventor David Rittenhouse.

As early American beer and whiskey makers multiplied, the demand for glass bottles grew. Beer-brewer and vineyard owner Thomas Jefferson courted glassmakers. Swiss immigrant financier Albert Gallatin, who would go on to become Jefferson's Treasury secretary, invested in a glasshouse in New Geneva, Pennsylvania. The entrepreneurial endeavors of the Founding Fathers were invaluable down payments on the future of glass in America. By the turn of the nineteenth century, Pittsburgh glassmaker Benjamin Bakewell and New England glass mogul Deming Jarves had launched remarkable, profitable ventures.

The son of English immigrants, Jarves received several patents for improvements in pressing techniques, mold design, furnace design, and methods of coloring glass. While European glassmakers had produced pressed glass before him, it is Jarves who "is due the credit for perfecting and putting into practical use the art of pressing glass." By the 1850s, his company had more than five hundred employees. Like other glass innovators before him, Jarves faced violent threats from "protective brotherhoods" of master glassmakers:

> The glass blowers on discovery that I had succeeded in pressing a piece of glass, were so enraged for fear their business would be ruined by the new discovery, that my life was threatened, and I was compelled to hide from them for six weeks before I dared venture in the street or in the glass house, and for more than six months there was danger of personal violence should I venture in the street after nightfall.

The very first tumbler produced from Jarves's labor-saving pressing device was put on public display at the Philadelphia Centennial Exhibition in 1876. The company expanded from production of exquisitely blown and cut tableware into chandeliers and fancy centerpieces, telegraph insulators, pharmaceutical ware, and door knobs. But with success came growing labor agitation, family disputes, and management conflicts, which prompted Jarves to separate from the company in 1858. He died in 1869. After a crippling national glass workers strike in 1887, the Boston and Sandwich Glass Company extinguished its furnaces and closed its doors forever.

But Jarves's legacy lived on in another company he had cofounded in 1818, the New England Glass Company, which would fatefully bring together two of the most important American giants in modern glass production: Michael Owens and Edward Libbey.

The Miner's Son and the Bookkeeper's Son

Michael Joseph Owens, still in his britches, skipped grade school and went straight to work. The third of seven children of poor Irish immigrants John and Mary, young Mike started toting lunch and water buckets to his father's coal mine at the age of nine.

"My father was a sort of genius. He could build anything, from a wheelbarrow to a boat," Owens reminisced. He would fly kites and attract gaggles of delighted children. But the lackadaisical elder Owens played when he should have been working and "worked at the thing he hated." Owens credited his father with passing on to him the "inventive instinct," but it was his mother who trained him with the "practical sense" and "great energy and purpose" he needed to succeed. At ten years old, the scrappy kid had his own full-time job. "I was born in Mason County, West Virginia, in 1859," he recounted, "and my father was a miner. I wasn't. But I worked at a job that I guess was just as hard. We moved to Wheeling when I was ten years old; and as my folks were poor and we had a large family, I went to work in a glass factory."

The name of that company was Hobbs, Brockunier, and Company, a flint glass factory founded by former employees of Deming Jarves's New England Glass Company (NEGC). John L. Hobbs was a glass-cutter. James Barnes was the furnace engineer who helped Jarves pioneer the "red lead" process. Hobbs and Barnes moved down to Wheeling, West Virginia, because of its cheap and abundant supplies of coal and natural gas—used to fuel the glass furnaces. The region also boasted railroad lines and the Ohio River, a valuable transportation hub. When Barnes died, Hobbs joined with Charles Brockunier, his new bookkeeper and company partner. Hobbs also brought in William Leighton, son of NEGC's Thomas Leighton, who had patented the "Boston silvered door knob" made of mercury glass for NEGC. Leighton served tirelessly as scientist and superintendent for the new venture. Hobbs's son, John H., also joined the company and succeeded his father upon his retirement in 1867. The company won industry renown for its perfection of lime glass, which could be produced much more cheaply than flint glass at the same high quality, as well as its fancy crackled, opalescent, and "Peachblow" colored art glasses.

Child labor was a staple of the glass industry. Girls worked in the packing rooms, polishing and wrapping glass products. "Blowers' dogs" or "dog boys" as young as eight served as workshop helpers. A glass-blower would remove a "gob" of molten glass from the furnace with a hollow iron blow pipe. He would expand the glass and shape it by blowing through the pipe and swinging it. A finisher would use a solid iron rod called a pontil and an assortment of wooden tools to work the glass into its final shape. Or the glass could be pressed into molds (as pioneered at the New England Glass Company). A shop of three skilled blowers and finishers would need three or four young boys. The "holding-mold boy" opened and closed iron molds for the glassblower. The "ketchin'-up boy" stood beside a presser "receiving tumblers from the large mold on a little tray and placing them on a little table at his side." The boy who grabbed the blown or pressed glassworks with a long iron rod and fired them in the reheating furnace for the adult finisher was the "sticker-up boy." And the lad who ferried the finished objects to the annealing oven was the "carryin'-in boy." Mike Owens described his own gritty duties maintaining the furnace flames:

"At that time, bottles were made by hand. The workman would blow a bottle, and then it had to be reheated so that the rim at the lip could be formed. To do this, the bottle was held with what were called snaps and thrust into a small round furnace in a pit. Boys were hired to feed the coal into this furnace. . . . That was my job when I was ten. I worked five hours in the morning; and when I came up out of the pit I was as black as that ink there. I went home, washed clean, ate my dinner, and went back for another five hours in the afternoon."

At many factories, an employee (the "knocker-upper" or "knocker-up") would be tasked with rousing snoozing workers. This would never have been a problem for the diligent Owens. During his rest periods, the indefatigable Owens worked even more. He used the precious down time to practice blowing glassware by imitating the masters he assisted. At eleven, he became a "carryin'-in boy" and then advanced to mold-holding. By 1880, some six thousand boys between the ages of ten and fifteen (one-quarter of the glassmaking workforce) were putting in ten-hour days, six days a week, for as little as thirty cents a day. Social welfare advocates and union leaders lobbied government authorities to crack down on the scourge of child labor in the glass industry, which exposed many to abuse, illness, and death. But Owens (whose manufacturing innovations would ultimately eliminate the problem in a way that no regulation could have ever achieved) had a decidedly different view of his early work experience.

"Work never hurt anyone!" he scoffed to a reporter. The conditions under which glass boys might work might hurt them, he acknowledged, "[b]ut the hard work I did as a boy never injured me. I went to bed early and I went to sleep without losing a minute. . . . In the factory, I went through all the jobs which boys performed; and I enjoyed every bit of the experience. I wanted to learn everything there was to be learned. And as there were no unions then to put obstacles in my way, I did learn every step of the process; and at fifteen I was a glass blower, working alongside of men two or three times my age."

A world away from the sooty furnaces of West Virginia's Hobbs, Brockunier, and Company, another teen was getting early training in the glass industry. Five years older than Owens, Edward D. Libbey got his first taste of the glass life as a "chore boy" at the Cambridge, Massachusetts, headquarters of Deming Jarves's New England Glass Company. Libbey's father, William, had joined the company as its bookkeeper after training as a corporate clerk in another of Jarves's businesses. He also served as manager of Jarves's Mount Washington Glass Works, where he learned the art-glass trade. The Libbey family, a combination of merchants and *Mayflower* stock, was well-to-do and well-connected. Young Edward had received rigorous academic train-ing first in Boston's superior public schools, then at the private Kents Hill Academy prep school in Maine. He studied Greek and Latin, poetry, rhetoric, philosophy, and business. Accounts vary as to whether Edward wanted to become a Methodist minister or whether that aspi-ration was more his parents' than his own. In any case, a damaging throat infection ended all plans for a career in public oration. Edward spurned college and instead returned to the glass factory to work. He had capitalism in his blood and didn't have time to waste.

In 1874, as self-taught fifteen-year-old Mike embarked on his glass-blowing tenure at Hobbs, Brockunier, and Company, twenty-year-old Edward took a position as a clerk at the New England Glass Company—from which Owens's employers had departed decades earlier. Though he was born wealthy, Libbey worked his way up from the bottom like any other apprentice. He traveled to Europe to study glass chemistry and history. He developed marketing plans, consulted on hiring de-cisions, maintained meticulous corporate records, and guarded the company's "batch book" of glass recipes. He immersed himself not only in the business and promotion of glass, but in the craft. He had the heart of an art collector and would pursue his aesthetic passions as he built an industrial glass empire until death. Libbey began his career amidst a devastating economic depression and mounting competition. In 1883, his father died and Libbey inherited the company—along with its skyrocketing fuel, labor, and shipping costs.

For a few rough years, Libbey kept the company afloat through the sheer force of his artistic, marketing, and entrepreneurial savvy. Thanks to patents the firm held on pioneering employee/inventor Joseph Locke's eye-catching Amberina and Peachblow colored art glass, the New England Glass Company found creative ways to boost sales in the high-end market. Locke also produced the patented Pomona, Agata, and Maize art glass for the company. Amberina was initially considered a failure by Libbey's father before he passed. The *Toledo Blade* reported: "One day a batch of glass came through that was merely amber instead of ruby in color. Rather than waste the batch, workmen sculpted the usual pieces of glassware from it, but when the elder Mr. Libbey saw the off-color glass he made some off-color remarks and rejected it completely. It was placed in a warehouse and written off as a complete and expensive loss."

Edward the aesthete, however, saw beauty in the accidental, two-toned creation, and he is credited with coining the name "Amberina." More important, he spotted a golden-ruby business opportunity. As Libbey biographer and University of Findlay business professor Quentin Skrabec told it, Libbey "created a market, and he had the genius to bring the market and the technology together." Libbey forged a licensing deal with Hobbs, Brockunier, and Company and other factories to manufacture Amberina, which was mixed with gold to produce a shaded ruby to amber gradient, in pressed glass. He then sold some of the company's Amberina inventory to friend and fellow glass pioneer Louis Tiffany (yes, as in Audrey Hepburn and *Breakfast at Tiffany's*). Amberina became all the rage in tableware and enjoyed several revivals during the next century. Libbey took out patents for other ornamental colored glass improvements and etched glass patterns as well, including his famous "Florence," "Corinthian," "Kimberly," and "Kite" motifs. He "aggressively defended his patents," Skrabec noted, and this vigilant commitment to the "defense of corporate intellectual rights was fundamental to the transformation of glassmaking from a craft to an industry."

Employed at companies with shared DNA in a fledgling industry, it was still highly unlikely that the poor miner's son from West Virginia and the privileged bookkeeper's son from Massachusetts would ever cross paths—let alone work side by side their entire adult lives revolutionizing the glass business. Their orbits were about to collide in a most uncanny way. One of America's most fruitful industrial partnerships emerged from economic hardship and labor turmoil. It was a convergence of two disparate business and mechanical geniuses who defied the historical forces of secrecy, obstructionism, and sabotage in their industry.

But before they stood with each other, Mike Owens and Edward Libbey stood *against* each other.

Libbey vs. Owens: Big Labor's "Wrecking Squad" Takes Aim

"OBEDIENCE TO THE MAJORITY."

That was the cardinal principle of the American Flint Glass Workers Union, which first allied itself with the militant Knights of Labor, a secret society of tradesmen dedicated to replacing capitalism with worker cooperatives. The AFGWU then became a charter member of the organized labor powerhouse that evolved into the American Federation of Labor. The AFGWU roped in makers of glass lamps, lamp chimneys, prescription bottles, pressed ware, clear-glass bottles, stoppers, and art-glass engravers and cutters. Like the ancient guilds and European protective associations that preceded them, the "Flints" sought tight control over the methods, output, factory conditions, wages, and workforce of the glass-making business. From its founding, the Flints' goal was to "equalize" the output and wages among all factories—regardless of differences in geography, demographics, and economics. They enforced draconian employment rules to repress nonunionism "that were stricter than those of almost any other national organization."

Organizers limited the number of apprentices permitted to be trained per workshop and punished workers who finished more pieces per half-day than were deemed acceptable by the union. At its first convention in Pittsburgh in 1878, the AFGWU proposed uniform production rates based on the "output of the least productive plants and slowest workmen. Later, the union passed a radical resolution "call[ing] upon the workingmen of the world to unite under the banner of international socialism. Manufacturers balked. The glass industry, one Pittsburgh factory owner complained, was run by unions "trying to do what the almighty did not see fit to do—prevent one man from making more than another man."

Agitation by the Flints and other glass-related labor unions swelled as organizers tried to dragoon workers at factories across New England, West Virginia, New Jersey, and Pittsburgh into their ranks. The Flints strong-armed nonunion workers in Massachusetts and led the strike that brought down the famed Boston and Sandwich Glass Company of Deming Jarves. The New England Glass Company was also on the Flints' hit list as they pressed for geographic wage parity.

Among those on the front lines of the AFGWU brotherhood: Mike Owens. He was young, combative, ambitious, and articulate. Always striving for self-improvement, the devout Irish-American Catholic had sought tutelage in public speaking from his family priest. He practiced oratory in what little spare time he had at a local debating club and showed natural leadership as a labor organizer. Owens's biographer Quentin Skrabec, Jr., notes that his commitment to the union "seemed more pragmatic than philosophical." He was looking for opportunities to advance his career. The local flint glass workers' union made him an officer and dispatched him to the convention of the national group in 1887 in Pittsburgh. The rank-and-file membership voted to strike at the New England Glass Company, and fiery Owens was credited as a key catalyst.

Libbey, under siege by these outside agitators infiltrating his factory, called the national committee "the wrecking squad." Determined not to suffer the same fate as the defunct Boston and Sandwich Glass Company, Libbey made a bold decision and adopted an escape plan:

It was time to go West or die.

The Toledo Turnaround

Once again, the story of glass became a story of survival. In a last-ditch effort to save his company from union saboteurs, Libbey relocated the New England Glass Company to Toledo, Ohio, and officially incorporated as Libbey Glass Company in 1892. The burgeoning and ambitious midwestern city aggressively courted the East Coast glassworks—offering land, homes for workers, and cash incentives, as well as convenient natural resources and transportation infrastructure. Natural gas was cheap and abundant. Coal was closer and more affordable. The region boasted high-quality sand deposits, Lake Erie (an ideal shipping route), and a major railroad hub. Now, Libbey needed to convince glassworkers to follow him.

A few hundred from East Cambridge reluctantly agreed to make the seven-hundred-mile journey by train with their families. Libbey widened his search. He placed newspaper advertisements in Wheeling, West Virginia, and traveled personally to interview candidates. Mike Owens recounted when the industrialist came to town on the recruitment drive that would transform both of their lives—and the world: Libbey "went to Wheeling for his workmen. I was one of them. A friend of mine, older than myself, was engaged as superintendent [in Toledo], but later decided to stay at Wheeling, so I wrote to Mr. Libbey and asked for the position myself." Despite his success as a union officer, Owens wanted more. He didn't want to stand in the way of progress. He wanted to lead the charge toward it. "I had become a glass-blower when I was fifteen. Now, thirteen years later, I was still a glass-blower. I didn't think much of *that* as progress," he explained. Work in Wheeling was irregular. He was tired of arbitrary production stoppages and precarious earnings. Libbey apparently didn't hold Owens's union organizing against him. While he rejected him for the superintendent's position, the New England capitalist took on the hot-tempered Owens as a glass-blower in 1888. The risk paid off.

Three months later, Owens had replaced an aging, incompetent plant supervisor and made his mark as a foreman in Toledo. He fired hundreds of glassworkers who were lazy and drinking on the job. An incurable workaholic who showed up to the plant before sunrise and went full-bore twelve hours daily, he expected his workers' energy and excellence to match his. Next, Owens took command as manager of Libbey's rented glass plant in nearby Findlay, Ohio. Libbey Glass had landed a crucial contract in 1891 to manufacture glass lightbulbs for Edison General Electric after a strike hit its primary supplier, New York–based Corning Glass, which was an "open shop" (nonunion).

Two noteworthy factors worked in the favor of the team in Toledo:

1. One of Libbey's top officials, Solon Richardson, had worked with Edison Electric on the East Coast, producing electric lightbulbs. After the move to the Midwest, Libbey Glass began producing bulbs for a few smaller electrical firms.
2. Owens had served as an officer with the striking Flints, who gave Corning glass employees the blessing to forgo their usual, mandated summer breaks and move temporarily to Toledo for work.

The hard-driving Owens oversaw the seventeen-month, high-stakes job, which reaped life-saving profits for Libbey Glass. Before the project, the firm "was suffering from a deficit of $3,000," glass historian Jack Pacquette found. Seven months after the Findlay operation fired up, "there was a surplus of $50,000, and by January 1, 1892—after 11 months of production—the total Libbey enterprise was $75,000 in the black."

Libbey enlisted Owens in a second, crucial entrepreneurial venture to secure the company's financial viability. Modeling it after the Gillinder & Sons glass exhibit Libbey admired with his late father on a visit to the 1876 Centennial Exhibition in Philadelphia, the aesthetic industrialist planned a spectacular glasshouse demonstration at the 1893 Columbian Expo in Chicago. His own board of directors opposed him, so Libbey raised money from private investors and put up his own personal funds. He secured exclusive rights to operate the only U.S. glass factory and pavilion at the fair. Libbey sent three hundred workers to staff the ten-pot furnace, including 150 glassblowers. Attendance was poor at first, until an employee suggested charging ten cents for admission (later raised to a quarter) and handing out souvenir stickpins decorated with Libbey glass bows.

The most popular displays and items featured at their palatial pavilion, which accommodated five thousand visitors at a time: a spun-glass dress made of Libbey Glass, keepsake inkwells blown on site, paperweights, and a room filled with sparkling glass furnishings. The Libbey pavilion's "crystal art room," lined with mirrors King Louis XIV–style, dazzled visitors with intricate cut-glass objects that glittered under bright light powered by George Westinghouse and Nikola Tesla's AC power. One enraptured reporter described it as a "room lined with diamonds." A brilliant gamble, the lavish exhibit of glass-making manned by Owens and his team created white-hot buzz about Libbey Glass and sparked a craze in fashionable crystal. The firm's cut-glass orders soared, as did its global reputation as the fair helped launch the "Brilliant Period" of American cut glass.

Libbey and Owens returned triumphantly to Toledo. Owens, of course, immediately went back to work. The management responsibilities Libbey conferred on his rough-and-tumble Irish union man soon set off the first revolutionary sparks of Owens's creative genius.

Though he couldn't draw or read blueprints, possessed zero experience in industrial design, and had never studied mechanical engineering (let alone any other formal academic subject past the third or fourth grade), Owens had the heart, soul, and mind of a classic American tinkerpreneur.

He was visionary, stubborn, and practical.

He surrounded himself with skilled, gifted builders.

He never, ever rested on his laurels.

And he found his greatest inspirations in adversity.

They Did It: The Age of Automation

A poem by Edgar Albert Guest served as Mike Owens's office motivational poster. Tacked to his wall, the paean to persistence was titled "It Couldn't Be Done":

Somebody said that it couldn't be done
But he with a chuckle replied
That "maybe it couldn't," but he would be one
Who wouldn't say so till he'd tried.
So he buckled right in with the trace of a grin
On his face. If he worried he hid it.
He started to sing as he tackled the thing
That couldn't be done, and he did it!
Somebody scoffed: "Oh, you'll never do that;
At least no one ever has done it";
But he took off his coat and he took off his hat
And the first thing we knew he'd begun it.
With a lift of his chin and a bit of a grin,
Without any doubting or quiddit,
He started to sing as he tackled the thing
That couldn't be done, and he did it.

There are thousands to tell you it cannot be done,

There are thousands to prophesy failure,

There are thousands to point out to you one by one,

The dangers that wait to assail you.

But just buckle in with a bit of a grin,

Just take off your coat and go to it;

Just start in to sing as you tackle the thing

That "cannot be done," and you'll do it.

"The dangers that wait to assail you." Given his limited schooling, it's unlikely Mike Owens was aware of just how much profound historical significance this line of his favorite poem carried. During the early years of the Industrial Revolution, the enemies of technological change targeted every conceivable machine that increased efficiency and productivity. The British legend of Ned Ludd romanticized working-class vandals who destroyed "Spinning Jenny" power looms and other textile equipment in wool factories across the English countryside. These anticapitalist anarchists were the Occupy Wall Street Movement of their time. Between 1811 and 1813, the so-called Luddites hacked away at thousands of wool-finishing machines with sledgehammers and axes, burned down warehouses, staged food riots, and murdered several factory owners and soldiers trying to quell the violence.

While America was spared such rampant and retrograde domestic terrorism, the Luddite virus manifested itself in other ways. Resistance was futile, but the Flints and other trade unions did their best to block or at least slow the adoption of automated devices and techniques in the glass industry. Owens and Libbey were not the first or only targets at the turn of the century. Big Labor devised multiple "antimechanization" strategies to protect their jobs, from fining rank-and-file union members who dared to use automated bottle-finishing machines to striking at chimney lamp factories that introduced a patented mechanical "crimper" to proposing the "highly unusual strategy of purchasing the exclusive licensing rights" of a patented device "in order to simply sit on the invention."

At the Libbey Glass factory in Findlay, as mold boys threatened to strike, Owens devised a semiautomated mold-opening device. He enlisted the plant blacksmith, James Wade, to help him build it. As described in his Patent No. 489,543, approved in January of 1893, they created an "apparatus for mechanically operating paste glass molds," which were used to mold fine glassware or lightbulbs and required wetting before each operation of molding. (At this point in the development of glass, human blowers were still needed in the manufacturing processes of products that hadn't been fully automated, including bulbs, tumblers, bottles, and lamp chimneys.) Instead of relying on mold boys to assist in opening the molds, Owens envisioned a foot pedal that could be used by the glass-blower. The innovation eliminated some twelve hundred mold boys industrywide and "brought the price of a sixteen-candle-power incandescent bulb down to eighteen cents [from about fifty cents], which helped bring electric lighting to the homes of average Americans." With the full faith and financial backing of his business partner Libbey, Owens secured several more patents for automated glass-making equipment—each growing in awesome complexity with applications for the manufacture of glass tumblers and lamp chimneys. In 1895, for example, Owens secured a patent for an "apparatus for blowing glass" that traded lung power for machine-blown air. He explained in his filing:

> Heretofore in the art of blowing glass, there has been a blower necessary, who manually blows the article into the desired form, there being a gathering boy to secure the gathering upon the pipe previous to blowing, and remove the moil after the article is formed and removed from the pipe.
>
> This invention has for its object to mechanically blow the glass and dispense with the blower, it only being necessary for

the gathering boy to secure the gathering upon the pipe and place it upon the apparatus and remove the same when the article has assumed the desired shape.

Soon after came an improved "mechanical glass-blower" that automated the movement and transfer of the blowpipe through a complicated system of cranks, shafts, levers, flexible tubes, movable shaping blocks, and movable pedestals mounted on cars that traveled on tracks connecting a glass factory's furnaces. Owens plainly spelled out the benefits:

It will be seen by the foregoing that in the use of mechanical means for carrying out the process of blowing glass the necessity of skilled labor is dispensed with, the work greatly facilitated, and the labor materially lightened by reason of the weight being sustained by the apparatus, and the use of one operator dispensed with.

Yet another breakthrough led Owens to invent a semiautomatic contraption that blew lightbulbs into carbon-coated molds. The machine featured five rotating arms, each with a mechanical blow pipe and a mold on the bottom. Here's how it mimicked hand-blown production:

A glob of molten glass would be picked up onto the pipe, the mold would surround it, and compressed air would blow the glass into the mold. The machine could produce 2,000 bulbs in five hours. While it actually took more workers to produce bulbs using this method, they no longer had to be skilled workers, thus reducing costs.

The molds could be varied and replaced, adaptable "to a great variety of uses," Owens disclosed. These would include glass tumblers and lamp chimneys. Key to later advancements in food, soft drink, alcoholic, and pharmaceutical packaging, the device ensured uniformity impossible to achieve through hand-blown, lung-powered glass manufacturing. By "means of the absolute control of the air-pressure," Owens wrote, "the quality of the work done by the machine is superior to that heretofore produced."

Owens and his engineers and designers formed an unprecedented industrial research and development team. Meanwhile, Libbey provided a top-notch legal team to defend and enforce the patents assigned to their company. He promoted innovative licensing and leasing arrangements that expanded the company's market penetration at home in the U.S. and abroad. As Owens's creations grew more sophisticated in size and operation, so did Libbey's corporate empire. In 1896, he formed the Toledo Glass Company as a spin-off of Libbey Glass to enable Owens to concentrate exclusively on inventing. The team scouted out like-minded glass inventors, making deals to buy their patents or bring them on board. This unleashed further inventive activity and breakthroughs by creating a market trade for patents. Economists Naomi Lamoreaux and Kenneth Sokoloff point out that this revolutionary ability to trade patents allowed creative individuals to make money off their ideas and use the returns to specialize in inventive niches.

Again, the unions attempted to intimidate adopters of new glass technology. They tried and failed to shut down a Pittsburgh company that purchased rights to an Owens lamp chimney machine. Undaunted, Owens moved on to bigger, better things.

What Owens lacked in formal education he made up for with four decades of total immersion in the tools, equipment, and processes of the glass industry. What he lacked in artistic ability and engineering skills he compensated for with the gifts of conceptualization and verbal communication. His renderings on paper and blackboard were crude and elementary. But the same oratorical prowess and forceful personality that vaulted him into union leadership helped him convey to his builders and makers the machinery in his restless mind. After dictating every last detail, he'd order the team to "Put it in iron." When the fantastic idea of a towering, fully automated contraption of iron and steel that could blow glass bottles at high speed came to him, Owens informed his boss and then paid a visit to share his new epiphany with Father Mullenbeck of St. Ann's Catholic Church.

Father Mullenbeck marveled at the meticulous, graphic description Owens provided and counseled him against telling too many outsiders:

"From what you've told me, I could go out and have this machine built."

For the next five years, Owens and his primary engineer, William Emil Bock, along with assistants Richard LaFrance, Bill Schwenfeier, his mechanic brother Tom, and others, toiled away at the design. Libbey put up $500,000 to support the research and patiently managed the rest of his often-squabbling executives and competing corporate interests. Team Owens built parts and prototypes whenever and wherever they could: at the office, in other Libbey-owned buildings, or in Bock's basement all hours of the day and into the midnight shift. "You would laugh at the first device we made," he joked with a journalist years later. "But the *basic idea* was there. The giant machines we build now have grown out of that idea." The biggest automation stumbling block involved the time-worn gathering process of retrieving molten glass from the furnace, which had been performed by gaffers and gathering boys since the glory days of crazy Tiberius. The team conceived and Owens improved a "sucker-upper" built on the concept of a bicycle tire pump to gather the glass in uniform quantities and inject it into molds forming the necks of bottles. Next, Owens had his makers transfer the gather into a body mold, where the "return stroke of the plunger blew the glass into proper shape."

The first successful product of the principle: a perfect, four-ounce jar for Vaseline petroleum jelly. He had his proof of concept. In 1903, Owens demonstrated a trial machine (known as "Number 4") that incorporated five of the bicycle pump–style arms ("heads") on a rotating circular frame. The device—which featured a whopping ten thousand parts—produced eight narrow-necked pint beer bottles in one minute. In 1904, Owens received his historic Patent No. 766,768 for the "glass shaping machine" that was "entirely automatic" and blew forms (be they bottles or anything else) "without the intervention of any labor whatever."

The usual obstructionists tried to prevent the spread of this efficient and astonishing technology, which, as the National Child Labor Committee acknowledged, had done more than any government regulation to end child labor abuses—not to mention its salutary effect on promoting safe and healthy packaging practices for beverages and drugs. American Luddites destroyed bottles produced at one Owens licensee's plant in Newark, Ohio. Union workers boycotted Toledo Glass and a new, Libbey-formed company, the Owens Bottle Company, which produced both the bottle-making machines and bottles.

But progress could not be stopped.

By 1900, fellow industrialist and inventor William Painter's Crown Cork & Seal was supplying stoppers for Owens bottles. The synergy revolutionized the beverage business. The success of the bottle-making venture yielded job creation and growth in myriad related manufacturing areas. Libbey acquired scores of businesses ranging from glass container plants to mold makers, to sand, paper box, and melting pot firms. He licensed the machines worldwide, with production in Canada, Mexico, England, Germany, Holland, Austria, Sweden, France, Denmark, Italy, Norway, Ireland, and Japan, for starters. Owens continued to tinker, refine, and improve the machines, producing hundreds of new versions at his eponymous bottle company. Owens had made clear in his patent filing that the glass-shaping machine was not limited to bottles. During the next decade, he would create adaptations to produce everything from glass prescription ware to gallon packers.

"We are still finding new steps to be taken," Owens said as business boomed. That is "the history of all achievement," after all. "Nothing is ever finished and done with," the tinkerpreneur mused.

The *Crockery and Glass Journal* reported that the firm's total market value in 1919 was $27 million after its initial incorporation with $500,000 preferred and $2.5 million common stock. "While making profit for stockholders, the company's product has reduced the price of bottles from twenty five to fifty per cent. The world as well the stockholders has profited." By 1923, just twenty years after the first successful trial of his original automatic machine, ninety-four of every hundred bottles manufactured in the U.S. were being produced mechanically—either by the Owens machinery or by semiautomatic equipment made by others.

And they *still* weren't done proving that what "couldn't be done," *could.*

Back to the Future: The Resurrection of *Vitrum Flexile*

Remember the legend of the hapless inventor who lost his head when he brought a sample of unbreakable glass to the ungrateful and insane emperor Tiberius? His workshop and recipes may have been destroyed, but his daring, inventive spirit infused the next two millennia of glass history. In 1922, another bold inventor held a demonstration of durable glass. It was Mike Owens. He held up a strip of one-foot-wide, three-feet-long glass for a reporter. "That is one of the most interesting developments in modern glass-making," he asserted. Explaining how a Pennsylvania chemist pioneered the process of laminated glass, Owens marveled: "The extraordinary thing about it is that it does not break and fly to pieces like ordinary glass. Let me show you."

Owens picked up a heavy paper cutter and slammed it into the glass a half-dozen times. Though some fine cracks appeared, the strip remained intact and nothing broke off. The implications for automotive safety were obvious.

The problem was that the lamination process, which involved inserting a celluloid layer between two panes of glass, required a radical new manufacturing method for flat glass. For two thousand years, artisans made windows by blowing cylinders of glass. "One side of the cylinder was then cut," Owens explained, then reheated and flattened, "and the glass rolled flat." Except it wasn't completely flat. The ancient, time-consuming, and unreliable techniques for producing window glass retained a problematic curve. It had to be eliminated. But could it be done?

The man who pioneered and patented true flat-glass production and automation was engineer and inventor Irving Colburn. His Eureka! moment for manufacturing glass in a continuous, single sheet came from . . . breakfast:

> Colburn's inspiration came to him while eating pancakes. He noticed that after cutting the pancakes, the syrup clung along the length of the knife blade as he lifted it. It occurred to him that a sheet of molten glass could be pulled up in a similar manner. In his machine, the glass was pulled from the tank by the bait (iron bars), then bent over a steel roller and propelled through the annealing lehr on rollers turned by electric motors.

Colburn faced the same kinds of financial difficulties and union obstructionism that Libbey and Owens overcame. But he didn't have their wherewithal. He had not forged the kind of critical business alliance Libbey and Owens had created. The clique of existing flat-glass manufacturers wanted no part of Colburn's monopoly-busting ideas. The Knights of Labor stood against him. He faced rejection from dozens of glass companies. After begging and borrowing to keep his dream alive, Colburn reached out to Owens, who eagerly embraced the revolutionary idea of this kindred glass maverick. Libbey once again defied the naysayers in his corporate empire and backed Owens and Colburn.

In 1912, they approved Owens's proposal to buy Colburn's machine and patents for $15,000. Owens zeroed in on key mechanical flaws in Colburn's design and embarked on a new, never-ending quest for improvement and perfection. The collaboration and close friendship with Colburn brought Owens full circle: He established a new sheet-glass production plant in his home state of West Virginia. Sadly, Colburn died in September 1917—one month before the plant went into full commercial production. But Owens and Libbey carried on.

The duo incorporated yet another new company, Libbey Owens Sheet Glass, and the sales team quickly and effectively spread word of the breakthroughs. Three years later, the company reported profits of $4.2 million, and European sales exploded. Millionaires many times over, Owens and Libbey separately pursued their passions (golfing and Catholic charity work for Owens; art collection and establishment of the world-class Toledo Art Museum, philanthropy, and travel for Libbey), but together continued in business until their deaths.

Owens died as he had lived: at work.

In December 1923 at a corporate board meeting of the Owens Bottle Company, as he passionately argued for new development proposals, he suffered a heart attack. Libbey paid generous tribute to his partner: "Self-educated as he was, a student in the process of inventions with an unusual logical ability, endowed with a keen sense of far-sightedness and vision, Mr. Owens is to be classed as one of the greatest inventors this country has ever known."

Libbey passed away two years later after a bout with pneumonia. After their deaths, Libbey-Owens Sheet Glass merged with the Edward Ford Plate Glass company to form the Libbey-Owens-Ford (L-O-F) company, which produced the world's first laminated auto safety glass for the Ford Motor Company's Model A. The incessant experimenters at L-O-F later introduced residential solar energy panels in the 1940s and manufactured the glass for the Empire State Building in New York.

The company also invented Thermopane insulated window glass. That's the protective, shatterproof glass used at the National Archives in Washington, D.C., to seal and protect original versions of the Declaration of Independence and Constitution—signed by the Founding Fathers who fought so tirelessly to promote the growth of American manufacturers and innovators in the useful arts.

Glass innovators faced mortal dangers and persistent existential threats from the days of Tiberius to Murano, through the Revolutionary War, and into postcolonial America. The mavericks of glass were assailed by naysayers who said it "couldn't be done" and by jealous competitors who inveighed that it *must not* be done. Edward Libbey and Michael Owens combined forces to demonstrate the timeless entrepreneurial formula for success: ambition, profit motive, creativity, resilience, and the never-ending quest for perfection.

9.

"PERFECT PARTNERSHIP":

Westinghouse, Tesla, and the Harnessing of Niagara Falls

Courtesy of the Tesla Memorial Society of New York

Niagara Falls almost killed my childhood dog, Boomer.

When I was eight or nine years old, my family visited the watery wonder on the New York side of the state park, which straddles the U.S.-Canada border. We boarded the famed *Maid of the Mist* ferry near Rainbow Bridge with our fluffy, white bichon frise in hand. As the tourist boat motored past the American Falls and into the basin of Horseshoe Falls, the mist morphed into a powerful spray. The souvenir plastic ponchos handed out by the crew did little to prevent us from getting soaked. I'll never forget the icy shock of the falls, so picturesque from afar, rudely pelting our faces—or the thunderous sound of waves crashing down violently in a thirteen-story cascade before our eyes.

About six hundred thousand gallons per second flow over the falls—and a few of those gallons nearly swallowed up our pet. Panicked by all the commotion or maybe just thirsty, he wriggled from my mother's grasp for a split second and was suddenly inches away from plunging over the boat railing and into the swirling vortex.

"Boomer!" we shrieked into the roaring oblivion. "Booooomer!"

A half-dozen hands reached out to pluck him back to safety. We disembarked with our shivering wet furball—awed, humbled, and scared out of our ponchos by the fearsome power of Niagara Falls.

The idea that this overwhelming force of nature could be controlled and commanded by man seemed utterly impossible to me as a child. It still does. Yet two great pioneers whose paths were destined to cross did indeed harness the falls. At Niagara, industrialist-inventor George Westinghouse and scientist-engineer Nikola Tesla spearheaded the first major hydroelectric plant and lit up the world. Each was prolific, genius, and visionary in his own right. Tesla joined Westinghouse and his talented team of engineers in the late nineteenth century to demonstrate the superiority of efficient, cheap, and commercially viable alternating-current electricity. When they combined their intellectual and entrepreneurial powers, revolutionary sparks flew.

The "War of the Currents," which pitted Westinghouse and company against direct-current promoter Thomas Edison and his fearmongering publicity machine, is well told and well known among history buffs. Team Edison had aggressively promoted his DC system (in which electricity flows in one direction) as the standard to distribute power. Team Westinghouse backed alternating current as a more efficient means of long-distance power delivery. Unlike DC, AC's variable current could be sent over cheap wires at high voltage and then easily "stepped down" to residential-use voltage levels with transformers. Threatened by AC's superiority, Edison launched a vengeful smear campaign against his rivals. (See, especially, Glenn Beck's *Miracles and Massacres* for the story of how Thomas Edison electrocuted animals as part of a horrific public relations attack on Westinghouse, Tesla, and AC electricity.)

What most schoolchildren never learn, however, is just how profoundly the profitable relationship between Westinghouse and Tesla benefited all of humanity. Private capital, individual initiative, personal integrity, and an abiding respect for intellectual property rights cemented the alliance between Westinghouse and Tesla. These two ambitious titans of business and innovation are exemplars not merely of American ingenuity, but most uniquely of *American capitalism.*

Tesla owned the key insights and patents on the AC electric induction motor. Westinghouse possessed the engineering know-how and industrial resources to transform Tesla's ideas into a practical system of AC electricity generation, transmission, conversion, and distribution. This "perfect partnership," as the Westinghouse company later called it, was both a strategic alliance and a personal bond that continues to bear limitless fruit today. Every time you plug a mundane appliance into an ordinary, duplex electrical outlet in your home—your bedside lamp, your alarm clock, your hair dryer, your vacuum—you enjoy Tesla's and Westinghouse's separate and joint legacies.

The road to Niagara Falls paved by these human dynamos is epic enough on its own. As you will see, the myriad unforeseen paths they opened up together are truly monumental—and their friendship, built on mutual respect, warm admiration, and impeccable character, was one for the ages.

"A Captain Among Captains"

Most biographical treatments start at the beginning of a subject's life. I want to skip forward for a minute to the end, with Tesla's eulogy and tribute to Westinghouse, who died on March 12, 1914, in New York City after battling a heart ailment. Tesla recalled the first time he met his friend, partner, and colleague for a special memorial issue of the journal *Electrical World & Engineer*:

> The first impressions are those to which we cling most in later life. I like to think of George Westinghouse as he appeared to me in 1888, when I saw him for the first time. The tremendous potential energy of the man had only in part taken kinetic form, but even to a superficial observer the latent force was manifest.

Westinghouse, like Tesla, was more than six feet tall. Physically imposing and physically fit for all but the last years of his astonishingly productive life, the Pittsburgh industrialist refrained from smoking and drinking. While Tesla enjoyed the dinner party scene and hobnobbed with literary and cultural celebrities of the day from Mark Twain to Rudyard Kipling to Antonín Dvořák, Westinghouse was more of a homebody. He enjoyed hosting his colleagues and coworkers, many of whom were young mentees. When Tesla visited, the two geniuses rose early to discuss business; in the evening, they enjoyed rare recreational time playing billiards. Tesla recalled his friend's ceaseless energy:

> A powerful frame, well proportioned, with every joint in working order, an eye as clear as a crystal, a quick and springy step—he presented a rare example of health and strength. Like a lion in a forest, he breathed deep and with delight the smoky air of his factories. Though past forty then, he still had the enthusiasm of youth. Always smiling, affable and polite, he stood in marked contrast to the rough and ready men I met.

He was a doting husband to wife Marguerite and a true gentleman. But as Tesla attested, Westinghouse's refined frame housed a warrior spirit:

Not one word which would have been objectionable, not a gesture which might have offended—one could imagine his moving in the atmosphere of a court, so perfect was his bearing in manner and speech.

And yet no fiercer adversary than Westinghouse could have been found when he was aroused. An athlete in ordinary life, he was transformed into a giant when confronted with difficulties which seemed insurmountable.

He enjoyed the struggle and never lost confidence. When others would give up in despair he triumphed. Had he been transferred to another planet with everything against him he would have worked out his salvation. His equipment was such as to make him win easily a position of captain among captains, leader among leaders.

By the time Tesla met Westinghouse in 1888, the "captain among captains" had already invented the railway frog, which allowed trains to cross other tracks smoothly; the car replacer, which guided derailed cars back onto the tracks; and the revolutionary, triple-valve railway air brake, which evolved from a "straight" version using air hoses to connect the cars, to the prevailing automatic system using air pressure to keep the brakes off, with subsequent improvements for quick-action use and electromagnetic power. He had also already founded the successful Westinghouse Air Brake Company, the Westinghouse Machine Company (which produced steam turbines and marine motors), and the Westinghouse Electric Company (which initially produced lamps and lighting systems), along with foreign subsidiaries and factories in France, England, and Germany. In addition, he had pioneered life-saving railroad signals and switching systems, formed the Union Switch and Signal Company, and patented friction draft gear to replace railcar coupling springs.

If all that weren't enough, Westinghouse in his "spare" time had immersed himself in the field of natural gas. After reading a newspaper article about the discovery of the new, clean-burning resource in Pittsburgh, he tackled the problems of distribution, metering, and safety in the emerging market. On his own estate, which he dubbed "Solitude," he started drilling with tools he built himself. To the dismay of his wife and neighbors, after one fiery experiment, he nearly burned down his house in an explosion. His trademark persistence and tinkering paid off not only for himself, residential customers, and factory consumers of natural gas, but also for the entire industry and science. He invented multiple safety devices to reduce dangerously high gas pressures, as well as valves, regulators, gauges, and drilling techniques; Westinghouse patented nearly forty products and improvements related to natural gas production and distribution. In 1884, he founded yet another venture, The Philadelphia Company, to provide natural gas in Pennsylvania and West Virginia. The utility supplied power for light, heat, and electricity in homes and businesses; produced and transported oil from fields in West Virginia; ran street railways in Pittsburgh; and oversaw a booming electric power and light business.

As a boy, Westinghouse had shown early talent in mechanics and engineering. Fooling around in his inventor father's machine shop, he constructed his own Leyden jar—a homemade capacitor, usually lined with metal foil, which stores static electricity charges between two electrodes inside and outside the container. (Benjamin Franklin had used glass Leyden jars in his famous kite-flying electrical experiments and in his electrocution studies on chickens and turkeys.) Westinghouse joined the Union army during the Civil War at age sixteen, serving in the infantry and cavalry before transferring to the navy as an engineer officer. Though his father offered to support him through college after he returned home from war, Westinghouse preferred to go straight to work. At nineteen, he secured his very first patent, for a rotary steam engine.

This combination of early hands-on exposure to machines, coupled with ingrained habits of mental discipline honed as a young soldier, provided Westinghouse a solid inventive and entrepreneurial foundation. "My early greatest capital was the experience and skill acquired from the opportunity given me, when I was young, to work with all kinds of machinery," he once explained, "coupled later with lessons in that discipline to which a soldier is required to submit, and the acquirement of a spirit of readiness to carry out the instructions of superiors."

But Westinghouse wouldn't follow others' orders for long. He was born to lead, and his commercial and managerial instincts are what set him apart. "He drove others," the editors of *Electrical World* observed, "but none so hard as himself. Outside of his own strong mind, his greatest asset was his ability to inspire others."

Tesla concluded his eulogy to the engineering captain's captain with a salute to Westinghouse's inventive impact:

> His was a wonderful career filled with remarkable achievements. He gave to the world a number of valuable inventions and improvements, created new industries, advanced the mechanical and electrical arts and improved in many ways the conditions of modern life.
>
> He was a great pioneer and builder whose work was of far-reaching effect on his time and whose name will live long in the memory of men.

Westinghouse would no doubt have agreed that this glowing description just as fittingly described his friend Tesla's own contributions to the world. Long after they had officially parted ways in business, Westinghouse supported his friend and kept up correspondence. Several Westinghouse engineers continued to consult and study with Tesla. And the company paid for the inventor's hotel room and board at the New Yorker Hotel at Thirty-Fourth Street and Eighth Avenue until Tesla's own death in 1943.

"The Greatest Electrician of the World"

Like Westinghouse, Tesla started tinkering with machinery at an early age in his hometown village of Smiljan, Croatia—taking apart clocks, fashioning a fishing rod and reel to catch frogs, inventing a pop-gun, fixing a hometown fire engine, fiddling with batteries, experimenting with water turbines, pumps, and motors. One of those mischievous motors involved strapping poor "May bugs" (June bugs in America) to a windmill-like contraption. Tesla amusingly recounted the invention's unfortunate demise:

> I would attach as many as four of them to a crosspiece, rotably arranged on a thin spindle, and transmit the motion of the same to a large disc and so derive considerable "power." These creatures were remarkably efficient, for once they were started they had no sense to stop and continued whirling for hours and hours and the hotter it was the harder they worked. All went well until a strange boy came to the place. He was the son of a retired officer in the Austrian Army. That urchin ate May-bugs alive and enjoyed them as tho they were the finest blue-point oysters. That disgusting sight terminated my endeavors in this promising field and I have never since been able to touch a May-bug or any other insect for that matter.

Young "Niko" was a math whiz with a photographic memory and a polyglot fluent in a half-dozen languages. His Serbian mother was a mechanically gifted homemaker who crafted her own appliances, including an eggbeater; his father was an erudite Serbian Orthodox clergyman who drilled him daily in literature and math to strengthen his reason and memory. After seeing a photo of the famed Niagara Falls, he told an uncle of his dream to place a gigantic water wheel underneath to harness its power. In his teens, Tesla contracted cholera and was bedridden for nearly a year. Doctors gave him up for dead at least three times. He later credited the captivating books of Mark Twain for pulling him through the illness.

Just a few decades later, Tesla would count Twain as a close friend, who "burst into tears" when the inventor told him how his novels saved his life. Not long after that, the Niagara Falls hydroelectric plant would become one of Tesla's signature achievements.

His path was far from straight and gilded. He admitted that a gambling addiction almost ruined him. He suffered hypersensitivity to sound and light and wrestled with nervous disorders that caused near breakdowns. The tortured Tesla described a boyhood affliction in which vivid images, "often accompanied by strong flashes of light," would transfix themselves before his eyes, and each would "persist despite all my efforts to banish it." This haunting mental phenomenon was a personal curse, but a blessing to the world. In 1882, Tesla experienced a visionary episode in a Budapest park during which the workings of the AC motor and its rotary magnetic field came to him. He wrote in his autobiography that:

> . . . the idea came like a flash of lightning and in an instant the truth was revealed. I drew with a stick on the sand the diagrams shown six years later in my address before the American Institute of Electrical Engineers.

After a stint as a traveling repairman for Thomas Edison's Paris branch, Tesla had constructed his first AC induction motor. Electric motors, of course, convert electrical energy into mechanical energy. When magnets attract and repel each other, they create force and rotational motion.

Here's a quick crash course in the "how" of motors:

At the heart of a motor lies the rotor or "armature," which is made by winding thin wire around two or more magnetic poles of a metal core. The rotor is mounted between two permanent and stationary field magnets that compose the "stator." Magnetic repulsion and attraction cause the rotor to, yes, rotate and produce torque (a steady rotating energy). Electrical current can flow constantly and in one direction (direct current or DC) or back and forth in an oscillating motion (alternating current or AC). DC motors use commutators (a pair of metal plates attached to the rotor by an axle) and brushes (metal or carbon pieces that come into contact with the commutator) to produce torque. In noninduction AC motors, slip rings are used to connect the rotor to an external circuit.

As Tesla explained, his AC induction motor solved a problem he had pondered since he was a college student back in Europe: the creation of dangerous sparks caused by the commutator. Instead of changing the magnetic poles of the rotor, Tesla altered the magnetic field in the stator and eliminated the need for a commutator altogether:

> The induction motor operates on alternating current. It has no commutator like a direct current motor, nor slip rings like an alternating current motor. Contrary to the two types just cited, the "field" current is not steady, but the current itself rotates constantly pulling around with it, by induction, the only moving part of the motor—the rotor or armature. Having no armature nor slip rings, the induction motor never sparks. It consequently knows no "brush" trouble. It needs no attention because of its ruggedness. Only the bearings wear out. Its efficiency too is higher.

Tesla planned to use a promised bonus from his work at Edison in France to establish a company to bring his brainchild to market. Somehow, perhaps as a result of inattention or naïveté or both, he was unceremoniously stiffed. Undaunted, he immigrated to America in 1884—with four cents, a book of poetry, and a letter of recommendation in his pocket—in search of opportunity. Edison lured him back to work on DC research in New York City. The ambitious immigrant threw himself into work. He turned out twenty-four types of machines for the company.

"For nearly a year my regular hours were from 10:30 a.m. until five o'clock the next morning without a day's exception," Tesla recalled.

Yet once again, Edison's company treated the genius shabbily. A promise to pay the inventor $50,000 for his labor "turned out to be a practical joke," he later wrote. He quit to found his own business, the Tesla Electric Light & Manufacturing Company, which built a municipal AC "arc lighting" system for the city of Rahway, New Jersey. Heartbreakingly, Tesla's investors had little interest in the real engine that drove the inventor—his AC motor—and before he knew it, Tesla had been booted out of his own company.

"It was the hardest blow I ever received," he confessed in his memoir. He suffered "terrible headaches and bitter tears," not to mention humiliating destitution. Tesla took a job as a ditch-digger for Western Union to make ends meet. It was there that he met a foreman interested in electricity, who introduced him to lawyers and businessmen tied to corporate banking magnate J. P. Morgan. At a fateful meeting, he convinced key investors to help him fund a new lab for his work on AC. The quick-thinking Tesla captured their imaginations with the story of the "Egg of Columbus."

Legend has it that Christopher Columbus came under fire from jealous noblemen in the Spanish court of Queen Isabella. The critics derided his discovery of the West Indies and scoffed that his achievement was insignificant since someone had been bound to run into the islands anyway. To illustrate how difficult tasks only looked easy after they had been accomplished, Columbus challenged the naysayers to stand an egg on one end without any props. After they all failed, Columbus made fools of them by simply picking up the egg, tapping it gently, and flattening one end by breaking the shell a bit. How easy it seemed . . . in hindsight. Afterward, Isabella allegedly pawned her jewels and provided Columbus with all the financial support she could muster.

Tesla seized on the visuals of the famous "Egg of Columbus" fable to show the moneymen how the principles of rotational magnetic fields worked in practice. He proposed to stand an egg upright like Columbus, but without causing a single crack.

"If you could do this we would admit that you had gone Columbus one better," the prospective investors told Tesla.

"And would you be willing to go out of your way as much as Isabella?" Tesla asked.

"We have no crown jewels to pawn," the lawyer responded, "but there are a few ducats in our buckskins and we might help you to an extent."

For his most important marketing demonstration to date, Tesla placed a copper egg on top of a wooden table. The egg represented the rotor of his AC two-phase induction motor. Underneath the table, Tesla attached four electromagnetic coils wrapped around a doughnut-shaped iron core. This rotating field ring created a magnetic force that caused the egg to spin faster and faster, until it stood, as promised, on its pointy major axis. Tesla delivered on his promise. The investors held up their end of the bargain, too. Tesla Electric 2.0 was born in a Manhattan lab building at 89 Liberty Street not far from rival Edison's.

In May 1888, after developing a polyphase induction motor incorporating multiple alternating currents, transformers, generators, transmission, and lighting, Tesla secured seven historic patents on his system. ("Polyphase" means the motor operated using multiple alternating currents that were not simultaneous—in other words the currents flowed "out of phase" with each other.) A few weeks later, to both professional and public acclaim, he delivered a milestone lecture on his discoveries and improvements before the American Institute of Electrical Engineers. The "wild man of electronics" had finally gained the respect, credit, and attention he was due.

But the work of the "greatest electrician of the world" to bring the benefits of AC into ordinary people's lives had only just begun. And it would take the century's greatest captain of engineers, patent lawyers, and mechanics to see the job through.

The Westinghouse Way

As both an individual inventor and a corporate organizer, Westinghouse was a lifelong believer in compensating creators for their labor and ideas. His team of patent lawyers worked scrupulously to protect and defend the company's own patents and trademarks—and just as diligently to respect others' claims. It was good business and the right thing to do. Thanks to the resources he had amassed as a result of his own inventive powers and commercial savvy, Westinghouse had the capital to reach out and support the creative output of promising tinkerpreneurs working toward the same goals.

Westinghouse Electric had already been conducting cutting-edge research and development on AC before Tesla entered the picture. In 1884, the company recruited William Stanley, who had established his own one-man lab where he designed a self-regulating dynamo, and an incandescent lamp with a carbon silk filament. At Westinghouse's Pittsburgh research shop, Stanley refined his AC ideas alongside Albert Schmid, Benjamin Lamme, Lewis Stillwell, Oliver Shallenberger, and Charles Scott.

Stanley developed the first commercial electrical transformer for Westinghouse in 1885–86 and crusaded for AC power over some inhouse critics. Transformers allowed easy changes in the voltage of power, which allowed power plants to transmit high-voltage AC power over long distances. Schmid oversaw the actual construction of machinery. Lamme secured 162 patents for improvements on everything from railway motors to rotary converters to induction motors. Stillwell invented a voltage regulator. Scott worked on transformers and power transmission. Shallenberger invented the electric meter after independently discovering the same electromagnetic principles of the induction motor that Tesla had harnessed months before him.

George Westinghouse, meanwhile, immersed himself in AC research and scientific literature as he oversaw his team's progress. In Europe, he was aware of the work on AC induction motors by Italian scientist Galileo Ferraris, who had independently developed a polyphase AC motor months before Tesla's patent approval and public speech to the AIEE in the spring and summer of 1888. Westinghouse also had knowledge of the pioneering work of Lucien Gaulard and John Dixon Gibbs on AC power distribution and transmission. In 1885, Westinghouse's legal team arranged to buy the American rights to Gaulard's and Gibbs's foreign patents. The Westinghouse engineers immediately set about improving their single-phase AC transformers for actual commercial use.

For Tesla, a deal with Westinghouse was win-win. After several months of negotiation, he went to Pittsburgh to finalize a cash, stock, and royalty deal for his AC patents worth an estimated $500,000 to $1 million. The royalty deal was an extremely generous $2.50 per horsepower on every motor. Tesla split the proceeds with the two key financial backers who made development of his motor and its components possible: lawyer Charles Peck and businessman Alfred Brown. As part of the arrangement, Tesla agreed to spend a year with the Westinghouse Electric team while they perfected the system and prepared it for commercial sale and distribution. Tesla's friend and advocate of American invention, Mark Twain, put the historical significance of the deal in perspective:

I have just seen the drawings and descriptions of an electrical machine lately patented by a Mr. Tesla, and sold to Westinghouse Company, which will revolutionize the whole electric business of the world. It is the most valuable patent since the telephone.

Author and technophile Mark Twain in Tesla's New York City laboratory

Inevitably, the eccentric Tesla clashed with some of the bright young engineers at Westinghouse's Garrison Alley lab in downtown Pittsburgh. They argued over phases and frequencies. They made design changes, including adding more copper wire to the rotor, substituting soft Bessemer steel for the iron in the motor's core, and developing a standard stator frame that could be cast and machined efficiently. Painstakingly, the team tinkered its way to commercial viability.

Impatient with the toil necessary to standardize and manufacture a practicable system, Tesla left on good terms after a year to return to New York. He moved on to patent yet more revolutionary methods and mechanisms for neon and fluorescent lights, high-frequency apparatus, oscillators, and the famed Tesla coil, which paved the way for radio, X-rays, and wireless power transmission. Striking photos of Mark Twain at Tesla's lab showed the novelist goofing around with phosphorescent photography and lighting a lamp by using a Tesla coil to pass electrical currents through his body. Tesla traveled to Europe with his dazzling light shows to lecture to awestruck crowds.

When he returned, Westinghouse enlisted Tesla's aid for their engineering triumph at the 1893 Columbian Exposition in Chicago. The Westinghouse AC central power plant in Machinery Hall generated more than twelve thousand horsepower of electrical energy to power the fair's 172,000 incandescent lamps, motors, and arc lighting systems. Their brilliant glow inspired the nickname "the White City." The Westinghouse crew oversaw installation of the entire exposition's wiring and circuits as well. With Tesla, Westinghouse also set up a complete, operational AC polyphase system with induction motors, generators, transformers, a rotary converter to DC power, and a railway motor. Tesla oversaw a separate exhibit featuring high-frequency-powered, wireless phosphorescent lights and also displayed his "Egg of Columbus"—which would become one of the fair's most popular attractions.

President Grover Cleveland presided at the opening ceremony on May 1, 1893.

"As by a touch the machinery that gives life to this vast Exposition is now set in motion," he announced, "so at the same instant let our

hopes and aspirations awaken forces which in all time to come shall influence the welfare, the dignity, and the freedom of mankind."

Cleveland pressed a button that activated the Westinghouse-Tesla machinery. Electric fountains and chimes sprang to life. More than seven hundred American flags unfurled. Cannons boomed. An orchestra played the "Hallelujah Chorus" from Handel's *Messiah* and then led the crowd in a rousing performance of the national anthem.

Westinghouse and Tesla were the toast of the world. But neither man, as ever, had time to rest on his laurels. Behind the scenes, Team Westinghouse had won the landmark contract to supply AC power for the Niagara Falls hydroelectric plant. The private venture was led by New York financier Edward Dean Adams of the Cataract Construction Company, backed by scions J. P. Morgan, John Astor and William Vanderbilt. An eminent group of scientists and engineers had chaired the commission overseeing construction proposals. Influential panelist Lord Kelvin, the famed British physicist, had sided with Thomas Edison in favor of DC power—until, that is, he visited the 1893 Columbian Exposition and World's Fair and witnessed Westinghouse's and Tesla's breakthroughs firsthand.

As Westinghouse biographer Henry Prout affirmed, "The best result of the Columbian Exposition of 1893 was that it removed the last serious doubt of the usefulness to mankind of the polyphase alternating current. The conclusive demonstration at Niagara was yet to be made, but the World's Fair clinched the fact that it would be made, and so it marked an epoch in industrial history."

Before they could electrify the falls at the U.S.-Canada border, though, the journeys of Westinghouse and Tesla took them on a critical side trip to the Rocky Mountain West.

The Telluride Test

According to local legend, the Colorado ski resort of Telluride didn't get its name from the mineral compound "tellurium" found in gold ore. The name is said to have originated from a catcall—"To hell you ride!"—shouted by knowledgeable residents to late-nineteenth-century fortune-seekers headed out on the treacherous path to the remote mining town in the southern San Juan Mountains. From the 1870s to the early 1890s, the high-altitude hamlet was heaven for gold-diggers who survived the tiring trek. Telluride mines teemed with gold, silver, lead, copper, and zinc. Burro trains gave way to a Rio Grande Southern Railroad stop in 1890, stimulating the economy further and increasing settlement.

One of the success stories of the Telluride rush was Ohio farmboy-turned-business-magnate Lucien L. ("L.L.") Nunn. The Oberlin College grad and law student seemed an unlikely frontiersman—he was balding, slight, and barely five feet tall. But Nunn was an entrepreneurial dynamo and a bit of a barroom brawler to boot, which came in handy in the heyday of the Wild West. He opened up restaurants in Leadville and Durango, earning extra money as a carpenter and cabin-builder. In 1888, as Westinghouse and Tesla were inking their landmark patent deal, thirty-year-old Nunn pitched a tent in Telluride. Living on oatmeal, he shingled roofs while getting his legal practice off the ground.

When he could afford a house, he built a tin tub in it and charged miners a dollar per soak. After building, renting, and selling tract homes for miners, he started buying commercial real estate and purchased lucrative water rights along the San Miguel River. Soon, he had saved enough to buy the San Miguel County Bank. Its vaults teemed with mining payrolls, which unfortunately attracted scheming criminals.

In 1889, a gang of thugs robbed Nunn's bank of nearly $21,000. The bandits' leader: Robert Leroy Parker, aka Butch Cassidy. It was the thief's first known heist.

Nunn bounced back from the holdup, but the farsighted town organizer realized that Telluride faced a much larger financial threat than Cassidy and his outlaws. Mining firms relied on small steam engines for drilling and milling ore. They had cleared all the surrounding timber for fuel and heat. Transporting coal or wood was prohibitively expensive. Nunn had been consulting for Telluride's Gold King Mine, a stamp ore-crushing mill on the verge of bankruptcy and desperately seeking energy alternatives. An Edison-style DC system wouldn't work. Copper prices were high and DC was a poor choice for long-distance transmission. Still in touch with East Coast friends and attuned to the news of the day, even from his remote mountaintop sanctuary, Nunn learned of Westinghouse and Tesla's groundbreaking work on AC generation and transmission. The news inspired a wild idea for his flagging Wild West hometown.

The Gold King Mine was located 2.6 miles from the San Miguel River, where Nunn held water rights. What if he could obtain a Westinghouse turbine and build an AC power plant using Mother Nature's natural resource? Nunn hired his brother Paul, an electrical engineer, to design an electrical station and transmission line. He took the blueprints and his moxie straight to Westinghouse headquarters for a last-ditch effort to save the Gold King Mine, and the rest of Telluride, for that matter.

The mountain man's daring offer: $50,000 in gold and $50,000 worth of his time and labor to build an AC generator and a one-hundred-horsepower motor in place of the mine's steam-powered plant.

"I'm willing to gamble that, gentlemen. What are you prepared to do?" Nunn challenged.

Just as Tesla's "Egg of Columbus" clinched his deal with the financial backers of his AC induction motor, Nunn's gutsy showmanship with the Westinghouse corporate board paid off. The company saw a (literally) golden opportunity to test and prove the viability of its generation, transmission, and distribution system in real-world conditions. The more rugged, the better. Nunn returned triumphantly to Telluride with an inked contract. Westinghouse tasked his engineers Charles F. Scott, Ralph Mershon, Lewis Stillwell, and V. G. Converse to help design and support the station.

With the help of young engineering students he hired from Cornell University, Nunn and his brother built the network of steel pipes, natural reservoirs, and a six-foot-diameter water wheel for the facility dubbed the Ames Hydroelectric Plant, near the outlying village of Ophir. (Ames was the name of a settlement located at the point in the San Miguel River where water was exploited for power.) Westinghouse provided two one-hundred-horsepower generators built by Tesla—one for power generation at the Ames station (really a wooden shack) and the other for the motor at the Gold King Mine nearly three miles away. Three miles of bare copper wire on thirty-foot-long poles carried three thousand volts of power. They labored through brutal snowstorms, thin air, avalanches, lightning, and windstorms to erect the line. Engineer and historian Alan Drew described the gold-letter day the electrical pioneers turned on the system:

On 19 June 1891, water from the San Miguel River was unleashed onto the 6-ft (1.83-m) Pelton water wheel. The wheel was attached by belt to the Westinghouse generator, whose armature began to rotate as the water wheel turned. The [AC] produced by the rotating armature was transmitted 3 mi (4.83 km) to successfully operate the 40-stamp ore crushing

mill at the Gold King Mine. This was arguably the first use of
[AC] for industrial use in the United States.

In 1988, the Institute of Electrical and Electronics Engineers designated the Ames plant as an official "milestone." A plaque erected at
the site notes that "this pioneering demonstration of the practical
value of transmitting electrical power was a significant precedent in
the United States for much larger plants at Niagara Falls (in 1895) and
elsewhere."

A team of fifteen to twenty attendants manned the Ames plant
around the clock. L. L. Nunn launched an educational program to
train staff. The early days of operation were perilous. Spectacular arcs
of electricity, six to eight feet long, would often be generated when
the plant went offline. Spectators would travel to watch the sparks fly.
Westinghouse engineers developed insulators, metal arresters, and automatic regulators as problems arose. The Telluride project's success,
coupled with Westinghouse's and Tesla's dazzling displays at the 1893
Columbian Exposition in Chicago, played a critical role in persuading
private investors and city leaders in Niagara Falls to move forward with
their AC hydroelectric generation and transmission proposal.

Seizing the day, the Nunns formed the Telluride Power Company,
the nation's first electric utility, to build stations for other mines and
supply lines to neighboring towns—starting with Telluride, of course.
Nunn partnered with Westinghouse Electric to conduct high-voltage
research and transformer development at the Ames plant for use in
building much longer-distance transmission lines and systems. As a
result of that research, the Nunns built a power plant in Provo, Utah,
that operated a safe maximum voltage of forty thousand volts. They
quickly extended their reach to Idaho, Montana, and Mexico. (Their
company still exists and operates today as Utah Power and Light; the
Ames station is still in operation, now owned by Xcel Energy and generating enough power for a town of four thousand.) Having passed
the Telluride test, both brothers would head back east to consult for

Westinghouse on the Niagara Falls project; Paul Nunn would oversee construction and operation of the Ontario power plant on the Canadian side of the cataract.

By electrifying the Gold King Mine, the Nunns had struck business gold for themselves and powered the West's commercial growth and wealth creation—just one more way in which the Westinghouse-Tesla team benefited others while in pursuit of its own industrial goals.

Let There Be Light(ning)

Tesla apparently never visited the Ames plant, but he did travel to Colorado on a separate research quest. With help from Westinghouse patent attorney Leonard Curtis, whose legal expertise was critical during the War of the Currents, Tesla set up a barnlike lab at East Pikes Peak and North Foote avenues in my adopted hometown of Colorado Springs. Curtis secured land for Tesla east of the city, paid for his lodging at the downtown Alta Vista Hotel, and arranged for the El Paso Power Company to supply AC power. Tesla also received private funding from hotel scion John Jacob Astor and other investors.

Our thin air at six-thousand-feet elevation provided the wizard a highly conducive environment. In 1899, Tesla built large air-core Tesla coils, high-frequency transformers, a tall tower, and large copper ball. He experimented with methods of measuring electrical waves from lightning, bouncing them back to earth, magnifying their power with a transmitter that created "resonant rise," and thereby charging the earth with electricity. The greatest electrician in the world created out-of-this-world displays of blue lightning arcs and bolts extending hundreds of feet—visible to the naked eye as far away as mining town Cripple Creek nearly fifty miles away.

During his groundbreaking tests on the wireless transmission of electrical energy, he knocked out power to the entire city for a week. Oopsie. Tesla returned to New York to conduct more studies, but a devastating fire burned down his lab. The Colorado Springs lab was also destroyed. Darkening financial clouds loomed. Sadly, the only visible traces left of Tesla's legacy in my city are a makeshift, one-room museum located in the basement of a bed-and-breakfast joint and a rusted historical marker obscured among a grove of trees at Memorial Park along East Pikes Peak Avenue. The stained sign reads: "It was at this facility on North Foote Avenue that Tesla felt he made his most important discoveries."

In a lengthy scientific journal article summarizing his Colorado Springs research, Tesla acknowledged that it would take time to gain public acceptance of his discoveries in wireless telegraphy and wireless energy transfer. Tesla wrote about resistance to his experiments using the Earth as an electrical conductor:

> Such reserve, and even opposition, of some is as useful a quality and as necessary an element in human progress as the quick receptivity and enthusiasm of others. Thus, a mass which resists the force at first, once set in movement, adds to the energy. The scientific man does not aim at an immediate result. He does not expect that his advanced ideas will be readily taken up. His work is like that of the planter—for the future. His duty is to lay the foundation for those who are to come, and point the way.

"What Modern Genius Has Accomplished"

At the turn of the century, both Tesla and Westinghouse would suffer heartache in the aftermath of nationwide financial panic beyond their control. But their joint victory at Niagara Falls and its impact on modernity were as irrevocable as their friendship.

After years of struggle, sacrifice, near-death experiences, nasty litigation, baseless fear-mongering, derision, and even, at one point, rumored industrial sabotage by pro-Edison spies, Westinghouse and the Garrison Alley engineers arrived at the precipice of Niagara Falls. In the summer of 1895, the Westinghouse team flipped the switch and turned on the power of the generator dubbed Dynamo No. 2. Nearly a month later, Dynamo No. 1 went online. The site incorporated ten Westinghouse-Tesla AC generators of five-thousand-horsepower capacity each, ignited by turbines turned by 430 cubic feet of water at 250 rpm. Westinghouse built all the auxiliary electrical apparatus, exciters, measuring devices, and switchers necessary for operation and power transmission.

Westinghouse-Tesla generators at Niagara Falls

Eventually, the plant would supply long-distance power for the cities of Buffalo, Tonawanda, Lockport, and beyond. Newspapers marveled at "what modern genius [had] accomplished" in taming the "mighty power of the great cataract." But they had barely begun to comprehend another extraordinary and unforeseen consequence of Westinghouse's and Tesla's partnership. The phenomenal success of their hydroelectric power system inspired dozens of companies in need of cheap, reliable power to move to Niagara. America's electrochemical and petrochemical industries relocated to the area, led by the Carborundum Company, Union Carbide, and the Pittsburgh Reduction Company.

Electrochemical wizard Charles Hall was yet another Oberlin College grad (like Telluride's Lucien Nunn) who benefited from the Westinghouse-Tesla alliance The incurable tinkerpreneur, obsessed with metals from childhood, had pioneered an efficient smelting method to extract aluminum from ore. Hall was just twenty-two years old when he made his discovery. The baby-faced inventor founded the Pittsburgh Reduction Company with steel scientist Alfred Hunt in 1888. Westinghouse, fascinated by metallurgy, supplied steam-driven dynamos for the operation and personally supervised their installation. Aluminum processing, however, required an unceasing supply of massive amounts of energy. The harnessing of Niagara Falls by Hall's Pittsburgh friend and neighbor provided the perfect solution. Alcoa's cheap, lightweight products helped revolutionize the automotive, aviation, and aerospace industries; the company is the third-largest supplier of aluminum in the world today.

A diverse range of manufacturers joined the electrochemical companies at Niagara, including the International Paper Company, Francis Hook & Eye & Fastener Co., Ramapo Iron Works, and International Acheson Graphite Co. Like Niagara Falls itself, one hydroelectric-powered innovation cascaded into another in a stupendous rush of creative industrial breakthroughs. Just one of countless examples: Buffalo historian Jack Foran noted that the graphite production process "was a serendipitous offshoot" of Carborundum Co. founder Edward Acheson's manufacturing process. Acheson realized that accidentally overheating carborundum produced an almost pure graphite. The product, made at the International Acheson Graphite Co. based near the Westinghouse-Tesla hydroelectric plant, became a critical component of lubricants, electrodes, electrotyping, paint pigments, lead pencils, and polishes.

In 1927, scientists displayed an automobile at a professional convention in New York with its parts meticulously labeled. Explanatory cards described the electrochemical processes and products required to manufacture each and every component of the car, from the engine to the brakes to the chassis. Over the display was a large sign that read: "Niagara Falls made Detroit possible."

A convention attendee explained, "We, as electrochemists, look upon the automotive industry as one of the by-products of the electrochemical industry." Of course, the electrochemical industry and automotive industries were beneficiaries and by-products of the hydroelectric industry—spearheaded by the founding fathers of industrial modernity, George Westinghouse and Nikola Tesla.

Legacy: "Let Me Never Falter"

The success of Niagara Falls, Tesla said in his speech "On Electricity" at a celebratory event for the plant, was a "signal for the utilization of water powers all over the world, and its influence upon industrial development is incalculable." His esteem for Westinghouse's heroic role only ripened with age. He later praised his partner as "the only man on this globe who could take my alternating-current system under the circumstances then existing and win the battle against prejudice and money power. He was a pioneer of imposing stature, one of the world's true noblemen of whom America may well be proud and to whom humanity owes an immense debt of gratitude."

For his part, Westinghouse memorialized Tesla in a most profound and sublime way. Each of the Niagara Falls generators bore a plate listing the patents that made the hydroelectric achievement possible. To Tesla belonged the greatest glory and credit—nine of the thirteen patents were his. Instead of working to exploit and crush Tesla, as Edison had attempted to do, Westinghouse threw his entire corporate weight behind the scientific visionary. Westinghouse paid him full and fair value for his patents, hired him to consult at Garrison Alley, supplied him with equipment and personnel, and vigorously promoted his name and innovations at the 1893 Columbian Expo. The pursuit of their individual self-interests yielded fruits far beyond either's imagination.

Westinghouse poured millions of dollars into these efforts to bring Tesla's innovations to market. He incurred the risks and wrath and litigious abuse of powerful enemies bent on destroying them both.

During the War of the Currents, business titan J. P. Morgan sought to manipulate the stock market in a bid to wipe out Westinghouse and gain control of the hydroelectric market. He used his deeply indebted house organ, the *New York Times*, and other newspapers to bash Westinghouse for poor financial management. The bitter grievances were long-standing. Morgan had backed Edison. After the financier ruthlessly stripped Edison of his company and formed General Electric, Westinghouse was at the top of the hit list. As part of a hostile takeover bid that stretched through the 1890s, Morgan and GE demanded that Westinghouse fork over control of the Tesla AC patents and sabotage the perfect partners' royalty agreement from 1888.

With his back to the wall, Westinghouse visited Tesla in 1897 to inform him of Morgan's scheme to starve his company. Westinghouse had spurned Wall Street and resisted relentless efforts to give in to Morgan, Edison, GE, and the electric trust. He refused to coordinate with other crony capitalists to raise his street light prices to pay "boodle"—political payoff money to aldermen and regulators. Now, his old Pittsburgh neighbors and purported friends—most notably, Morgan man Henry Frick—had abandoned him. Westinghouse was bleeding cash. Tesla agreed to tear up the royalty agreement and instead accepted a lump sum payment of $216,000 in place of royalties valued then at an estimated $12 million.

It was an astounding act of magnanimity that provided invaluable financial relief and ultimately preserved the company.

Tesla asked if Westinghouse would remain committed to bringing the AC polyphase system online.

"I believe your polyphase system is the greatest discovery in the field of electricity," Westinghouse told him. He vowed: "It was my efforts to make it available to the world that brought on the present difficulty. But I intend to continue, no matter what happens, with my original plans to put the country on an alternating-current basis."

As every electrical outlet in your house attests, Westinghouse kept his promise. But in the end, Tesla's sacrifice for his friend did not prevent Morgan from stripping away Westinghouse's post as captain among captains. He was forced out of the corporate empire that bore his name and died in 1914.

After Westinghouse passed, Tesla encountered a last bitter reminder of why his great friend detested "New York bankers."

Years earlier, Morgan had tossed in money to support Tesla's Colorado Springs research and thrown in another $150,000 to subsidize Tesla's wireless transmission research and construction of the Wardenclyffe Tower in Long Island, an early wireless transmission tower designed by Tesla. But Tesla was a pawn and a nuisance in Morgan's crony capitalist games. Morgan threw him under the bus after Edison-backed Guglielmo Marconi successfully received Morse code radio signals by wireless transmission over a four-mile distance in 1896. The wealthy and politically connected Marconi, who went on to receive the Nobel Prize, had used Tesla coils and studied Tesla's wireless work from at least a year beforehand. Morgan ignored Tesla's protests. He blew off the wireless communications wizard's pleas to pay him money owed (just as Edison had done at the very start of his career), abandoned Wardenclyffe, and instead invested in Marconi America (which later became Radio Corporation of America, aka RCA). While he cashed in, the billionaire manipulator "purposefully scuttled any future ways Tesla could raise money."

The U.S. Supreme Court ruled that Marconi's Morgan-backed company had indeed infringed Tesla's patents—but not until after Tesla had died.

For Edison and Morgan, corrupted capitalism was a means to control others and increase their own power.

For Tesla and Westinghouse, free-market capitalism was a means to do well for themselves while unleashing power to the rest of the world.

Tesla, even in darkest despair, refused to yield or retire. To illustrate the indefatigable tinkerpreneur's raison d'etre, he recited from Goethe's "Hope":

Daily work—my hands' employment,
To complete is pure enjoyment!
Let, oh, let me never falter!
No! there is no empty dreaming:
Lo! these trees, but bare poles seeming,
Yet will yield both food and shelter!

Ultimately, despite their opponents' ugliest efforts to stop them, the story of Tesla and Westinghouse is one of enduring American optimism and faith. Their heroic risk-taking and unceasing commitment to technological advancement and virtuous free enterprise defined the Age of Progress.

From 1880 to 1890, his friend and biographer Henry G. Prout summed up, Westinghouse "took out 134 patents, an average of over one patent a month, and he stimulated and directed the work of many other inventors." Over the course of forty-eight working years, Westinghouse continued to take out a patent every month and a half until death. The last fifteen of his more than four hundred patents were awarded posthumously, ranging from marine turbines to the automobile air spring to improvements on an automatic train control, which was the subject of his last patent, granted in November 1918—

four years after his death! On one occasion in the twilight years of his career, an acquaintance told Westinghouse he had earned more wealth than most other men on earth and should take a break from working.

"No, I do not feel that it would be right to stop here," Westinghouse replied. "I feel that I have been given certain powers to create and develop enterprises that other men can find useful and profitable employment."

Westinghouse's reply—and the boundless fruits of his partnership with Tesla—stand as a timeless rejoinder to capitalism-bashers and clueless ingrates who believe that "at a certain point you have made enough money."

PART IV

PAST, PRESENT, FUTURE

The very first official thing I did, in my administration—
and it was on the very first day of it too—
was to start a patent office.

—HANK MORGAN IN MARK TWAIN'S *A CONNECTICUT YANKEE IN KING ARTHUR'S COURT*

10.

SMART LIMBS:
The Next Generation of American Tinkerpreneurs

At the turn of the prolifically inventive nineteenth century, the A.A. Marks Company of New York City took out a newspaper advertisement touting its award-winning artificial limbs. The ad, headlined "LEGS AND ARMS with rubber feet and hands," featured an illustration of a double-amputee performing a miraculous task:

Climbing a ladder.

"[H]e has two artificial legs substituting his natural ones, which were crushed by a railroad accident and amputated," the manufacturers explained. "With his rubber feet he can ascend or descend a ladder. He can walk and mingle with persons without betraying his loss; in fact he is restored to his former self for all practical purposes."

The Marks family founded its medical equipment company in 1853 "for the purpose of relieving and helping the maimed and deformed." The company sold its patented products—which also included crutches and wheelchairs—by mail order. Unlike clunky, wooden peg legs that hadn't evolved for centuries, A.A. Marks pioneered a new generation of prosthetics made of rubber. The company hailed the advent of indefatigable Charles Goodyear's vulcanization process, which allowed it to add a springy, sponge rubber to their artificial hands and feet. Goodyear probably never imagined that the gum elastic he originally used for mundane valves, galoshes, and mailbags would be incorporated in life-enhancing prosthetics.

A.A. Marks also determined through research and experimentation that the key to increasing usability and durability lay in improving the construction of the ankle joints. Within a few decades, the company had custom-fit and sold more than nine thousand prosthetic devices to amputees across the country. Marks's son, George Edwin, studied civil engineering before joining his father. He patented six important improvements in the design and manufacture of artificial limbs. The Marks family published several tomes and treatises, including the *Manual of Artificial Limbs* and *A Treatise on Artificial Limbs*, which became industry bibles. Their technological advancements earned praise from physicians, patients, and scientific panels, including a committee of the Franklin Institute, which honored the inventors with a prestigious medal.

At the 1893 Columbian Exposition in Chicago, the company's representatives displayed a wide array of fifty different limbs and prosthetic parts. They weren't alone. "In a testament to the demand for prostheses," a medical historian reported, "no fewer than nine manufacturers of artificial limbs had assembled on this occasion to display their wares."

Another family-owned prosthetics firm, the Winkley Company of Minnesota and Wisconsin, later bought out A.A. Marks. Albert Winkley was a farm boy who lost his left leg in a horrible lawn mower accident at age eleven. As a young man dissatisfied with his stiff and painful prosthetic, he invented and patented an adjustable artificial limb with a slip socket. "We began as a result of one man's struggle to be more comfortable walking in an artificial limb," Winkley's president, Greg Gruman, told me. "Given the advances of today's prosthetics it might seem primitive, but was typical for the time."

Winkley partnered with savvy businessman Lowell Jepson, who had befriended Winkley after purchasing horses from him. The Winkley Company, founded in 1888, reached out to the railroad industry and offered hope to amputees who had lost limbs in occupational accidents. Winkley covered its willow-wood prosthetics with rawhide leather to strengthen them. Custom-made machines smoothed the wooden parts; workers hand-forged and pounded out steel joints. Women in the knitting department manufactured special stump stockings. Winkley, now in its fifth generation of family ownership, is still in business today after more than 125 years.

The overwhelming number of soldiers who lost limbs during the Civil War—thirty thousand Union and forty thousand Confederate—spurred even more entrepreneurial Americans to put their time and talents into this market. Engineering student James Edward Hanger led the pack. After dropping out of school to join his brothers in the Confederate Army, eighteen-year-old Hanger suffered life-threatening leg wounds at the Battle of Philippi in West Virginia. Hanger had been saddling his horse in a stable when a cannonball ripped through the building and tore through his limb. Leaving a crimson-spattered trail, the desperate young man crawled up to the barn loft to hide. And die.

Union troops discovered Hanger drifting in and out of consciousness while hemorrhaging blood in the hay. Surgeon James D. Robison performed the first battlefield amputation on the young man with no anesthesia or sterilized tools. The Union doctor and his assistants removed Hanger's shredded limb from above the knee with dirty saws and knives, then transported him to a medical facility.

"I cannot look back upon those days in the hospital without a shudder," recalled Hanger. "No one can know what such a loss means unless he has suffered a similar catastrophe. In the twinkling of an eye, life's fondest hopes seemed dead. I was the prey of despair. What could the world hold for a maimed, crippled man!"

Despair Begets Ingenuity

Hanger returned home with an unwieldy peg leg and hobbled upstairs to his bedroom. He summoned puzzled relatives to bring supplies—wood, household scraps, tools—and locked himself away. After three months, he fulfilled a promise to himself not to emerge until he could walk downstairs to his family. Triumphantly, he tossed the peg leg aside and descended with ease wearing the "Hanger Limb"—his first-of-a-kind prosthetic fashioned from oak barrel staves, rubber, and metal bits. The design was hinged at both the ankle and knee to improve mobility.

"I am thankful for what seemed then to me nothing but a blunder of fate, but which was to prove instead a great opportunity," Hanger reflected. He secured several patents, opened up his first store in Richmond, incorporated J.E. Hanger Company in 1906, and vigorously promoted his products to fellow amputees.

Five of Hanger's six sons joined the thriving business. In constant pursuit of improvement, Hanger traveled to Europe after World War I to study new techniques in amputation surgery. After he died in 1919, the sons, their in-laws, and several cousins turned the family enterprise into a corporate powerhouse. The company gradually expanded to Atlanta, Philadelphia, Pittsburgh, St. Louis, London, and Paris. Government subsidies for disabled veterans brought in lucrative contracts after World War I. But Hanger's success derived from the founding vision and private initiative of an intrepid teenage soldier who staved off death and hopelessness to pursue his American Dream.

After more than 150 years in business, Hanger Orthopedic Group, Inc., is the oldest and one of the largest prosthetics and orthotics companies in the world—with patient care, manufacturing, and distribution divisions dedicated to "enhancing human potential." (Prosthetics replace lost limbs and other body parts; orthotics support or correct deformed or damaged limbs.) CEO Ivan Sabel consolidated and modernized the company. With venture capital funding, Hanger made nearly one hundred acquisitions that increased the reach and scope of its device development and distribution. The for-profit conglomerate generated more than $1 billion in revenue in 2013, and employs more than three thousand employees in forty-three states, along with twenty-five offices across Europe. A philanthropic foundation by Sabel supports thousands around the world who have suffered debilitating injuries as a result of disease, accidents, or violence.

Hanger has remained at the forefront of innovation. The Hanger clinics provide devices for infants with head deformities known as plagiocephaly and orthotics for children with cerebral palsy and other conditions. They also supply insoles and footwear for diabetics, neck braces and spinal orthoses for patients with chronic diseases or injuries, burn masks, and postmastectomy forms and bras. At the Northwest Hanger Clinic's National Upper-Extremity division in Tacoma, Washington, inventor Ryan Blanck is now leading research and development for clients with trauma-related amputations and limb injuries. Blanck cared for hundreds of wounded American soldiers at the Center for the Intrepid, Brooke Army Medical Center (BAMC) in Fort Sam Houston, Texas. While there, he devised the Intrepid Dynamic Exoskeleton Orthosis (IDEO), a carbon and fiberglass ankle-foot orthotic custom-molded for each warrior. Thanks to Hanger's purchase of Blanck's patent rights (which he had waived for the military), his products will now be widely available to civilians. He also worked on Segway inventor Dean Kamen's DEKA Arm System, or "Luke Arm," with the Department of Defense. DEKA's robotics engineers have partnered with New England–based Next Step Orthotics and Prosthetics and Southern California–based Biodesigns, Inc., on the project.

The Marks family, Albert Winkley, and James Hanger would undoubtedly be amazed and proud of how far their American successors have taken the industry to improve the human condition. Austin-based Hanger Orthopedics was just one of the U.S. companies supporting victims of the 2013 Boston Marathon terrorist attack. Sixteen innocent men, women, and children lost limbs in the double bombing that sent nails, shrapnel, and metal scraps flying. Two lost both legs. By the first anniversary of the attack, the amputees had each faced scores of surgeries, skin grafts, and grueling rehab.

Eight of the survivors use carbon-fiber sockets manufactured by United Prosthetics, a small, family-owned business in Dorchester, Massachusetts. Italian immigrant Philip Martino, originally a shoemaker, founded the company as United Limb and Brace in 1914 after working at a prosthetic company in Boston. Martino's two partners were former patients and amputees themselves. Within a decade, Martino had patented a cushioned socket for thigh legs using sponge rubber. Next, he invented and patented a socket improvement for patients with above-the-knee amputations. The sockets connect to artificial knees or other parts manufactured separately by different companies. When Martino died, his World War II hero son took over and established close relationships with local hospitals and nursing homes. A redevelopment push by Boston city officials wielding eminent domain powers forced the company out of its workshop and offices. The resilient family found new digs and kept going. Four generations of Martinos have worked in the business, now based in a two-story brick warehouse in Dorchester.

Dorchester is also the hometown of Jane Richard, age seven, the youngest Boston Marathon bombing victim. Her brother Martin, age eight, died in the attack. Jane also lost a leg from beneath the knee, and now walks on an artificial limb designed by her neighbors at United Prosthesis. The family had never heard of the company until tragedy struck.

From Ribbons to Robotics

There are thousands of unsung private businesses like United Prosthetics humming along unnoticed in small towns across America. Just as the nineteenth century brought inventors out of the woodwork to address the needs of wartime and occupational amputees, so has the twenty-first century spurred entrepreneurial innovation from the depths of adversity. The wars in Iraq and Afghanistan created a new generation of wounded warriors in need of artificial limbs. These days the materials of choice are no longer oak wood, leather, and sponge rubber, but lightweight carbon-fiber composites and advanced plastics.

Who builds them?

Meet the Bally Ribbon Company, just one of countless American companies that supply prosthetic manufacturers with their material foundations. Yarn salesman Herbert Harries founded his Berks County, Pennsylvania–based business in 1923. He built massive looms that wove an eclectic variety of fabrics for garter belts, hat bands, suspenders, and blanket bindings. Harries used his machines to manufacture Purple Heart ribbons and nearly six hundred other types of military decorations. During World War II, the company adapted its industrial processes to produce woven webbing, tapes, and specialty fabrics for the military. Bally Ribbon next diversified from textiles and defense work to aerospace, safety, automotive, and medical applications.

The firm's design engineering division dove into the composites industry in the 1990s with 2D and 3D structural fabrics. These are advanced textiles that combine disparate materials to add strength without adding weight. Fiberglass, carbon fiber, or natural fibers, for example, can be mixed with plastic resins to create reinforced composites. Bally workers spin nylon, polyester, aramid, graphite, glass, quartz, ceramic, and silicon carbide into watchbands, backpack straps, parachutes, and spacesuit components. The company's weavers and engineers produce the tubular materials used to make stents and grafts for patients with damaged aortas. They've also innovated implantable ligature tape, dental materials, and monofilament material used in blood filtration, aspirating devices, and bone marrow transplants.

In the 1970s, the company developed biomedical webbing and braided carbon graphite materials for the manufacture of the world's most advanced artificial limbs. Hundreds of employees use everything from original shuttle looms to the most advanced software for manufacturing work. The company installed large braiding machines in the past fifteen years that produce carbon yarn tubular products used for the fabrication of artificial legs. Bally recently celebrated more than ninety years in business and is in its fourth generation of family ownership. When I asked Bally vice president Bert Harries, grandson of founder Herbert Harries, what the company's secret to success was, he told me: "Our willingness to work and our openness to everything. We never said no to an opportunity." He added: "American small businesses are incredible generators of ideas, hard workers and wealth for this country. Bally has great people and a next generation that is working hard and interested in continuing our innovative history. Their great-grandpa would be amazed at the technology at Bally today, but it's probably what he would have expected."

Another American small business success story, the Willow Wood Company in rural Mt. Sterling, Ohio, shares a similar story of perseverance and evolution. Founder William Edwin Arbogast lost both legs in a railroad accident in 1901. He spent 212 days in a hospital, recovering. Like other amputee tinkerpreneurs, he was unhappy with the state of prosthetic technology. Arbogast used the willow wood grown on his family farm to carve himself better limbs than those available on the market. In 1907, he established the Ohio Willow Wood Company, Inc. The business grew steadily, but the Great Depression forced its leaders to find creative ways to survive. Willow Wood diversified into the manufacture and sale of wooden polo mallets and balls.

The Arbogasts were tested again when a factory fire struck and destroyed the entire company plant in 1933. The founder's $40,000 in life savings went up in flames with it. But Willow Wood stood fast. The *Pittsburgh Post-Gazette* reported at the time:

It takes more than the loss of both legs at the knees, the washing away of all his winter's cutting of valuable red willow and the destruction by fire of his willows wood factory to discourage William E. Arbogast, president of the Ohio Willow Wood Factory here. Although his entire factory was wiped out by fire on June 15, he is already in the field with his products and his new fireproof factory plans are practically complete.

During World War II, Willow Wood made parts for the Navy's PT boats and the Army's B-17 bombers. But their core business remains prosthetics. Willow Wood sells products ranging from stump socks to cushion heels to gel liners. Their "vacuum suspension systems" improve the seal between a prosthetic socket and the artificial limb's liner. The company has also been at the forefront of computer-assisted design and computer-assisted manufacture (CAD/CAM) with its "OMEGA Tracer" system. It incorporates handheld scanners that capture images of a patient's body and digitize the files, which are then used with milling machines to carve and manufacture parts.

"From Bench to Bedside"

Prosthetics can now be controlled by other parts of the body connected by cables, external motors, and sensors that pick up electrical signals emitted by muscle movements. They no longer clunk and clink. They listen and "think" with embedded microprocessors that gather data on mobility and motility to improve functionality.

Climbing a ladder is kid's play compared to the activities enabled by modern artificial limbs—from Olympic running to rumba dancing, skiing, and mountain climbing.

There aren't just one or two large prosthesis makers in America, but hundreds of all sizes and specialties. Many of the new tinkerpreneurs themselves are amputees, just like the leading nineteenth-century prosthetic pioneers. Others are still in their teenage years or barely out of them, just like James Hanger and Albert Winkley before them.

Bob Radocy, who lost his left hand in a car accident, runs an eight-person small business in Boulder, Colorado, called Therapeutic Recreation Systems Inc. He self-financed his start-up in 1979 and now manufactures an estimated one thousand specialized prosthetics a year for clients who have lost hands and arms. "In addition to dozens of prosthetic sports attachments," the *Boulder County Business Report* noted, "40 percent of the company's business comes from prosthetic crawling devices for infants born without hands or feet. The company also makes specialized attachments for individuals all over the world, such as well-known amputee and Boulder resident Aron Ralston, who made headlines after self-amputating one arm after a climbing accident in a slot canyon in Utah."

The founder of for-profit Flex Foot, Inc., Van Phillips, lost his left leg below the knee after a motorboat collided with him in a grisly water-skiing accident His athletic experience helped propel prosthetics technology into a new era with a deceptively simple insight: The devices, he concluded, needed an energy source. From the hind legs of kangaroos and cheetahs, Phillips observed how limbs store power and muscle energy. He constructed an artificial leg of carbon graphite— stronger than steel, lighter than aluminum—whose springy C-shape stored kinetic energy with every step. Phillips owns more than one hundred American and foreign patents. Users of his famous "Cheetah" legs range from elite Paralympic athletes to grade-school amputee Jane Richard, the seven-year-old Boston Marathon bombing survivor.

As a child, Phillips built his own tree houses and constructed elaborate ice forts. "Anything you can think of, you can create," the tech titan urges schoolchildren with the enduring optimism of the tinkerpreneur.

Some of the most cutting-edge developments in twenty-first-century prosthetics involve "neural interfacing" with an implanted brain chip and sensor that communicate with robotic limbs. With such a system, quadriplegics may one day be able to control prosthetics with their thoughts. BrainGate, a privately held company based in Boston and Los Angeles, owns more than thirty patents related to neural interfacing technology. A consortium of academic researchers first pioneered the brain-to-consumer interface. One of them, tinkerpreneur Jeff Stibel, used money from the sale of his start-up Simpli.com (an Internet behavior analysis tool), to form a for-profit venture to bring the BrainGate system to market. Blackrock Microsystems LLC, a privately held Utah company, manufactures the implantable hardware. Many of the company's other devices and tools are driving the "next generation of such key areas as auditory prosthesis, bladder control, pain, epilepsy, pharma research, and treatments for arrhythmia and heart failure."

MIT researcher Hugh Herr started his own company, BiOm, which manufactures and sells the "world's first bionic foot-and-calf system." Herr is a double amputee who lost both legs in a climbing accident. MIT described how his invention works:

> Using battery-powered "bionic propulsion," two microprocessors and six environmental sensors adjust ankle stiffness, power, position, and damping thousands of times per second, at two major positions: First, at heel strike, the system controls the ankle's stiffness to absorb shock and thrust the tibia forward. Then, algorithms generate fluctuating power, depending on terrain, to propel a wearer up and forward. . . .
>
> Among other things, the system restores natural gait, balance, and speed; lowers joint stress; and drastically lowers the time required to acclimate to the prosthesis (which can take weeks or months with conventional models).

Boston Marathon attack survivor and professional ballroom dancer Adrianne Haslet-Davis, who lost her left leg below the knee in the bombing, demonstrated Herr's system in an unforgettable way: Near the end of Herr's presentation at a TED (Technology, Education, and

Design) talk in Vancouver, Canada, in March 2014, Haslet-Davis took the stage with her dance partner. Dressed in a sparkling white mini-dress, she performed underarm turns, hip rolls, dramatic dips, and open breaks in a sensual, rhythmic rumba.

In less than a year, Herr reported, he and his team had pro-grammed Haslet-Davis's prosthetic to perform the fundamentals of dance: "In 3.5 seconds, the criminals and cowards took Adrianne off the dance floor. In 200 days, we put her back."

Herr is passionately committed to the successful commercializa-tion of his ideas. BiOm continues to develop new products with an esti-mated $50 million in grants and venture capital from firms including WFD Ventures, General Catalyst Partners, Sigma Partners, and Gilde Healthcare Partners. "I'm always thinking about minimizing the time and investment to get from bench to bedside," Herr has said. "Starting a company is one way of enhancing that efficiency" and fueling "com-mercial progress."

Not just one way. The *best* way. As Nobel Prize–winning economist Milton Friedman summed up human experience: "So that the record of history is absolutely crystal clear: There is no alternative way, so far discovered, of improving the lot of the ordinary people that can hold a candle to the productive activities that are unleashed by a free en-terprise system."

"The Fuel of Interest"

America's brightest young minds are now at work on their own pat-ented solutions and improvements in prosthetics.

At age sixteen, Katherine Bomkamp, daughter of a retired Air Force colonel, invented a pain-free socket using the concept of ther-mal biofeedback to help eliminate the problem of "phantom pain" in amputees. She was exposed to the issue while she and her father visited Walter Reed Army Hospital in Washington, D.C. The condition occurs when the brain continues to send signals and commands to missing limbs. "I started looking into what phantom pain was," Bomkamp explained, "and quickly found that there was no medication available on the market for treatment." Commonly prescribed antipsychotics and barbiturates cause serious side effects. "For my tenth-grade science project that year," Bomkamp says, "I decided to do something about it."

Bomkamp theorized that using controlled heat to stimulate an amputee's severed nerve endings would divert the brain into concentrating on the temperature instead of sending the signals that caused phantom pain. She cold-called prosthetics experts and forged a relationship with Jake Godak of wholesale distributor Cascade Orthopedic Supply in California. He built the first socket and prosthetic leg based on her ideas. Bomkamp secured a patent on her invention and established her own company, Katherine Bomkamp International LLC. Katherine told me, "Securing the patents has been absolutely vital." She has retained a patent attorney and is licensing her invention as "the best route" to get it to market. Her advice for budding tinker-preneurs? "Surround yourself with people who know more than you do. I found mentors in the industries I wanted to work in, and they added a lot of credibility to what I was trying to do."

Massachusetts Institute of Technology student David Sengeh, twenty-seven, has a patent pending on artificial limbs using magnetic resonance imaging and 3D printing. A grad student at MIT's Media Lab, Sengeh began working on prosthetic socket design as a result of his experience growing up in war-torn Sierre Leone, where brutal terrorists chopped off innocent civilians' arms and legs to induce fear and quell civil unrest. Sengeh plans to start his own company.

Eric Ronning designed a 3D printable prosthetic hand while a junior mechanical engineering student at the University of Wisconsin–Madison. He started his own company, called "Re," to manufacture the low-cost devices he calls "ReHands."

And then there are the Girl Scouts in Iowa who call themselves the

"Flying Monkeys." In 2011, they secured a patent for a low-cost prosthetic hand made of Lego building blocks. The girls, ages eleven to thirteen, created the device for a three-year-old toddler born without fingers on her right hand. Dubbed the "BOB-1," the scouts' invention is made of moldable plastic, Velcro, and a pencil grip—all at a cost of ten dollars to build.

"I think it would be cool if we had, like, our own company and then we made BOBs," twelve-year-old Zoe Groat, aka "Monkey 1," told ABC News.

"I hope to make lots of them," twelve-year-old Gaby Dempsey ("Monkey 3"), added. "It could go nationwide. A lot of people could use them. It would help people."

"It's a really big deal to be getting a patent," thirteen-year-old Kate Murray, aka "Monkey 2," explained to a reporter. "Almost no one at our age has one and it's very special. It means our invention is really worth it."

Young Kate is right. America's patent process is a "big deal" indeed. As the stories of the successful tinkerpreneurs in this book illustrated time and again, the securing of patents and protection of intellectual property were critical keys to commercial success—and will be essential to securing America's inventive future.

CONCLUSION

America's founders knew that progress would come not merely at the hands of "great" inventors pioneering extraordinary breakthroughs, but by the widespread invention and improvement of ordinary and "small" contrivances and advancements. In 1790, they created and refined a decentralized, market-based patent system "based on the conviction that individual effort was stimulated by higher expected returns." The promise of financial reward was the "fuel of interest" that stokes the "fire of genius," in the words of America's only president to hold a patent, Abraham Lincoln.

The very first article of the U.S. Constitution gave Congress the explicit mandate "to promote the Progress of Science and the useful Arts, by securing for limited Times to Authors and Inventors the exclusive Right to their respective Writings and Discoveries." Most Americans don't realize just how unique and revolutionary the modern, market-based U.S. patent system is in world history. At the time of its creation and development through the nineteenth century, it was the first of its kind, the most generous to inventors, and the most conducive to progress. The original builders of America recognized a utilitarian purpose for patent laws in which "[t]he public good fully coincides . . . with the claims of individuals." Congress and the early courts provided for expansive and generous protection of inventors' intellectual property rights, as George Mason University law professor Adam Mosoff has extensively documented.

The U.S. patent system first began as an intimate process during which three high-level White House officials—the attorney general, the secretary of war, and the secretary of state—reviewed each patent application. As the population exploded, so did the nation's inventive spirit. In 1836, major patent reforms were adopted, including the creation of the U.S. Patent Office and its bureau of trained, professional examiners. Our farsighted forefathers created tradable assets for inventors that they could sell, license, or assign to others for monetary gain. In return, inventors agreed to public disclosure of their ideas and expiration of the patent after a limited time period. The tradeoffs allowed broad dissemination of technical knowledge and catalyzed even more innovation and invention.

Thomas Jefferson, the first patent examiner of the United States and one of the godfathers of American invention, is often credited with (or blamed for) framing the Constitution's intellectual property protection exclusively as a "special monopoly privilege" of the government. But many modern foes of intellectual property rights in academia have twisted Jefferson's writings and whitewashed America's grounding in natural rights philosophy. Primary historical sources, congressional documents, and colonial-era courts—as well as early patent statutes and nineteenth-century patent case law—reveal that patents have been construed as *basic civil rights in property* since America's first days.

Statesman and constitutional lawyer Daniel Webster said it best during a floor speech before the U.S. House of Representatives in 1824:

> [T]he right of the inventor is a high property; it is the fruit of his mind—it belongs to him more than any other property— he does not inherit it—he takes it by no man's gift—it peculiarly belongs to him, and he ought to be protected in the enjoyment of it.

Webster vigorously defended patent cases, including the valiant battles on behalf of Charles Goodyear. You'll remember that Goodyear's vulcanized rubber process made possible, among so many other beneficial things, the prosthetics breakthroughs of A.A. Marks. Goodyear was forced to prosecute thirty-two infringement cases involving patent pirates all the way to the U.S. Supreme Court. After years of litigation and costs that left both near bankruptcy, Webster and Goodyear prevailed. Webster declared in his winning Supreme Court argument for Goodyear that the Constitution does not create out of whole cloth, but *secures* the inventor's natural, pre-existing, inherent right to his or her intellectual property. This right, Webster posited, was "more clear than that which a man can assert in almost any other kind of property."

Legal controversies about intellectual property abound between the utilitarian and natural rights camps. But here's the bottom line: Rather than denigrate the profit motive, the patent and copyright clause of the Constitution celebrates and encourages "individual effort by personal gain [as] the best way to advance public welfare through the talents of authors and inventors." Free-market capitalism, so maligned in today's culture and mainstream politics, was at the heart of our founding intellectual property rights infrastructure.

The Patent Office in D.C. was open to the public and provided inspiration to hundreds of thousands of visitors. The stately building displayed thousands of patent models in glass cases arranged by subject matter. The miniature models, no larger than twelve inches by twelve inches by twelve inches, were required as part of the application process from 1790 to 1880. This allowed tinkerers who didn't have the ability, education, or means to describe their ideas on paper to demonstrate them in a concrete, mechanical way. *Scientific American* ran regular feature articles on patentees and myriad advertisements promoting patent advice. *Popular Mechanics* ran its own "Patent Bureau" offering consultation and legal services to aspiring inventors.

Nineteenth-century inventors and entrepreneurs were the cultural heroes and pop icons of their day. President Lincoln not only defended the intellectual property rights of clients, but personally encouraged technological innovation. The mechanically inclined pioneer was an early adopter of the telegraph. He tested the Henry and Spencer repeating rifles on the White House lawn. He assisted weapons inventors George H. Ferriss, James Holenshade, Isaac Diller, and James Woodruff—fostering the development of new machine guns, cannons, explosives, gunpowder, and fireproofing methods. Lincoln also delivered lectures on the history of discoveries, inventions, and patent laws. He took his young son to visit the Patent Office in Washington. And he practiced what he preached.

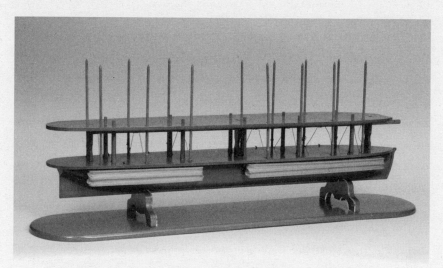

A patent model reproduction of Lincoln's device for buoying vessels over shoals
Courtesy of the National Park Service

As a young flatboat operator in Illinois, Lincoln was involved in an accident that grounded the vessel. The impact sent hogs and barrels, which he had been hired to transport, overboard. Years later, while traveling home along the Detroit River from Washington, where he was serving in Congress, he witnessed a steamboat run aground. It triggered his quest to invent a flotation device to buoy a grounded ship over sandbars or other obstructions without discharging all of its cargo. He constructed a miniature model (now housed at the Smithsonian Institute), wrote up a description, applied for a patent, and paid the same thirty-dollar fee every other aspiring patentee was required to file. On May 22, 1849, the U.S. Patent Office approved his invention and issued Patent Number 6,469 for his "device for buoying vessels over shoals." Though he did not pursue commercialization of his product (Lincoln was, after all, preoccupied with more pressing matters), scholar Jason Emerson notes that the president's ideas "may have advanced the creation of modern ship salvaging and submarine construction."

The great American novelist Mark Twain—patent holder on three inventions (a self-adhering scrapbook, a memory game, and an elastic strap for clothing), technology investor, and friend of inventive genius Nikola Tesla—venerated our patent system in his novel, *A Connecticut Yankee in King Arthur's Court*. Transported from the nineteenth century back to the Middle Ages, Twain's time-traveling protagonist, Hank Morgan, set out to modernize sixth-century society. "The very first official thing I did, in my administration—and it was on the very first day of it too—was to start a patent office," Hank says, "for I knew that a country without a patent office and good patent laws was just a crab and couldn't travel anyway but sideways and backwards."

The fuel of interest—that is, the opportunity to profit from one's ideas—induced a large number of diverse people to turn their attention to inventing, innovating, and improving. As one official at a celebration of the patent office centennial quipped in 1891, the patent office stimulated Americans to "turn their thinking into things." From 1863 to 1913, an estimated 800–1,200 patents were issued to black inventors. Between 1790 and 1895, some 3,300 women secured more than 4,100 patents. Frontier and rural women patented important devices and improvements in dairy farming and food preservation. New England and East Coast women pioneered manufacturing innovations in everything from elevator safety to sewing machines and paper bags.

Between 1870 and 1930, economist B. Zorina Khan's research shows, 21 percent of all patentees were foreign-born inventors; foreign-born residents accounted for between 10 and 14 percent of the total population.

Throughout this book, the American tinkerpreneurs who successfully commercialized both "ordinary" and "extraordinary" inventions and innovations extracted financial gains from their patents. They defended, acquired, and traded on their patents unapologetically. Glass industrialists Michael Owens and Edward Libbey licensed their bottle-making equipment. Nikola Tesla sold his key alternating current patents to George Westinghouse, who had the capital and know-how to bring Tesla's work to market. Disposable bottle cap pioneer William Painter, who had been the victim of intellectual property theft early in his career, armed himself with aggressive patent lawyers. So did Westinghouse, disposable razor inventor King Gillette, and Maglite inventor Anthony Maglica. Fending off intellectual property thieves was vital to a budding tinkerpreneur's survival.

For more than two centuries, these founding principles and institutions have yielded the most innovative nation in the world. As the many examples in this book have shown, American tinkerpreneurs are also among the world's most generous philanthropists. Profit and the public good go hand in hand. But the twenty-first century has ushered in dangerous threats to the time-tested patent system and American innovation. Under the guise of "reform," transnationalists and anti-traditionalists have undermined inventors' rights and U.S. sovereignty.

As part of his radical bid to "fundamentally transform" America, President Obama signed the Orwellian-titled America Invents Act (AIA) in 2011. If truth-in-advertising laws applied to politicians who front massively complex bills that do the *opposite* of what they proclaim to do, these hucksters would be jailed for their patently fraudulent "reform" legislation. Cosponsored by Sen. Pat Leahy (D-VT) and Rep. Lamar Smith (R-TX), the law was marketed as a job-creation vehicle that would relieve a backlog of an estimated seven hundred thousand patent applications and crack down on patent "trolls" supposedly abusing the system through frivolous litigation against alleged infringers. In truth, the AIA is a special-interest boondoggle that enriches corporate lawyers, Big Business, and federal bureaucrats at the expense of independent inventors and fledgling innovators the American patent system was created to protect and encourage.

The AIA's primary agenda? "Harmonizing" our patent laws with the rest of the world to reward paper-pushers who are "first to file" at the Patent Office, instead of those who are "first to invent." These and other measures enacted by President Barack Obama threaten to drive garage tinkerers and small inventors—the designers, engineers, and builders of American prosperity—out of the marketplace. Longtime venture capitalist Gary Lauder notes that the first-to-file system has suppressed solo and small business innovation in Europe and Japan. "The US gets ten times the angel and venture capital of Western Europe—which recently declared an 'innovation emergency,'" Lauder observes, "so why are we harmonizing with them? They should be harmonizing with us." Amen and hallelujah! If only American politicians spoke up for American inventors with such force and clarity.

Large multinational entities benefit most from the European patent system of "first to file." Solo do-it-yourself-ers and small start-up shops—like the ones highlighted throughout this book—don't have armies of high-priced attorneys on retainer to race to the patent office for every last brainchild. Steve Perlman, prolific inventor and holder of more than one hundred patents on inventions ranging from Quicktime to WebTV to MOVA Contour 3-D special effects imaging, tried to teach Congress how the time-tested, uniquely American "first to invent" system had allowed him to create successful businesses that supported thousands of American jobs. "A large part of invention is trying out a vast number of ideas," he explained in an open letter to leading senators. To develop MOVA Contour, a digital facial motion capture system used most famously to reverse-age Brad Pitt in *The Curious Case of Benjamin Button,* Perlman experimented with one hundred unique inventions over five years of research and development. He ended up patenting only a half-dozen ideas after the necessary trial-and-error tinkering.

The original inventor-friendly process, enshrined by founding constitutional principles, allowed inventors to wait and vet quality patent applications until they'd fully developed and tested quality inventions. Cash-strapped start-ups could defer patent filing expenses until they decided they were good and ready. Under the old American way, as long as Perlman kept proper documentation, he retained priority over his ideas from the date he conceived them:

> It typically costs us $20,000–$30,000 to obtain a commercial-grade patent. As you can imagine, in a First-to-File country, as a startup, we could only file patents on a small fraction of the inventions at the time of conception. . . . [T]he inventions that looked the most promising at the outset turned out to be dead ends. Had we filed patents on them, it would have been wasted money, while the inventions that mattered would not have been patented at all, potentially making it impossible to fund the company. It is no surprise that the [U.S.] is by far the leading nation in the world when it comes to startups and, since its earliest days (when "First-to-Invent" was established), America has been known as a mecca for invention.

No more, thanks to Team Obama's wrecking crew. The European-style "first to file" now in place in America is a "*forced* to file" regime that incentivizes a hasty stampede to the federal patent office. In the name of global harmony, we now reward paper-pushing attorneys—whether or not they're representing true first inventors. Instead of "streamlining" the application process and reducing paperwork backlogs, the AIA induces corporations to inundate patent examiners with incomplete, placeholder applications that will inevitably need to be amended, refined, and reconsidered. This is not patent "reform." It's a Big Business Patent Lawyers' Full Employment Act.

Like Obamacare, the sheer size and complexity of the AIA nullify the dubious benefits the White House and its statist lobbying pals claim it will bring. University of Virginia law professor John Duffy points out that the law is 140 pages long, "more than twice the length of the entire federal patent statute" since its last recodification in 1952. Stuffed with earmarks and bribes for the banking industry, Michigan Democrats who lobbied for a new satellite patent office in Detroit, and other well-connected cronies, the AIA's thirty-seven sections are intentionally complex. Its sloppy drafting will result in "cases interpreting the law going to the courts for twenty years before lawyers really know how to advise clients," patent lawyer David Boundy predicts. Also buried in the law: a new pay-for-play scheme, dubbed "Fast Track for Fat Cats" by indie inventors, which allows large companies to expedite their applications by forking over a $4,800 fee. Southern California small business inventor Bryan Pate, who founded an elliptical training bike company in 2005, states the obvious: "Having to spend more money to speed up the process favors big companies, not small ones."

Crony favoritism is a feature, not a bug, of President Obama's radical initiatives—from Obamacare to the Dodd-Frank financial "reform" monstrosity to the federal stimulus package (aka porkulus) to Patentcare. It's no coincidence that the AIA's chief Senate cheerleader, Democratic Senator Pat Leahy, championed President Obama's first PTO nominee, David Kappos, a former Big Biz corporate lawyer for IBM. As head of the PTO, Kappos lobbied aggressively for passage of the AIA. Kappos then resigned from the White House to take a cushy lobbying job with New York firm Cravath, Swaine, and Moore, which Kappos had worked closely with when his former employer IBM retained them. Kappos is now paid handsomely to advise deep-pocketed clients on how to navigate the intellectual property rules and complex patent regulations that he implemented at taxpayer expense. Nice revolving-door work if you can get it.

To add insult to small-size inventors' injury, the bipartisan, corporate special interests behind the AIA are the same ones selling American workers and patriotic job creators like Tony Maglica down the river through rampant outsourcing and systemic importing of cheap, temporary foreign labor. But that's the subject of another book.

Classics scholar and historian Arnold Toynbee is best remembered for arguing that "civilizations die from suicide, not by murder." Global competitors certainly pose serious external threats to America's leading role as an innovation leader. But we face grave existential threats within our own borders: homegrown ignorance, apathy, and downright hostility toward the principles and institutions that made America great. Real "reform" begins with the repeal of the innovation-stifling "America Invents Act," a return to first constitutional principles that maintain a level playing field among tinkerpreneurs of all sizes, and a rhetorical and policy ceasefire by Beltway class warriors who've recklessly demonized our nation's most productive and creative members for their own political gain.

Liberty, not government, is the world's most powerful wellspring of innovation. The stories I've told here are but a small confirmation that free human beings, acting in their own self-interest, also best serve the public good. This revolutionary idea is a hallmark of American exceptionalism. French historian Alexis de Tocqueville reported that the doctrine of enlightened "self-interest rightly understood" was a part of America's DNA from its founding. It was a tenet held and practiced fiercely not just by elites, but by everyone. "You may trace it at the bottom of all their actions, you will remark it in all they say. It is as often asserted by the poor man as the rich," de Tocqueville observed. Author Charles Murray adds that the Founders promoted industriousness—"something more than working hard." Murray describes it as "the bone-deep American assumption that life is to be spent getting ahead through hard work and thereby making a better life for oneself and one's children." He points to German social historian Francis Grund, a contemporary of de Tocqueville's, who observed firsthand America's insatiable willingness to work. "Active occupation is not only the principal source of happiness, and the foundation of their natural greatness, but they are absolutely wretched without it. . . . Business is the very soul of an American," he wrote in 1837.

Entrepreneurial industriousness was in the soul of businessman Charles Hires, who turned dirt into dollars and twigs into root beer. It was in the souls of the Scott brothers, who went from selling butcher paper on the streets to building a corporate powerhouse selling toilet paper and paper towels. It drove William Painter, who achieved great wealth, but kept working until he could work no more. It bound business partners Willis Carrier and J. Irvine Lyle, Westinghouse and Tesla, and Libbey and Owens, whose engineering feats and business endeavors still benefit the world today. It was in the souls of the Roebling family, who gave limbs and lives to fulfill their American Dream. It was in the souls of the mom-and-pop shop owners and indomitable amputees who pioneered artificial limbs in the nineteenth century. And it's in the souls of their twenty-first-century successors from New England to West Virginia, Iowa, Colorado, and California.

Our founders understood at the dawn of the Age of Progress what the Girl Scouts in Ames, Iowa, who secured a patent for their Lego limb, now appreciate: *The power to make money is the power to do good.*

When one tinkerpreneur's dream is fulfilled, unimaginable new opportunities arise. One new industry begets myriad others. Through voluntary associations between and among countless producers and consumers, private advancement and social progress are made.

These are the results of one of humankind's most marvelous innovations of all. It guides millions of individual makers and risk-takers to pursue their own profits and happiness while enhancing the public good—including all of the tinkerpreneurs I've profiled. It's the same ineluctable force that brings complete strangers together to produce cars, planes, trains, electricity, pharmaceuticals, smartphones, dumb-waiters, diapers, pencils, prosthetics, and yes, this book.

No one can see or touch it, but modern American life and all of its wondrous amenities wouldn't exist without this freedom-powered device:

The invisible hand.

ACKNOWLEDGMENTS

Behind every story, there's another story. Behind the stories of *Who Built That*, there are even more stories of providence, patriotism, entrepreneurship, friendship, and family.

In April 2010, Glenn Beck and his staff asked if I could offer a "unique experience" item for their celebrity charity auction to benefit the Special Operations Warrior Foundation. I proposed to take the top bidders on a train up the Cog Railway in Colorado Springs. It's a historic ride to the top of Pikes Peak, more than fourteen thousand feet above sea level. The breathtaking views there inspired schoolteacher Katharine Lee Bates to pen the words to "America, the Beautiful" in 1893.

The winning bid for the train ride was placed by an energetic, freedom-loving couple from Oklahoma, Scott and Debbie McEachin. Scott is also a railroad history buff; his enthusiasm was infectious. After our trip, my curiosity was sparked: *Who built that?* The groundbreaking Cog Railway, I discovered, was the result of one man's private initiative. Wisconsin inventor and entrepreneur Zalman Simmons, who made a fortune from the coil-spring mattress company that still bears his name today, spearheaded the project against all odds. In the late 1880s, Simmons had traveled by mule to check on insulators for telegraph wires that he had installed at the top of Pikes Peak for the army signal station. The irrepressible businessman vowed to build a better transportation alternative up the steep mountainside. Simmons incorporated the Manitou & Pike's Peak Railway Company, invested his own capital, recruited engineers, and spent two years overseeing construction. In 1891, the railway's first passenger car—carrying a church choir from Denver—ascended the nine-mile track and reached the summit. Nearly 125 years later, the privately funded railway that Simmons built is still in business today.

In 2013, I shared that story with Glenn and we talked about our mutual love of American tinkerers. Our discussion of my book idea— a "fateful meeting of geek minds," I called it—evolved into one of the most satisfying research endeavors of my writing career. My thanks to Glenn, Kevin Balfe, and the staff at Mercury Ink for their belief in this project. Thanks to Scott and Debbie for their stimulating company and continued camaraderie. And thanks to Zalman Simmons for his mountain-traversing inspiration!

Thanks to Simon & Schuster's Threshold Editions editorial director Mitchell Ivers and assistant editor Natasha Simons for their keen insights and masterful guidance on shaping the manuscript.

Thanks to the staff members at the Lincoln Home National Historic Site, Allegheny Portage Railroad National Historic Site, National Park Service, Lower Merion (Pennsylvania) Historical Society, the University of Toledo's Ward M. Canady Center, Heinz History Center, and Westinghouse Electric Company for their assistance.

I can't thank Tony Maglica enough for sharing his invaluable time and insights with me. Thanks also to Mag Instrument, Inc., in-house general counsel Jerry Reilly and all of Tony's employees who took a few moments out of their busy day to explain their work.

Thanks to Greg Gruman of the Winkley Company, Katherine Bomkamp of Katherine Bomkamp International, and Bert Harries of Bally Ribbon Company for sharing information about their remarkable businesses.

Big thank-you bouquets to Cindy McNew for her sharp eyes and editing feedback; to my Colorado Springs friends Tina Cox and Mark Connell for their techno-engineer-y expertise and review of several chapters of the book; and to Jacob Bunn for his assistance in manuscript prep.

Deepest thanks to my dear in-laws, Carole and Dick, for their constant encouragement and trenchant editing suggestions every step of the way. It was a special privilege and blessing to receive support from Carole, an accomplished novelist and superlative storyteller who gave her time so generously as she bravely battled cancer. Her spirit lives on in my heart and these pages.

And as always, the best for last: Unending thanks and praise for my husband and rock, Jesse, and my children, Veronica and Julian, for their love and support. Kids, one of the most important themes of this book is my life lesson for you: *Nihil boni sine labore.*

NOTES

EPIGRAPHS AND INTRODUCTION

vii   "The great glory of the Americans is in their wondrous contrivances—in their patent remedies for the usually troublous operations of life." Anthony Trollope, *North America 1863* (Philadelphia: J.B. Lippincott & Co., 1863), p. 127.

vii   "So I suppose all those great works built themselves!" Francis Ellington Leupp, *George Westinghouse: His Life and Achievements* (Boston: Little, Brown, and Company, 1918), p. 274.

2   "The Scrap Heap—that inarticulate witness of our blunders, and the sepulchre of our blasted hopes." "Memoir of Don Juan Whittemore," *Transactions of the American Society of Civil Engineers* (New York: ASME), Vol. 82, 1918, p. 1658.

3   ". . . every single great idea that has marked the twenty-first century, the twentieth century and the nineteenth century has required government vision and government incentive." Matt Welch, "Biden: Every Great American Idea 'has required government vision and government incentive," Reason.com blog, October 27, 2010, accessed May 14, 2014, http://reason.com/blog/2010/10/27/biden-every-great-american-ide, and Tad DeHaven, "It Ain't So, Joe," Cato.org blog, October 27, 201, accessed May 14, 2014, http://www.cato.org/blog/it-aint-so-joe.

3   ". . . the core responsibilities of the financial system to help grow our economy." Barack Obama, "Remarks by the President on Wall Street Reform

in Quincy, Illinois," White House transcript, April 28, 2010, accessed May 14, 2014, http://www.whitehouse.gov/the-press-office/remarks-pres ident-wall-street-reform-quincy-illinois.

3 ". . . at a certain point you have made enough money." Ibid.

4 "If you've got a business—you didn't build that. Somebody else made that happen." Jake Tapper, "Did Obama say, 'If you've got a business, you didn't build that'?" ABC News, July 16, 2012, accessed May 14, 2014, http://abcnews.go.com/blogs/politics/2012/07/did-obama-say-if-youve -got-a-business-you-didnt-build-that/.

4 "The Obama campaign and its media defenders argued that his re- marks were taken 'out of context'." Glenn Kessler, "An unoriginal Obama quote, taken out of context," *Washington Post*, July 23, 2014, accessed May 14, 2014, http://www.washingtonpost.com/blogs/fact-checker/post /an-unoriginal-obama-quote-taken-out-of-context/2012/07/20/gJQA dG7hyW_blog.html.

4 ". . . straight from the White House transcript." Barack Obama, "Remarks by the President at a Campaign Event in Roanoke, Virginia," White House transcript, July 13, 2012, accessed May 15, 2014, http://www.whitehouse .gov/the-press-office/2012/07/13/remarks-president-campaign-event -roanoke-virginia.

4 ". . . Article I, Section 8, Clause 8, of our Constitution." U.S. Constitution, art. I, sec. 8, cl. 8, accessed May 14, 2014, http://www.constitution.org/js /js_319.htm.

5 ". . . candidates and operatives in *both* political parties derided private equity and venture capitalism as 'vulture capitalism.'" See, for example, Fe- licia Sonmez, "Rick Perry doubles down on 'vulture capitalist' criticism of Romney," *Washington Post*, January 11, 2012, accessed May 14, 2014, http:// www.washingtonpost.com/blogs/post-politics/post/rick-perry-doubles -down-on-vulture-capitalist-criticism-of-mitt-romney/2012/01/11/gIQA ziWqqP_blog.html, and John Nichols, "Romney still reaps huge profits from Bain's vulture capitalism," *The Nation*, July 16, 2012, accessed May 14, 2014, http://www.thenation.com/blog/168899/romney-still-reaps-huge -profits-bains-vulture-capitalism.

5 "President Obama routinely indicted 'millionaires and billionaires.'" Jeanne Sahadi, "Billionaires with 1% tax rates," CNN.com, accessed May 15, 2014, http://money.cnn.com/2011/12/07/news/economy/obama _taxes/.

5 "Anticapitalism saboteurs organized wealth-shaming protests at corpo- rate CEOs' private homes." Mark Trumbull, "Occupy Wall Street: Who

are the targets of millionaires' march?" *Christian Science Monitor,* October 11, 2011, accessed May 15, 2014, http://www.csmonitor.com/USA /Politics/2011/1011/Occupy-Wall-Street-Who-are-targets-of-millionaires -march.

5   "Paul Krugman (a former high-paid adviser to corrupt energy company Enron) whipped up hatred against the 'plutocrats.'" Paul Krugman, "Plutocrats feeling persecuted," *New York Times,* September 27, 2013, accessed May 14, 2014, http://www.nytimes.com/2013/09/27/opinion/krugman -plutocrats-feeling-persecuted.html?_r=0.

5   "Democratic strategist Donna Brazile publicly endorsed an incendiary protest slogan embraced by so-called progressives." "Eliminationist retweet by Donna Brazile: 'Prune the top 1$,'" Twitchy.com, accessed May 14, 2014, http://twitchy.com/2014/04/24/eliminationist-retweet-by -donna-brazile-prune-the-top-1/.

5   "New York State lawmakers received threatening mail saying it was 'time to kill the wealthy.'" Tim Mak, "E-mail: 'Time to kill the wealthy,'" Politico .com, October 6, 2011, accessed May 15, 2014, http://www.politico.com /news/stories/1011/65307.html.

5   ". . . from a disgruntled state government worker." Nicholas Confessore, "State police investigating e-mail to lawmakers," April 1, 2011, accessed December 25, 2014, http://cityroom.blogs.nytimes.com/2011/04/01/state -police-investigating-e-mail-to-lawmaker/?_r=0.

6   ". . . even as private venture capital has grown from 'the pilot light of American industry' to its 'roaring glass furnace.'" Rushworth M. Kidder, "Venture capital: fuel for new inventions," *Christian Science Monitor,* January 13, 1983, accessed May 15, 2014, http://www.csmonitor.com /1983/0113/011337.html.

6   "In *The Money of Invention,* business professors Paul Gompers and Josh Lerner noted." Paul Gompers and Josh Lerner, *The Money of Invention: How Venture Capital Creates New Wealth* (Boston: Harvard Business Review Press, 2001), p. 67.

6   "Kleiner Perkins 'made more than 475 investments, generating $90 billion in revenue and creating 275,000 jobs.'" Maggy Bruzelius, "Venture Capitalist Launches a Superyacht—and a Novel," MIT Alumni Association *Infinite Connection News & Views,* Alumni Profiles, 2006, accessed May 15, 2014, https://alum.mit.edu/news/AlumniProfiles/Archive/Tom _Perkins_-2753.

7   "In January 2014, Tom Perkins wrote a passionate letter to the *Wall Street Journal.*" Thomas Perkins, "Progressive Kristallnacht coming?" *Wall Street*

Journal, January 24, 2014, accessed May 15, 2014, http://online.wsj.com /news/articles/SB10001424052702304549504579316913982034286.

7 "'Any time the majority starts to demonize a minority, no matter what it is, it's wrong. And dangerous. And no good ever comes from it.'" Ibid.

8 "'It's absurd to demonize the rich for being rich and for doing what the rich do, which is get richer by creating opportunity for others.'" Ibid.

10 "... eighteenth-century philosopher and political economist Adam Smith's famous free-market theory." Adam Smith, *An Inquiry into the Nature and Causes of the Wealth of Nations* (London: Methuen & Co., Ltd.), 5th edition, Edwin Cannan, ed., 1904, Section IV.2.9., available online through the Library of Economics and Liberty, accessed May 14, 2014, http://www.econlib.org/library/Smith/smWN.html.

PART I

13 "We had faith and enthusiasm in our enterprise, with loyalty to each other and to a common cause." Margaret Ingels, *Willis Haviland Carrier: Father of Air Conditioning* (Garden City, N.Y.: Country Life Press, 1952), p. 47.

CHAPTER 1: MAGLITE'S TONY MAGLICA: TORCHBEARER OF THE AMERICAN DREAM

All details about the Maglica and Jurcan families' lives on Zlarin come from *The Winds of Ruza and Borovica: A story about the Zlarin Families—Jurcan and Maglica.*

18 "compensated instead with a bit of fish for lunch or a small carafe of wine." Dusko Dean, *The Winds of Ruza and Borovica: A Story About the Zlarin Families—Jurcan and Maglica* (self-published, 1993).

18 "Irving Berlin and Albert Einstein." "Home," Red Star Line Museum, accessed May 7, 2014, http://www.redstarline.be/en; "A Philadelphia Quaker and Fabric Row," The PhillyHistory Blog, March 21, 2013, accessed May 7, 014, http://www.phillyhistory.org/blog/index.php/2013/03/a -philadephia-quaker-and-fabric-row/.

18 "desperately selling apples for a nickel apiece." "Timeline of the Great Depression," Public Broadcasting Service, accessed May 7, 2014, http://www .pbs.org/wgbh/americanexperience/features/timeline/rails-timeline/.

20 "Germans executed nearly 270 Croats in the village of Lipa." John Peter Kraljic, "Croatian Inmates in German Concentration Camps," Croatian World Network, accessed May 7, 2014, http://www.croatia.org/crown

/articles/6261/1/E-Croatian-Inmates-in-German-Concentration-Camps
.html.

21 "'amazing stories' the company has collected from first responders, soldiers, sportsmen, and ordinary housewives." All the letters come from
Maglite archives. I've edited the text only for spelling and grammar.

26 "atomic bomb project parts during World War II." "Mag Instrument, Inc.
Business Information, Profile, and History," JRank Articles, accessed
May 7, 2014, http://companies.jrank.org/pages/2592/Mag-Instrument
-Inc.html; "History Milestones," A. O. Smith, accessed May 7, 2014, http://
www.aosmith.com/About/Detail.aspx?id=130.

26 "I modified the machines I had." Kemp Powers, "Anthony Maglica," CNN
Money, September 1, 2004, accessed May 7, 2014, http://money.cnn.com
/magazines/fsb/fsb_archive/2004/09/01/8184669/index.htm.

27 "bulbs were inefficient and could not produce a steady stream of light."
"Flashlight Museum," Wordcraft.net, accessed May 7, 2014, http://www
.wordcraft.net/flashlight.html.

28 "establishing the famous Lionel Train Company in 1902." "Lionel And
Railroads In America," Lionel, accessed May 7, 2014, http://www.lionel
.com/CentralStation/LionelPastAndPresent/.

28 "torches became a national sensation." Invention Geek, "Let There Be
Light!—Invention of the Flashlight," Patent Plaques, March 8, 2011, accessed May 7, 2014, http://www.patentplaques.com/blog/?p=2071.

28 "advertised the flashlights using the biblical phrase, 'Let There Be Light.'"
"Flashlights 101: Flashlight History," Energizer, accessed May 7, 2014,
http://www.energizer.com/learning-center/Pages/flashlight-history
.aspx.

28 "so you get a better connection." Powers, "Anthony Maglica: Mag Instrument."

29 "Tony put it bluntly." Paul B. Brown, "Magnificent Obsession," *Inc.*,
August 1, 1989, accessed May 7, 2014, http://www.inc.com/magazine
/19890801/5754.html.

30 "essentially the Maglite® of computers." "The Mag Instrument Story,"
Maglite, accessed May 7, 2014, http://www.maglite.com/history.asp.

30 "We have worked hard to earn our reputation." "Mag Instrument Inc.
Prevails In Patent Infringement Lawsuit," PR Newswire, August 12, 1999.

31 "selling Maglite look-alikes," Mag Instrument Inc. Major Historical Events,
Maglite, accessed May 7, 2014, http://www.maglite.com/eventtimeline.asp.

31 "products that embody those technologies and bear those marks." "Strengthening American Manufacturing," Maglite, accessed May 7, 2014, http://www.maglite.com/strengthen.asp.

32 "unabashedly 'Made in America.'" W. Lidwell and G. Manacsa, *Deconstructing Product Design: Exploring the Form, Function, Usability, Sustainability, and Commercial Success of 100 Amazing Products* (Minneapolis: Rockport Publishers, 2011), pp. 115–16.

32 "If I can do it, anyone can! This is America!" Peter Whoriskey, "Lightbulb factory closes: End of an era for U.S. means more jobs overseas," *Washington Post*, September 8, 2010, accessed May 7, 2014, http://www.washington post.com/wp-dyn/content/article/2010/09/07/AR2010090706933.html.

CHAPTER 2: THE WIZARDS OF COOL: AIR-CONDITIONING INNOVATORS WILLIS CARRIER AND IRVINE LYLE

36 "the atmosphere exerts a pressure of about fifteen pounds per square inch." Margaret Ingels, *Willis Haviland Carrier: Father of Air Conditioning* (Garden City, N.Y.: Country Life Press, 1952), p. 4.

37 "My mother told me to go to the cellar and bring up a pan of apples." Ibid, p. 3.

37 "Lyle played varsity football for the school and joined Sigma Chi (the social fraternity) and Tau Beta Pi (the honor society for engineers)." University of Kentucky College of Engineering, Engineering Alumni Association, "Joel Irvine Lyle," accessed May 12, 2014, https://www.engr.uky.edu/alumni/hod/joel-irvine-lyle/.

38 "After he researched electricity and magnetism at the U.S. Patent Office and Library of Congress, Cornell concluded that he needed to fix faulty cable insulation problems." Corey Ryan Earle, "Ezra Cornell's legacy of innovation and entrepreneurship lives on," *Ezra: Cornell's Quarterly Magazine*, Volume IV, Number 3, Spring 2012, accessed May 12, 2014, http://ezramagazine.cornell.edu/SPRING12/CornellHistory.html.

38 "Morse hired him to string up the overhead line between Washington and Baltimore, through which the inventor delivered his famous 'What hath God wrought?' message." Cornell University, "I Would Found an Institution"; The Ezra Cornell Bicentennial, "The Telegraph," accessed May 12, 2014, http://rmc.library.cornell.edu/ezra/exhibition/telegraph/.

38 "An intrepid capitalist, Cornell took a large part of his pay in stock and became Western Union's largest stockholder." The Business of the Tele-

graph; Ezra Cornell: A Nineteenth-Century Life, accessed May 12, 2014, http://rmc.library.cornell.edu/Ezra-exhibit/EC-life/EC-life-6.html.

38   "Buffalo Forge, cofounded by a Cornell grad, made blacksmith's forges, upright drills, steam engines, heaters, dust collectors, blowers, and band-saws." VintageMachinery.org, "Buffalo Forgo Co.," accessed May 12, 2014, http://vintagemachinery.org/mfgindex/detail.aspx?id=129.

39   "The 'catch' must be edible or I don't try for it. I only fish for edible fish and test for useful data." WillisCarrier.com, "The Launch of Carrier Air Conditioning Company," accessed May 12, 2014, http://www.williscarrier .com/m/1903-1914.php.

39   "'MANY ARE HEAT STRICKEN IN SUDDEN TORRID WAVE,' the Brooklyn (N.Y.) Daily Eagle reported in late May of that year." "MANY ARE HEAT STRICKEN IN SUDDEN TORRID WAVE," The Brooklyn Daily Eagle, Volume 62, Number 144, May 25, 1902, p. 58, accessed May 12, 2014, http://reference.insulators.info/publications/view/?id=4978.

39   "President Theodore Roosevelt escaped from the sweltering Washington, D.C., swamp to the cooler confines of his Sagamore Hill beach home on Oyster Bay, New York." Lawrence L. Knutson, Theodore Roosevelt's Summer White House (Washington, D.C.: White House Historical Association, 2011), accessed May 12, 2014, http://www.whitehousehistory.org/blog /wp-content/uploads/2011/08/theodore-roosevelt-summer-white-house .pdf.

39   "A team of thirty-five employees operated the plant's twenty-five steam-power presses and forty hand presses at all hours to meet grueling dead-lines." History and Commerce of New York, 1891, Second Edition (New York: American Publishing and Engraving Co., 1891), p. 115.

40   "The magazine's most famous cartoonist: Theodor 'Dr. Seuss' Geisel, who was hired at age twenty-three as a writer and artist in the late 1920s. An-other famous Judge alumnus, Harold Ross, left in 1925 to found The New Yorker." Thomas Fensch, The Man Who Was Dr. Seuss: The Life and Work of Theodor Geisel (New Century Exceptional Lives Series) (Sharon's Books), December 1, 2001.

41   "By July 17, 1902, as New York sweated out the heat wave, Carrier had drawn up plans for what would be the world's first scientific air-conditioning system." Margaret Ingels, Willis Haviland Carrier: Father of Air Conditioning, op. cit., p. 17. The term was first coined by textile engineer Stuart Cramer, who invented special humidifiers in North Carolina to keep yarn fibers moist in dry factory air. He dubbed the humidity control process "air-conditioning"; later, the term incorporated temperature control as well.

41   "The air is cooled by blowing it over a set of cold pipes called an evaporator coil." Ashrae.org, "Top Ten Things About Air Conditioning," accessed May 12, 2014, https://www.ashrae.org/resources—publications/free-resources/top-ten-things-about-air-conditioning.

42   "Carrier engineer Margaret Ingels marveled at the scope of her bosses' breakthroughs." Margaret Ingels, *Willis Haviland Carrier: Father of Air Conditioning*, op. cit., p. 18.

42   "A year later, they replaced the compressor at Sackett & Wilhelms and Lyle reported back to Buffalo Forge that 'the cooling coils which we sold this company have given excellent results during the past summer.'" Ibid., p. 19.

43   "Those in a position to know give to J. I. Lyle the credit for a large measure of the commercial success of the Carrier Air Conditioning Company." "Organization of Carrier Engineering Corporation," *The Heating and Ventilating Magazine*, Volume 12, 1915, p. 51.

43   "He once jetted off on a business trip only to discover that his suitcase contained nothing but a handkerchief." Margaret Ingels, *Willis Haviland Carrier: Father of Air Conditioning*, op. cit., pp. 35–36.

43   "Here is air approximately 100 percent saturated with moisture." Ibid., p. 21.

44   "Carrier realized in that foggy moment that he could dry air by *wetting* it—passing it through water and using the spray as the condensing surface." WillisCarrier.com, "The Launch of Carrier Air Conditioning Company," op. cit.

44   "The mist also helped cleanse and purify the air of dust." T. A. Heppenheimer, "Cold Comfort," *American Heritage*, Spring 2005, Volume 20, Issue 4, accessed May 12, 2014, http://archive.today/iEMad#selection-1203.341-1207.

45   "Dubbed 'Carrene-2,' it became the basis for Carrier's own refrigerants for centrifugal compression." Ibid.

45   "Carrier's relentless theoretical research affected not only air-conditioning, but also agriculture, aeronautics, food engineering, pharmaceuticals, meteorology, weather reporting, and more." Donald P. Gatley, "Psychrometric Chart Celebrates 100th Anniversary," *ASHRAE Journal*, Vol. 46, No. 12, November 2004, pp. 16–20.

45   "The application of this new art to many varied industries has been demonstrated to be of greatest economic importance." Willis H. Carrier,

"Rational Psychrometric Formulae," *Journal of the American Society of Mechanical Engineers*, Volume 33, July 1911, pp. 1311–49.

46 "Workers flocked to the stemming room for relief from the humidity, heat, and dirt." Margaret Ingels, *Willis Haviland Carrier: Father of Air Conditioning*, op. cit., pp. 37–39.

47 "During World War II, the military took advantage of Carrier's top engineering talent and produced classified machinery and parts, including airplane engine mounts, sight hoods for guns, tank adapters, and anti-submarine bomb dischargers." WillisCarrier.com, "The Launch of Carrier Air Conditioning Company," op. cit.

48 "Zukor served as treasurer for Loew's Inc., which later became the parent company of Metro-Goldwyn-Mayer Pictures." Albin Krebs, "Adolph Zukor Is Dead at 103; Built Paramount Movie Empire," *New York Times*, June 11, 1976, accessed May 12, 2014, http://www.nytimes.com/learning/general/onthisday/bday/0107.html.

48 "The budding showman wanted to produce movies with glamorous celebrities and lasting artistic value beyond the short one-reel features then in vogue. In 1912, he established his own production company. Among his founding partners: feature-length film pioneer Jesse Lasky and director Cecil B. DeMille." Bernard F. Dick, *Engulfed: The Death of Paramount Pictures and the Birth of Corporate Hollywood* (Lexington, Ky.: University Press of Kentucky, 2001).

49 "Among the most famously luxe entertainment edifices of the time: the Chicago Theater in Illinois, Loew's Penn in Pittsburgh, and impresario Sid Grauman's Chinese and Egyptian theaters in Los Angeles." Lucy Fischer, ed., *American Cinema of the 1920s: Themes and Variations* (New Brunswick, N.J.: Rutgers, The State University of New Jersey, 2009).

49 "Enter the entrepreneurial engineers. Inventor Walter Fleisher attempted to cool the Folies-Bergère theater in New York City with a primitive air washer, but lack of mechanical refrigeration doomed it." "The Story of Comfort Air Conditioning," accessed May 12, 2014, http://www.hevac-heritage.org/electronic_books/comfort_AC/8-CAC2.pdf.

49 "At Chicago's Central Park and Riviera Theaters, impresarios Barney and Abe Balaban and Sam and Maurice Katz unveiled a new, carbon dioxide–based cooling system devised by Frederick Wittenmeier that blew chilled air out of 'mushroom' vents at the feet of moviegoers." David Balaban, *The Chicago Movie Palaces of Balaban and Katz* (Charleston, S.C.: Arcadia Publishing, 2006).

49 "Carrier engineers were initially mocked by theater snobs for their 'upside down system.'" "The Story of Comfort Air Conditioning," op. cit.

50 "This sophisticated machinery was the first practical means of cooling large spaces." WillisCarrier.com, "The Launch of Carrier Air Conditioning Company," op. cit.

50 "Traditional 'reciprocal compressor' devices were large units that operated like back-and-forth pistons on a locomotive." T. A. Heppenheimer, "Cold Comfort," op. cit.

50 "The entire system of electric transmission has been developed from nothing to an enormous industry with relatively simple motors that are high-speed rotative equipment." Margaret Ingels, *Willis Haviland Carrier: Father of Air Conditioning*, op. cit., p. 55.

52 "It takes time to pull down the temperature in a quickly filled theater on a hot day, and a still longer time for a packed house." Ibid., pp. 64–67.

52 "The Rivoli's main marquee blared 'REFRIGERATING PLANT' and the doorway entrance sign boasted 'COOLED BY REFRIGERATION.'" Mark H. Huston, "Brief History of Centrifugal Chillers," *ASHRAE Journal*, Vol. 47, No. 12, December 2005, p. 25.

52 "The theater was more than just a picture palace. It had become an 'ideal summer resort.'" "Rivoli Air Conditioning Advertisement, 1925," *New York Times*, accessed May 12, 2014, http://www.nytimes.com/interactive /2012/09/02/nyregion/a-history-of-new-york-in-50-objects.html?src=se &_r=0#/?gridItem=02-fifty-objects-slide-DC1Y.

52 ". . . generating year-round profits and patrons thanks to the 'marvelous equipment which absolutely assures a temperature that is just right.'" WillisCarrier.com, "The Launch of Carrier Air Conditioning Company," op. cit.

53 "The company also installed its system at the famed Roxy theater in New York, a fifty-nine-hundred-seat palace billed as 'the cathedral of the motion picture.'" Matthew Steigbigel, "'Playing the Palace': A History of Motion Picture Palaces," April 15, 2013, accessed May 12, 2014, http:// www.thecredits.org/2013/04/playing-the-palace-a-history-of-motion -picture-palaces/.

53 "By 1930, Carrier had installed three hundred air-conditioning systems in movie theaters across the country." Margaret Ingels, *Willis Haviland Carrier: Father of Air Conditioning*, op. cit., p. 68.

53 "The inventive genius and capitalist ambition of Carrier, Lyle, and their crew transformed summertime, once a box-office bomb, into Holly-

wood's most profitable season." Seth Abramovitch, "Forever 74 Degrees: How Movie Theaters Keep Cool During Summer's Scorching Months," *The Hollywood Reporter,* July 1, 2013, accessed May 12, 2014, http://www .hollywoodreporter.com/news/forever-74-degrees-how-movie-578120.

54 "Dr. Couney, who did not charge parents for his medical services, took the show on the road, treating babies at World's Fairs and European expositions, the Atlantic City Boardwalk." Fans of the HBO television show *Boardwalk Empire* will remember the scene featuring baby incubators from the premiere episode. See more at: pressofAtlanticCity.com, "For 'Boardwalk Empire'-era Atlantic City, babies in incubators were a sideshow attraction," accessed May 12, 2014, http://www.pressofatlanticcity.com/blogs /scott_cronick/for-boardwalk-empire-era-atlantic-city-babies-in-incu bators-were/article_89b9eb56-d992-11df-bdf7-001cc4c03286.html.

54 "San Francisco, Omaha, Chicago, Denver, Rio de Janeiro, and Mexico City." Neonatology on the Web, "Coney Island Sideshows," accessed May 12, 2014, http://www.neonatology.org/pinups/coneyislandnurses.html.

54 "As Carrier Air Conditioning Company of America engineer T. A. Weager explained in 1916, this 'sort of oven' was 'kept at a uniform temperature.'" T. A. Weager, "Successful Baby Incubator Installation," *Hospital Management*, Volume 1, February 1916, p. 9.

54 "Carrier used the same downdraft distribution and bypass techniques it applied in theaters . . ." Ibid.

55 "He received a patent in 1851 for the 'first machine ever to be used for mechanical refrigeration and air conditioning,' but was unable to create a viable business out of the invention." John Gladstone, "John Gorrie, the Visionary," *ASHRAE Journal*, December 1998, accessed May 12, 2014, https:// www.ashrae.org/File%20Library/docLib/Public/200362795143_326.pdf.

55 "Gorrie's ice maker 'made enough ice to chill bottles of champagne for a party but could not get the financial support he needed to develop his idea commercially,' *American Heritage* magazine observed." T. A. Heppenheimer, "Cold Comfort," op. cit.

55 "By the late 1950s virtually all new hospitals were installing airconditioning." Raymond Arsenault, "The End of the Long Hot Summer: The Air Conditioner and Southern Culture," *The Journal of Southern History*, Volume 50, Number 4, November 1984, pp. 597–628.

55 "Keeping the test tubes alone sealed tightly against contaminating bacteria, yeast and mold found in ordinary air would have slowed down their work considerably." "Air Conditioners Vital to Salk Vaccine Output," *Sarasota Herald-Tribune*, May 15, 1955.

56   "Temperature and humidity controls were the most important factors in rearing mosquitos successfully." *Manual for Mosquito Rearing and Experimental Techniques*, published by the American Mosquito Control Association, Inc., AMCA Bulletin Number 5, January 1979, accessed May 12, 2014, http://www.mosquitocatalog.org/files/pdfs/048499-0.pdf.

56   "A few years later, Carrier engineers traveled to Rome, Italy, to install a centrifugal chiller at Laboratori Palma, a subsidiary of American pharmaceutical company Squibb." Mauro Capocci, "'A chain is gonna come.' Building a penicillin production plant in post-war Italy," *Dynamis*, Volume 31, Number 2, 2011.

57   "By 1927, they had turned their initial investment into a $1.35 million business." Margaret Ingels, *Willis Haviland Carrier: Father of Air Conditioning*, op. cit., p. 47.

58   "We had faith and enthusiasm in our enterprise, with loyalty to each other and to a common cause." Ibid.

CHAPTER 3: ROEBLING: THE FAMILY THAT BUILT AMERICA'S MOST FAMOUS BRIDGES

60   *"Lector, si monumentum requiris, circumspice."* "Reader, if you are seeking his monument, look around you." The Latin inscription is carved on famed architect Christopher Wren's tomb beneath the dome of St. Paul's Cathedral. The British Museum, "Christopher Wren, *Design for the Dome of St. Paul's Cathedral*, a drawing in brown ink over pencil," accessed May 13, 2014, http://www.britishmuseum.org/explore/highlights/highlight_objects/pd/c/christopher_wren,_st_pauls.aspx. See also: Merriam-Webster's dictionary: "The phrase is generally used to describe a person's legacy—and can be taken to mean that what we leave behind (including intangible things like relationships) best represents our life." See Merriam-Webster, "Top 10 Latin Words to Live By: #9: Si Monumentum Requiris, Circumspice," accessed May 13, 2014, http://www.merriam-webster.com/top-ten-lists/top-10-latin-words-to-live-by/si-monumentum-requiris,-circumspice.html.

60   "Have you ever tried building a popsicle stick truss bridge?" See Garrett's Bridges for great tutorials on how to build truss bridges: http://www.garrettsbridges.com/.

62   "The drawing depicts two rope-makers spread apart, facing each other while twisting stretched yarns, with a third in the middle regulating the tension of the final twist." Emily Teeter, "Techniques and Terminology of Rope-Making in Ancient Egypt," *Journal of Egyptian Archeology*, Volume 73, 1987, pp. 71–77.

62 "Though one may be overpowered, two can defend themselves. A cord of three strands is not quickly broken." BibleGateway, Ecclesiastes 4:12 (New International Version), accessed May 13, 2014, http://www.biblegateway .com/passage/?search=Ecclesiastes%204:12.

62 "In China, ingenious workers made cable out of bamboo, which they used to tow boats up the Yangtze River and construct the world's first suspension bridges." Guadua Bamboo, "Bamboo Cables," accessed May 13, 2014, http://www.guaduabamboo.com/bamboo-cables/.

62 "Before you conjure up images of the Founding Fathers rolling doobies with parchment paper." North American Industrial Hemp Council, Inc., "Distinguishing Hemp from its cousin?" accessed May 13, 2014, http:// naihc.org/hemp_information/content/hempCharacter.html.

62 "Virginia's colonial leaders required each family to grow one hundred plants for cordage; the governor himself grew five thousand plants." *Manufactures of the United States in 1860; Compiled From the Original Returns of The Eighth Census under the Direction of the Secretary of the Interior* (Washington D.C.: Government Printing Office, 1865).

62 "At present we are like separate filaments of flax before the thread is formed, without strength because without connection. But union would make us strong." Benjamin Franklin, *The Works of Benjamin Franklin, L.L.D.*, Vol. 3 (London: Macmillan Company, 1905).

63 "It took a 1,000-foot-long path to produce a 100-fathom (600 foot) rope." Mystic Seaport: The Museum of America and the Sea, "Plymouth Cordage Company Ropewalk," accessed May 13, 2014, http://www.mysticseaport .org/locations/village/ropewalk/.

63 "By the end of the eighteenth century, there were 14 major rope walks in Boston; by 1810, 173 rope walks were in operation from Maine to Kentucky." *The Story of Rope: The History and the Modern Development of Rope-Making* (North Plymouth, Mass.: Plymouth Cordage Company, 1916).

63 "Then a school-boy, with his kite/Gleaming in a sky of light." Henry Wadsworth Longfellow, *The Poetical Works of Henry Wadsworth Longfellow, With Bibliographical and Critical Notes In Six Volumes*, Volume III (Boston: Houghton, Mifflin and Company, 1886).

64 "In the long building, a roper spun hemp, backing slowly away from a revolving hook turned by an apprentice manning a crank." Edward Tunis, *Colonial Craftsmen: And the Beginnings of American Industry* (Baltimore, Md.: Johns Hopkins University Press, 1999), pp. 114–15.

64 "The roper wrapped a bundle of hackled." A "hackle" was a board with sharp steel teeth, which was used to comb out the "tow," or matted fiber, from the hemp.

64 "To make a yard for each yarn in a one-inch-diameter rope the length of a football field, spinners would have to walk several miles backward." Bill Hagenbuch, "The Story of Rope," ropecordNEWS, Volume VX, Number 1, Spring 2006, accessed May 13, 2014, http://www.ropecord.com /cordage/publications/cordage_news/Spring2006.pdf.

64 "But guild workers 'resented the employment of any hands who had not served a regular apprenticeship at the trade, and there was bitter opposition to the introduction of machinery.'" Frederick Converse Beach, ed., *The Encyclopedia Americana* (New York: The Americana Company, 1904).

64 "By the mid-1790s, George Parkinson and John Pittman had filed the first U.S. patents for flax- and hemp-spinning machines to manufacture cordage." *Manufactures of the United States in 1860*, op. cit.

65 "These were literally historic steps forward, because the new machinery replaced backward-walking spinners with upright, rotating devices that could spin several thousand feet of rope in just a few square feet of space." Frederick Converse Beach, ed., *The Encyclopedia Americana*, op. cit.

65 "Kentucky led domestic production of hemp by the 1850s, with a peak of forty thousand tons produced annually." Kentucky Department of Agriculture, "History of hemp in Kentucky," accessed May 13, 2014, http:// www.kyagr.com/marketing/history-of-hemp-in-Kentucky.html.

65 "Johann Sebastian Bach served there briefly as an organist at age twenty-three, composing his first cantata." Daniel R. Melamed, "The text of 'Gott ist mein König,'" *Bach*, Volume 32, Number 1, 2001, pp. 1–16.

66 "But mother Friederike, a natural go-getter and domestic CEO—who 'made everybody work, managed her household, family, the business and her quarter of town besides.'" Donald Sayenga, ed., *Washington Roebling's Father: A Memoir of John A. Roebling* (Reston, Va.: American Society of Civil Engineers, 2009).

66 "There, professors nurtured his passions for algebra and geometry, architecture, bridge and building construction, and hydraulics." Kathryn E. Harrod, *Master Bridge Builders: The Story of the Roeblings* (New York: Julian Messner, Inc., 1958), pp. 26–27.

66 "On the bank of the Regnitz River, young Röbling squatted with notebook and drafting pencil in hand as he sketched the iron bar chains, stone towers, and majestic arc of this "miracle bridge." Ibid.

66 "No decisions could be made, no actions taken." Johann August Roebling, *Diary of My Journey to American in the Year 1831* (Trenton, N.J.: Roebling Press, 1931), p. 113.

66 "Should he remain in the fatherland, tied down to the strict rules of semi official life." Donald Sayenga, ed., *Washington Roebling's Father: A Memoir of John A. Roebling*, op. cit.

67 "All of the German immigrants survived the seventy-eight-day journey except a one-year-old girl, who died after contracting a cold and diarrhea and was buried at sea in a box weighted with iron." Robert W. Grosse, ImmigrantShips.net, accessed May 13, 2014, http://www.immigrantships .net/v6/1800v6/augustedward18310808.html#Robbling. See also: Roebling, *Diary of My Journey to American in the Year 1831*, op. cit., p. 85.

67 "When the waters were calm." Donald Sayenga, ed., *Washington Roebling's Father: A Memoir of John A. Roebling*, op. cit.

67 "Röbling also helped build safer and more humane restroom facilities on board the ship." Roebling, *Diary of My Journey to American in the Year 1831*, op. cit. pp. 18–19.

67 "In his diary, the business-minded Röbling frequently noted that such disputes could have been minimized by a clearly defined, thorough contract." Ibid., pp. 36–37.

68 "I believe we can reasonably allow ourselves the hope of arriving in America in good time to celebrate the anniversary of the Declaration of Independence (the Fourth of July) with the free citizens of the United States." Ibid., p. 50.

68 "The Fourth of July, as the day of the fifty-fifth anniversary of the Declaration of Independence, was hailed by us with sympathy and celebrated in our thoughts." Ibid., p. 87.

69 "How long have we not been without the sight of land and vegetation!" Ibid., p. 98.

69 "After undergoing mandatory health inspections at the Lazaretto quarantine station, where immigrants with infectious diseases were detained." ExplorePAhistory.com, "Lazaretto Quarantine Station Historical Marker," accessed May 13, 2014, http://explorepahistory.com/hmarker .php?markerId=1-A-302.

69 "The numerous hindrances, restrictions, and obstacles, which are set up by timid governments and countless hosts of functionaries against every endeavor in Germany, are not to be found here." Roebling, *Diary of My Journey to American in the Year 1831*, op. cit., p. 112.

70   "But there was no going back or looking back. Johann Röbling was exactly where his mother had sacrificed everything for him to be—in the land of the free, home of the brave." Donald Sayenga, ed., *Washington Roebling's Father: A Memoir of John A. Roebling*, op. cit.

70   "He, his brother, and another Mühlhausen family traveled by wagon over the Appalachian Mountains to western Pennsylvania." Roebling, *Diary of My Journey to American in the Year 1831*, op. cit.

70   "He and his fellow immigrants were 'frightened away from the South by the universally prevailing system of slavery.'" Ibid., pp. 117–19.

70   "He expressed hope for slavery's eventual abolition." Ibid.

71   "We now live as *free* men . . . we live in a section of the country where nature is beautiful and where every diligent person can easily earn a livelihood." John A. Roebling, "Opportunities for immigrants in Western Pennsylvania in 1831," *The Western Pennsylvania Historical Magazine*, Vol. 18, No. 2, June 1935, p 75.

71   "So much remains correct and always true: the Americans now are the most enterprising people on earth and in time will become the most powerful and the most wealthy." Karl Arndt and Patrick Brostowin, "Pragmatists and prophets: George Rapp and J. A. Roebling versus J. A. Etzler and Count Leon," *The Western Pennsylvania Historical Magazine*, Vol. 52, No. 1, January 1969, p. 180.

72   "If one plan won't do, then another must." David McCullough, *The Great Bridge: The Epic Story of the Building of the Brooklyn Bridge* (New York: Simon & Schuster, 1972).

72   "Drawn back to Philadelphia and the waters around it, Roebling patented an improved boiler for steamships and a safety gauge for a steam-boiler flue." Andreas Kahlow, "Johann August Röbling (1806–1869): Early Projects in Context," accessed May 13, 2014, http://www.arct.cam.ac.uk/Downloads/ichs/vol-2-1755-1776-kahlow.pdf, p. 1761.

73   "The latter journal was edited by Dr. Thomas Jones, a physician, engineer, and patent solicitor for the U.S. Patent Office, who later served as Roebling's patent agent." Donald Sayenga, ed., *Washington Roebling's Father: A Memoir of John A. Roebling*, op. cit., see note 27 on p. 37.

73   "Two years later, when Roebling aligned himself with another engineer." Clifford W. Zink, *The Roebling Legacy* (Princeton Landmark Publication), 2011, pp. 30–31.

73   "English inventors Andrew Smith and Robert Newall were separately testing their own wire rope designs and machinery in London." Donald

Sayenga, "Modern History of Wire Rope," accessed May 13, 2014, http://atlantic-cable.com/Article/WireRope/Sayenga/wirerope4.htm.

74   "My mother fed them; they commenced work in summer at 5 a.m., came to breakfast at 6:30 . . ." Donald Sayenga, ed., *Washington Roebling's Father: A Memoir of John A. Roebling*, op. cit., p. 75.

75   "Townsend's Quaker ancestors sailed to America from England with William Penn on the good ship *Welcome* in 1682." *History of Beaver County, Pennsylvania* (Philadelphia: A. Warner & Co., 1888).

75   "The Townsend company manufactured rivets, nails, fasteners, and telegraph wire, in addition to supplying Roebling with wire for his early experiments and projects." J. M. Townshend, "The Townshend Company," *Milestones*, Volume 25, Number 1, May 1919, accessed May 13, 2014, http://www.bchistory.org/beavercounty/BeaverCountyTopical/Industry/Town sendCompany/Townsendcompany.html.

75   "And the Sligo Iron Works made charcoal 'blooms' for Roebling wire—large blocks cast from molten iron and later steel." *The American Engineer*, Volume V, 1883, p. 308.

75   "He secured U.S. Patent 2,720A in July 1842 for 'A Method of and Machine for Manufacturing Wire Ropes,' which described his plan for spinning wire rope while maintaining uniform tension on all of its strands." U.S. Patent Office, "Method of and machine for manufacturing wire ropes," patent number US 2720 A (July 16, 1842).

75   "(It's housed today at the Smithsonian's Museum of American History.)" National Museum of American History, "Machine for Wrapping Wire-Rope, Patent Model," accessed May 13, 2014, http://americanhistory.si .edu/collections/search/object/nmah_1403809.

77   "with tears of joy rolling down his cheeks, his only reply was *'God is good!'* " "How John A. Roebling's Wire Rope Got Its Start," *The Bulletin of the American Iron and Steel Association*, Volume 20, Number 1, January 6, 1886, p. 275.

78   "My father often told me when referring to the [Pittsburgh] Suspension aquaduct [*sic*] that he never would have been allowed to build such a structure in Prussia . . ." Donald Sayenga, ed., *Washington Roebling's Father: A Memoir of John A. Roebling*, op. cit.

78   "The *Pittsburgh Daily Gazette* praised the 'noble structure' and effused." Gibbon, "How Roebling Did It," *JOM*, op. cit.

78   "The spans were supported by two four-and-one-half-inch cables made on land separately for each span; they were hoisted in place from flatboats." Niagra Falls info, "John Augustus Roebling," accessed May 14, 2014, http://

www.niagarafallsinfo.com/history-item.php?entry_id=1406&current
_category_id=219.

79 "Cooper was an extraordinary manufacturer and inventor in his own
right." Debbie Sniderman, "Peter Cooper," ASME.org, accessed May 14,
2014, https://www.asme.org/career-education/articles/entrepreneurship
/peter-cooper.

79 "The Roeblings' ethos and ubiquity inspired their newly adopted hometown's motto: 'Trenton makes, the world takes.'" Delaware River Heritage Trail, "The Roebling Company's Kinkora Works," accessed May 14,
2014, http://www.delrivgreenway.org/heritagetrail/Roebling-Companys
-Kinkora-Works.html.

80 "When Roebling was well enough to travel again." Donald Sayenga, ed.,
Washington Roebling's Father: A Memoir of John A. Roebling, op. cit.

81 "Roebling and his workers finished them all in two years' time by 1850."
Ibid.

81 "Currier & Ives, the famed nineteenth-century 'printmakers to the
American people,' celebrated the scenic wonder in a series of lithographs
depicting the falls from various vantage points." SpringfieldMusuems,
"Niagara Falls, From Goat Island," undated, accessed May 14, 2014,
http://www.springfieldmuseums.org/the_museums/fine_arts/collection
/view/7-niagara_falls_from_goat_island.

81 "Roebling's old nemesis, Charles Ellet, boasted he could build a suspension bridge 'safe for the passage of locomotives and freight trains,
and adapted for any purpose for which it is likely to be applied.'" Pierre
Berton, *Niagara: A History of the Falls* (Albany, N.Y.: State University of New
York Press, 1992), p. 81.

81 "He won the initial contract on a $190,000 bid for an eight-hundred-foot-
span bridge featuring two carriageways, two footways, and a central railroad track with a due date of May 1, 1849 right before the summer tourist
season kicked off." Ibid., p. 83.

82 "Ellet lost his job when the thievery was discovered. He then lost a bid to
sue the bridge sponsors, who paid him a five-figure sum to go take a hike
off a short bridge." Pierre Berton, *Niagara: A History of the Falls*, op. cit.,
pp. 46–47.

82 "He eagerly drew up plans to improve on Ellet's flawed design . . ." American Society of Civil Engineers, "Roebling, John Augustus," accessed
May 14, 2014, http://www.asce.org/PPLContent.aspx?id=2147487354.

82   " 'You say in your last' communication, he wrote to his close friend and factory manager Charles Swan, that '*Mrs. Roebling and the child* are pretty well. This takes me by *surprise*, not having been informed at all . . . what do you mean?' " Aymar Embury II, "An American 'Forsyte Saga,' " *The Princeton Alumni Weekly*, Volume 32, Number 10, pp. 206–7.

83   "When his Niagara Bridge opened in 1855, Roebling attained international fame." American Society of Civil Engineers, "Roebling, John Augustus," op. cit.

84   "I shall do all that may be in my power to promote a peaceful settlement of all our difficulties. The man does not live who is more devoted to peace than I am." "The Receptions at Trenton; Speech of Mr. Lincoln in the Senate. Speech in the Assembly. Speech to the People." *New York Times*, February 22, 1861.

84   "In Fredericksburg, Maryland, Washington rebuilt a strategic bridge destroyed by a flood in two weeks' time. His father helped supply maps to Union generals and donated $100,000 to support the cause." Donald Sayenga, ed., *Washington Roebling's Father: A Memoir of John A. Roebling*, op. cit., p. 192.

85   "a striking example of what can be accomplished by one man overcoming great difficulties." Ibid., p. 210.

85   "The span . . . was renamed in his father's honor in 1983." Covington-Cincinnati Suspension Bridge Committee, "A Quick History of the Roebling Suspension Bridge," June 2004, accessed May 14, 2014, http://roeblingbridge.org/content/quick-history-roebling-suspension-bridge.

85   "He worked hard all day out in the winter weather, losing a meal now and then." Donald Sayenga, ed., *Washington Roebling's Father: A Memoir of John A. Roebling*, op. cit.

85   "She died of a protracted illness in Trenton while he was working in Cincinnati in 1864." David McCullough, *The Great Bridge: The Epic Story of the Building of the Brooklyn Bridge*, op. cit.

86   "The massive device was designated a national historic mechanical engineering landmark in 1981." The American Society of Mechanical Engineers, Greater Trenton Section, *Roebling 80-Ton Wire Rope Machine*, October 21, 1989, accessed May 14, 2014, https://www.asme.org/get media/7ff4baee-6655-4ca7-afab-867080380992/139-Roebling-80-ton -Wire-Rope-Machine.aspx.

86   "Washington and Charles both studied engineering at Rensselaer Polytechnic Institute. Ferdinand studied at Columbian College (now George

Washington University) and Polytechnic College of Philadelphia." Roeb-
lingMuseum.org, "Ferdinand Roebling," accessed May 14, 2014, http://
roeblingmuseum.org/about-us/ferdinand-roebling/. See also: David Mc-
Cullough, *The Great Bridge*, op. cit.

87   "More than science, more than art, Roebling proclaimed, the bridge
would stand as a patriotic symbol and structural tribute 'to the energy,
enterprise and wealth of that community which shall secure its erection.'"
Charles Beebe Stuart, *Lives and Works of Civil and Military Engineers of
America* (New York: D. Van Nostrand, 1871).

87   "As he had been when he was a child, faithful eldest son Washington was
at his father's side when disaster struck." Donald Sayenga, ed., *Washington
Roebling's Father: A Memoir of John A. Roebling*, op. cit.

88   "One of his sketches dated March 1857 depicts a hulking Egyptian pylon
with a winged lion's head looming over the roadway entrance to his Manhattan and Brooklyn Bridge." Mary J. Shapiro, *A Picture History of the Brooklyn Bridge with 167 Prints and Photographs* (New York: Dover Publications,
Inc., 1983).

88   "The *New York Times* obituary reported that up until three o'clock in the
morning before the day he died, Roebling had 'continued to direct his
attendants.'" "OBITUARY: John A. Roebling, the Engineer," *New York
Times,* July 23, 1869.

88   "Roebling's deathbed condition was a horrifying seizure known as 'opisthotonos,' in which the patient leaps from the mattress, shoulder blades
drawn back with the body contorted." John L. Phillips, *The Bends: Compressed Air in the History of Science, Diving, and Engineering* (Chelsea, Mich.:
BookCrafters, 1998).

89   "Daily and hourly, I was the miserable witness of the most horrible ti-
tanic convulsions . . ." Donald Sayenga, ed., *Washington Roebling's Father: A
Memoir of John A. Roebling*, op. cit.

89   "'Here I was at the age of 32,' Washington later recounted, 'suddenly put
in charge of the most stupendous engineering structure of the age! The
prop on which I had hitherto leaned had fallen.'" Donald Sayenga, ed.,
Washington Roebling's Father: A Memoir of John A. Roebling, op. cit., p. 232.

90   "Several shafts in the roofs of the caissons, equipped with iron hatches,
would allow passage of workers and materials." "Building Bridge Caissons," *New York Times,* March 28, 1897.

91   "'She has very much captured your brother Washy's heart at last,' he confessed in a giddy letter to his sister Emily. 'It was a real attack in force.'"

Clifford W. Zink, *The Roebling Legacy* (Princeton Landmark Publication, 2011), p. 62.

91 "Emily came from a prominent *Mayflower*-descended family that was socially connected, though not wealthy. She was polished, patriotic, and educated in rhetoric and grammar, algebra, French, and piano." Roebling Museum, "Emily Warren Roebling," accessed May 14, 2014, http://roeblingmuseum.org/about-us/emily-warren-roebling/.

92 "Again, Washington had to tweak his father's plans by enlarging them." "The East River Bridge," *New York Times*, December 16, 1879.

92 "It was Dante's *Inferno* in a pressurized box, master mechanic E. F. Farrington recounted, 'with half-naked bodies, seen in dim, uncertain light.'" Ibid.

92 "In the bare shed where we got ready, the men told me no one could do the work for long without getting the 'bends.'" EyeWitness to History, "Sandhog: Building the Brooklyn Bridge, 1871" (2005), accessed May 14, 2014, http://www.eyewitnesstohistory.com/brooklynbridge.htm.

93 "During the sinking of the caissons, 'he never left Brooklyn, not even for an hour,' the *American Engineer* reported, 'and at all hours of the day and night, he visited the work going on under the water.'" *American Engineer*, Volume V, 1883, op. cit.

93 "The know-nothings in the media had the chutzpah to accuse Roebling of 'stupidity.'" Donald Langmead, *Icons of American Architecture: From the Alamo to the World Trade Center* (Westport, Conn.: Greenwood Publishing Group, 2009).

93 "They derided him for being an inferior engineer . . ." Ibid.

94 "In December 1870, a careless workman held a candle too close to the oakum caulking of a wooden seam inside the Brooklyn caisson." "The Caisson of the East River Bridge on Fire—The Works Damaged to the Extent of $20,000," *New York Times*, December 3, 1870.

94 "He labored with the crew for twelve hours straight through the night, then came down with a painful case of the bends as he ascended." W. P. Butler, "Caisson disease during the construction of the Eads and Brooklyn bridges: A review," *Undersea and Hyperbaric Medical Society*, Volume 31, Number 4, 2004.

94 "Three other bridge workers died of the awful disease and more than one hundred others suffered nonfatal occurrences of the decompression syndrome as caisson work continued." Ibid.

94   "the emotional pain caused by ignorant criticism, fraudulent contractors, the virulent opposition of the press, and interference by trustees with neither ability nor vision, hurt him far more." Donald Langmead, *Icons of American Architecture: From the Alamo to the World Trade Center*, op. cit.

94   "'I thought I would succumb to disease,' Washington later wrote in his memoirs, 'but I had a strong tower to lean upon, my wife, a woman of infinite tact and wisest counsel.'" Donald Sayenga, ed., *Washington Roebling's Father: A Memoir of John A. Roebling*, op. cit.

95   "it was common gossip that hers was the great mind behind the great work." David McCullough, *The Great Bridge: The Epic Story of the Building of the Brooklyn Bridge*, op. cit.

95   "When bids for the steel and iron work for the structure were advertised for three or four years ago, it was found that entirely new shapes would be required." "Mrs. Roebling's Skill," *New York Times*, May 23, 1883.

95   "Schemers spread false rumors that Washington was paralyzed or 'really as one dead.'" David McCullough, *The Great Bridge: The Epic Story of the Building of the Brooklyn Bridge*, op. cit.

95   "I think it can be said of us in this time, our time, whatever may have been the subjection and insignificance of women in other days." "Mrs. Washington Augustus Roebling"; In: . . ." Elroy M. Avery, ed., *Daughters of the American Revolution Magazine*, Volume 18, July–December 1900, pp. 246–50.

96   "Iron manufacturer and New York mayor Abram Hewitt hailed the bridge as 'an everlasting monument to the self-sacrificing devotion of woman, and of her capacity for that higher education from which she has been too long barred.'" Ibid.

96   "enfranching cable, silvered by the sea." Marianne Moore, "Granite and Steel," *The New Yorker*, July 9, 1966, p. 32.

96   "Poet Walt Whitman 'returned to his beloved city and saw the nearly complete bridge,' the Academy of American Poets noted . . ." "Poetry Landmark: The Brooklyn Bridge in New York City," accessed May 14, 2014, http://www.poets.org/poetsorg/text/poetry-landmark-brooklyn-bridge-new-york-city.

96   "Crossing Brooklyn Ferry." Walt Whitman, "Crossing Brooklyn Ferry," accessed May 14, 2014, http://www.bartleby.com/142/86.html.

97   "He spent the next two years laboring on his ambitious, modernist epic tribute of fifteen lyric poems, 'The Bridge.'" "Hart Cranes The Bridge: A Digital Resource," accessed May 14, 2014, http://sites.jmu.edu

/thebridge/. See also: Lawrence Kramer, "Hart Crane's 'The Bridge,'" accessed May 14, 2014, https://muse.jhu.edu/books/9780823248735.

97   "Complex, sweeping, and controversial, it was Crane's attempt to connect the Roeblings' monument to his own metaphysical 'bridgeship.'" John T. Irwin, *Hart Crane's Poetry: "Appollinaire lived in Paris, I live in Cleveland, Ohio"* (Baltimore, Md.: Johns Hopkins University Press, 2011).

97   "To Brooklyn Bridge." Hart Crane, "To Brooklyn Bridge," accessed May 14, 2014, http://www.poets.org/poetsorg/poem/brooklyn-bridge.

97   "Upon publication of his book-length series, Crane discovered that he had been living in the same apartment building at 100 Columbia Heights where Washington Roebling supervised the span's construction from his bed." Clive Fisher, *Hart Crane: A Life* (New Haven, Conn.: Yale University Press, 2002).

98   "He built a fine mansion with his wife, traveled with her when his health permitted, and amassed a fortune estimated at $29 million." David Mc-Cullough, *The Great Bridge: The Epic Story of the Building of the Brooklyn Bridge*, op. cit.

98   "'bridge builder in petticoats.'" Carol Simon Levin, "Bridge Builder in Petticoats: Emily Warren Roebling," accessed May 14, 2014, http://bridge builderinpetticoats.com/.

98   "She was one of forty-eight women pioneers who earned a law degree from New York University in 1899." "The Woman's Law Class," *New York Times*, March 31, 1899.

98   "She penned a biography of her husband, historical essays on the Brooklyn Bridge construction, legal papers on giving money to charity and the 'value of being your own executor.'" Elroy M. Avery, ed., *Daughters of the American Revolution Magazine*, op. cit.

98   "And though the years aiding her husband had taken a physical toll, Emily traveled to Russia, shared tea with Queen Victoria, and organized relief efforts for U.S. troops returning from the Spanish-American War." Bernardsville Public Library, "Bridge Builder in Petticoats: Emily Warren Roebling & the Brooklyn Bridge," nj.com, February 5, 2014, accessed May 14, 2014, http://blog.nj.com/somerset_county_announcements /2014/02/bridge_builder_in_petticoats_e.html.

PART II

101   "Alexis de Tocqueville," *Democracy in America and Two Essays on America* (London: Penguin Books, 2003), p. 644.

CHAPTER 4: I, TOILET PAPER

This chapter was inspired by Foundation for Economic Education founder Leonard Read's classic essay "I, Pencil," first published in 1958.

103   "I, Toilet Paper." Leonard E. Read, "I, Pencil: My Family Tree as told to Leonard E. Read," Irvington-on-Hudson, N.Y.: The Foundation for Economic Education, Inc., 1999, Library of Economics and Liberty, accessed May 1, 2014, http://www.econlib.org/library/Essays/rdPncl1.html.

104   "8.6 sheets of me per restroom visit." "The Toilet Paper Encyclopedia," Consumers Interstate Corporation, Norwich, Conn., accessed May 1, 2014, http://encyclopedia.toiletpaperworld.com/toilet-paper-facts/toilet -paper-quick-facts.

104   "$8 billion per year." Richard Smyth, *Bum Fodder: An Absorbing History of Toilet Paper* (Souvenir Publishing, October 2012), p. 1.

105   "mashed-up mulberries, old rags, and hemp fibers," "The Toilet Paper Encyclopedia," Consumers Interstate Corporation, Norwich, Conn., accessed May 1, 2014, http://encyclopedia.toiletpaperworld.com/toilet -paper-history/complete-historical-timeline.

106   "Inventive great grandson David Rittenhouse constructed a model watermill." "University of Pennsylvania University Archives and Records Center," Penn Biographies, David Rittenhouse, accessed May 1, 2014, http://www.archives.upenn.edu/people/1700s/rittenhouse_david.html.

106   "eight generations of the Rittenhouse family." "William Rittenhouse," Paper Discovery Center, accessed May 1, 2014, http://www.paperdiscovery center.org/williamrittenhouse/.

106   "RittenhouseTown." James Green, *The Rittenhouse Mill and the Beginnings of Papermaking in America* (The Library Company of Philadelphia and Friends of Historic RittenhouseTown, 1990).

106   "only active printer south of Boston." Green, *The Rittenhouse Mill and the Beginnings of Papermaking in America*, p. 5.

106   "brown paper for wrapping at two shillings a ream," Edward Tunis, *Colonial Craftsmen: And the Beginnings of American Industry* (Johns Hopkins University Press; reprint edition, June 17, 1999), p. 132.

106   "journalist who partnered with Benjamin Franklin." "Benjamin Franklin: Writer and Printer," The Library Company of Philadelphia, accessed May 1, 2014, http://www.librarycompany.org/bfwriter/publisher.htm.

106   "to publish books." "William Bradford, Colonial Printer Tercentenary Review," American Antiquarian Society, accessed May 1, 2014, http://www.americanantiquarian.org/proceedings/44604985.pdf.

106   "mill outside Chestnut Hill, Pennsylvania." "William Rittenhouse 1644–1708," Immigrant Entrepreneurship, accessed May 1, 2014, http://www.immigrantentrepreneurship.org/entry.php?rec=9.

107   "excellent commercial facilities, and optimum manufacturing conditions." "William Rittenhouse 1644–1708," accessed May 1, 2014, http://www.immigrantentrepreneurship.org/entry.php?rec=9.

107   "eighteen of these early American paper mills." F. C. Huyck & Sons and Perry Walton, *Two Related Industries* (Albany, N.Y.: F. C. Huyck & Sons, 1920), p. 17.

107   "Franklins also ran their own lucrative wholesale paper business." John Bidwell, American Paper Mills, *1690–1832: A Directory of the Paper Trade with Notes on Products, Watermarks, Distribution Methods, and Manufacturing Techniques* (Hanover, N.H.: Dartmouth College Press, 2012), accessed May 2, 2014, https://muse.jhu.edu/books/9781611683165; "Benjamin Franklin, Entrepreneur," The Benjamin Franklin Tercentenary, accessed May 2, 2014, http://www.benfranklin300.org/etc_article_entrepreneur.htm.

107   "Revere even stabled his horses at the Crane mill." "History of Crane Paper Company," Crane & Co., accessed May 2, 2014, http://www.crane.com/about-us/learn-more/history.

107   "Crane's sons and grandsons." J. T. White and Company, *The National Cyclopedia of American Biography*, 1906, p. 69.

107   "internationally renowned fine stationery." "About Us," Crane & Co., accessed May 2, 2014, http://www.crane.com/about-us.

107   "leading pioneer in currency security technology." Ylan Q. Mui, "Crane Has Provided the Paper for U.S. Money for Centuries; Now It's Going Global," *Washington Post*, December 13, 2013, accessed May 2, 2014, http://www.washingtonpost.com/business/economy/crane-has-provided-the-paper-for-us-money-for-centuries-now-its-going-global/2013/12/13/9aa4190a-5c39-11e3-be07-006c776266ed_story.html.

109   "patent for preventing the paper pulp from becoming burned or discolored by adding calcium to the mixture." Charles W. Carey, Jr., and Ian C. Friedman, Tilghman, Benjamin and Richard, *American Inventors, Entrepreneurs, and Business Visionaries*, Revised Edition, American Biographies. New York: Facts On File, Inc., 2011, *American History Online*, accessed Feb-

ruary 24, 2014, http://www.fofweb.com/activelink2.asp?ItemID=WE52&i
Pin=AIE0237&SingleRecord=True.

109   "Wood pulp mills sprouted up in poplar-abundant Maine." "History of
       Papermaking," Maine Pulp and Paper Association, accessed May 2, 2014,
       http://www.pulpandpaper.org/history.shtml.

109   "$30,000 to establish a paper mill in Neenah, Wisconsin, in 1872."
       "Kimberly-Clark Corporation," Harvard Business School Historical Col-
       lections, accessed May 2, 2014, http://www.library.hbs.edu/hc/lehman
       /company.html?company=kimberly_clark_corporation; "Product Evolu-
       tion," Kimberly-Clark Corporation, accessed May 2, 2014, https://www
       .kimberly-clark.com/ourcompany/innovations/product_evolution.aspx.

110   "two of the Fortune 500 company's billion-dollar brands." "Kimberly-
       Clark's Kotex Brand Achieves Billion-dollar Status," Kimberly-Clark
       Corporation, accessed May 2, 2014, http://investor.kimberly-clark.com
       /releasedetail.cfm?ReleaseID=649875.

110   "Hoberg died in a tragic machinery accident at the factory." "Procter
       & Gamble History," *Southeast Missourian*, September 4, 2009, accessed
       May 2, 2014, http://www.semissourian.com/story/1567637.html.

111   "tearing off a considerable part of the contiguous sheet." "Toilet-paper
       Roll," All Over Albany, accessed May 2, 2014, http://alloveralbany.com
       /images/1891patent.pdf; "Toilet Paper Was Invented In {Albany}," All
       Over Albany, accessed May 2, 2014, http://alloveralbany.com/archive
       /2010/03/15/toilet-paper-invented-in-yep-albany.

111   "Clogged pipes with consequent impure air and disease prevented." "Per-
       forated Paper The Standard," The Virtual Toilet Paper Museum, accessed
       May 2, 2014, http://nobodys-perfect.com/vtpm/exhibithall/informa
       tional/1886_APW_ad.jpg.

111   "morphed into cart-pushing delivery boy by afternoon." M. E. Dixon, *The
       Hidden History of Delaware County: Untold Tales from Cobb's Creek* (History
       Press, 2010), pp. 64–65.

111   "executive at the Curtis Publishing Company (publisher of the *Ladies'
       Home Journal*)." Sons of the Revolution, Pennsylvania Society, *Annual Pro-
       ceedings* (The Society, 1901), p. 39.

111   "James Hoyt, inspired them with his patented." US333073 A, Decem-
       ber 22, 1885, Google Patents, accessed May 3, 2014, http://www.google
       .com/patents/US333073.

111   "enclosed bathroom tissue container in 1885." "Manufacturing: Tissue
       Issue," *Time*, August 22, 1938, accessed May 4, 2014, http://www.time.com

/time/magazine/article/0,9171,788421-1,00.html. Here's a photo of the Hoyt holder: "Tagyerit.com," accessed May 4, 2014, http://www.tagyerit .com/images/tp/1885hoytholder1.jpg.

112 "roll of toilet paper!" Jenny Knodell, "The Bathroom Was an Uncomfortable Place before Cardboard Tubes," *IQS Newsroom*, accessed May 4, 2014, http://blog.iqsdirectory.com/packaging/the-bathroom-was-an-uncom fortable-place-before-cardboard-tubes/.

112 "packaged for either commercial or residential sale." "Toilet Paper," How Products Are Made, accessed May 4, 2014, http://www.madehow.com /Volume-6/Toilet-Paper.html.

112 "merchants wouldn't display it and publications wouldn't advertise it." "The Roll That Changed History: Disposable Toilet Tissue Story," Kimberly-Clark Corporation, accessed May 4, 2014, http://www.cms .kimberly-clark.com/umbracoimages/UmbracoFileMedia/ProductEvol _ToiletTissue_umbracoFile.pdf.

113 "company's first branded product." Catherine Earley, "The Greatest Missed Luxury," The Pennsylvania Center For the Book, Fall 2010, accessed May 4, 2014, http://pabook.libraries.psu.edu/palitmap/TP .html.

113 "a small, single picture." Bernice Kanner, "The Soft Sell," *New York*, Vol. 15, No. 38, September 27, 1982, p. 14.

113 "machine for tightening rolls of paper." "Machine For Tightening Rolls of Paper," US806847 A, December 12, 1905, Google Patents, accessed May 4, 2014, https://www.google.com/patents/US806847?dq=ininventor:%22A rthur+H+Scott%22&hl=en&sa=X&ei=-qUGU9XqHoXaoASMvYDwAQ&v ed=0CE4Q6AEwBQ.

113 "supporting device for toilet paper packages." "Supporting Device For Toilet Paper Packages," US865436 A, September 10, 1907, Google Patents, accessed May 4, 2014, https://www.google.com/patents/US865436?dq=i ninventor:%22Arthur+H+Scott%22&hl=en&sa=X&ei=mgQMU5-pCInly QH6h4GIBw&ved=0CEkQ6AEwBA.

113 "several toilet paper cabinets." "Ininventor: 'Arthur H. Scott,'" Google Search, accessed May 4, 2014, https://www.google.com/search?tbo=p&tb m=pts&hl=en&q=ininventor:%22Arthur+H+Scott%22.

113 "cheap towel formed from paper and adapted for all general uses." "Paper Towel," US 1141495 A, June 1, 1915, Google Patents, May 4, 2014, http:// www.google.com/patents/US1141495.

114　"prevent students from infecting each other." "One Teacher's Fight Against Germs: The Disposable Paper Towels Story," Kimberly-Clark Corporation, accessed May 4, 2014, http://www.cms.kimberly-clark.com /umbracoimages/UmbracoFileMedia/ProductEvol_PaperTowel_um bracoFile.pdf.

114　"In 1995, Kimberly-Clark bought Scott Paper for $9.4 billion," Glenn Collins, "Kimberly-Clark to Buy Scott Paper, Challenging P.& G." *New York Times*, July 18, 1995, accessed May 4, 2014, http://www.nytimes .com/1995/07/18/business/kimberly-clark-to-buy-scott-paper-challeng ing-p-g.html.

114　"and *in the absence of any human master-minding!*" Leonard E. Read, "I, Pencil: My Family Tree as told to Leonard E. Read" (Irvington-on-Hudson, N.Y.: The Foundation for Economic Education, Inc., 1999), Library of Economics and Liberty, accessed 4 May 2014, http://www.econ lib.org/library/Essays/rdPncl1.html.

CHAPTER 5: CROWNING GLORY: HOW WILLIAM PAINTER'S BOTTLE CAPS BECAME A $9 BILLION BUSINESS

116　"the brainchild of William Painter." "Hall of Fame: Inventor Profile," National Inventors Hall of Fame, accessed April 23, 2014, http://www.invent .org/hall_of_fame/292.html. The only material difference now is that the cork liner has been replaced with modern plastic, the corrugated teeth cut from twenty-four to twenty-one, and the cap's skirt shortened in height.

116　"boyhood aspiration always and ever had been to 'make something.'" From William Lewis's tribute to Painter in Orrin Chalfant Painter, *William Painter And His Father Dr. Edward Painter: Sketches and Reminiscences* (Baltimore: The Arundel Press, John S. Bridges Td Co., 1914), p. 53.

117　"discharged by a piston operated by the thumb, upon unsuspecting observers." Ibid., p. 14.

117　"Whoopee Cushion." The Whoopee Cushion was invented by a Canadian rubber firm in the 1930s and sold by the American novelty mail-order giant Johnson Smith Company.

117　"Son Orrin joked that Painter earned his degree from the 'University of Hard Knocks.'" Painter, *William Painter And His Father Dr. Edward Painter: Sketches and Reminiscences*, op. cit., p. 28.

117   "patent leather." Is defined as "a type of leather that has a hard and shiny
       surface," "Patent Leather," Merriam-Webster.com, accessed May 12, 2014,
       http://www.merriam-webster.com/dictionary/patent_leather.

117   "manufacturing shop of Pyle, Wilson & Pyle." J. T. Scharf, *History of Dela-
       ware: 1609–1888: Local history* (Philadelphia: L.J. Richards & Co., 1888),
       p. 793.

117   "reportedly appropriated the device (along with the financial rewards)
       as his own." Ibid. Schar credits Pyle—Painter's own uncle—as the "inven-
       tor of the invaluable 'softening' machine now in use at the factory." See
       also "U.S. Patent 15816 A," Google Patents, accessed May 12, 2014, http://
       www.google.com/patents/US15816.

118   "Nobody should ever get the best of him again by putting clothes on the
       children of his brain and endowing them with his or her name." Painter,
       William Painter And His Father Dr. Edward Painter: Sketches and Reminiscences,
       op. cit., p. 54.

118   "Painter would surely have been an enthusiastic user of Post-it Notes, in-
       vented by 3M engineers in the 1970s." Nick Glass and Tim Hume, "The
       'Hallelujah Moment' Behind Invention of the Post-it Note," CNN, April
       4, 2013, accessed May 12, 2014, http://edition.cnn.com/2013/04/04/tech
       /post-it-note-history/.

118   "he would rise, dust off his pants, and walk on, oblivious of everything and
       everyone around him." Painter, *William Painter And His Father Dr. Edward
       Painter: Sketches and Reminiscences*, op. cit. p.31.

118   "he'd walk several blocks past his downtown Baltimore mansion on Cal-
       vert Street." Jacques Kelly, "The Ivy hotel was once home to prominent
       city businessman," *Baltimore Sun*, December 13, 2013, accessed May 12,
       2014, http://www.baltimoresun.com/news/maryland/baltimore-city/bs
       -md-ci-kelly-column-ivy-hotel—20131213,0,6940720.column.

119   "Add sixteen pounds of sugar, and ten ounces of tartaric acid." "Miss
       Beecher's Domestic Receipt Book," Internet Archive: Digital Library of
       Free Books, Movies, Music & Wayback Machine, accessed May 12, 2014,
       http://archive.org/stream/missbeechersdome01beec/missbeechers
       dome01beec_djvu.txt.

119   "is a most valuable agent for checking nausea and vomiting." Ibid.

119   "John Mathews and his namesake son, quickly went to work manufac-
       turing commercial soda fountain equipment." C. M. Depew, *1795–1895:
       One Hundred Years of American Commerce . . . a History of American Com-
       merce by One Hundred Americans, with a Chronological Table of the Important*

Events of American Commerce and Invention Within the Past One Hundred Years (D. O. Haynes & Company, 1895), p. 470.

120   "patent medicine." Defined as "a packaged nonprescription drug which is protected by a trademark and whose contents are incompletely disclosed," "Patent Medicine," Merriam-Webster.com, accessed May 12, 2014, http://www.merriam-webster.com/dictionary/patent_medicine.

120   "a woodsy medicinal syrup." "Charles E. Hires Company 1870–present Philadelphia, Pennsylvania," Federation of Historical Bottle Collectors, accessed May 12, 2014, http://www.fohbc.org/PDF_Files/HiresRootBeer_DonYates.pdf.

120   "marketed as 'root beer' at the 1876 Philadelphia Exposition." Eileen Bennett, "Local historians argue over the root of the story of how Hires first brewed beer that made millions," *Press of Atlantic City* (N.J.), June 28, 1998, cited on Cumberland County, New Jersey, website, accessed May 12, 2014, http://www.co.cumberland.nj.us/content/163/241/597.aspx.

120   "Pemberton famously introduced Coca-Cola to customers at an Atlanta, Georgia, drugstore in 1886." Joe Nickell, "'Pop' Culture: Patent Medicines Become Soda Drinks," Committee For Skeptical Inquiry, January/February 2011, accessed May 12, 2014, http://www.csicop.org/si/show/pop_culture_patent_medicines_become_soda_drinks/.

120   "Paris-based Compagnie de Limonadiers served up a lemonade-flavored syrupy beverage in the seventeenth century." "Soft drink," *Encyclopedia Britannica*, accessed May 12, 2014, http://www.britannica.com/EBchecked/topic/552397/soft-drink.

120   "aciduous soda water . . . prepared and sold in London by a Mr Schweppe," "American Druggist and Pharmaceutical Record" (American Druggist Publishing Company, 1903), Vol. 42, p. 258.

120   "the same Schweppe whose name you still see on your ginger ale can." Schweppe's, the very same maker of tonic water and ginger ale, is now part of the Plano, Texas–based Dr Pepper Snapple Group.

120   "he invented the national beverage." J. Parton, *Life of Thomas Jefferson: Third President of the United States"* (J. R. Osgood, 1874), p. 498.

120   "should be stored upside down, 'well corked, and cemented.'" "Impregnating Water with Fixed Air," Today In Science History, accessed May 12, 2014, http://www.todayinsci.com/P/Priestley_Joseph/PriestleyJoseph-Making CarbonatedWater1772.htm.

121   "rubber gasket held between two metal plates attached to a wire spring loop." "Bottle Closures," Antique Soda & Beer Bottles, accessed May 12,

2014, http://mysite.verizon.net/vonmechow/closures.htm. See also "Bottle Finishes & Closures," Society for Historical Archaeology, accessed May 13, 2014, http://www.sha.org/bottle/closures.htm#Hutchinson_Spring _Stopper.

121   "U.S. Patent Office had approved an estimated fifteen hundred bottle stopper patents." "The Crown Cork Cap and Crown Soda Machine 1892 and 1888," The American Society of Mechanical Engineers, May 25, 1994, accessed May 12, 2014, https://www.asme.org/getmedia/917b2933-3e75 -4207-b26e-ca0f62b41644/174-Crown-Cork-Soda-Filling-Machine.aspx; "Who Invented the Crown Cap Lifter?" Bullworks.net Virtual Corkscrew Museum and Flower Frog Gazette, accessed May 12, 2014, http://www .bullworks.net/virtual/infopages/crowncork.htm.

123   "the closures (for either carbonated or fermented, 'still' drinks) could be manufactured cheaply and economically." The disks cost only twenty-five cents per gross versus two dollars or more for the Hutchison closures. Riley, 1958, "Bottle Finishes & Closures."

123   "the Bottle Seal sold at twenty-five cents per gross." Painter, *William Painter And His Father Dr. Edward Painter: Sketches and Reminiscences*, op. cit., p. 57.

123   "the makers of a New England soft drink called 'Moxie.'" Jim Baumer, "A Somewhat Brief History of Moxie," *I Am Jim Baumer*, January 25, 2010, accessed May 13, 2014, http://www.jimbaumer.com/2010/01/25/a-some what-brief-history-of-moxie/. According to Merrill Lewis, president of the New England Moxie Congress, and Wayne T. Mitchell, Penobscot Nation representative to the Maine state legislature, the word "moxie" comes from the Wabanaki Algonquin dialect and means "dark water." See "A Brief History of 'Moxie,' *Esquire*, May 6, 2010, accessed December 29, 2014, http://www.esquire.com/style/answer-fella/define-moxie-0510.

123   "this health-and-vigor beverage gave rise to the familiar expression, 'You've got a lot of Moxie.'" "The History of Moxie," Moxie Beverage Company, accessed May 13, 2014, http://www.drinkmoxie.com/history .php, and Nickell, op. cit.

124   "summed up the selling points in five words: 'Pure, clean, neat, tight, cheap.'" "William Painter Bottle Stopper," Hutchinson Bottle Collectors' Association, accessed May 13, 2014, http://www.hutchbook.com /Painter%2009-29-1885/default.htm.

125   "I have devised metallic sealing-caps embodying certain novel characteristics which render them highly effective and so inexpensive as to warrant throwing them away after a single use thereof, even when forcible displacement, as in opening bottles, has resulted in no material injury to

the caps." "Bottle-sealing Device," US Patent 468258 A, Google Patents, accessed May 13, 2014, http://www.google.us/patents/US468258.

128   "restless energy and indomitable perseverance." Painter, *William Painter And His Father Dr. Edward Painter: Sketches and Reminiscences*, op. cit., p. 44.

129   "send a cargo of crown-capped beer to South America and bring it back." S. Van Dulken, *Inventing the 19th Century: 100 Inventions That Shaped the Victorian Age from Aspirin to the Zeppelin* (New York University Press, 2001), p. 68.

129   "threw a welcome back party and invited Charm City reporters to witness the taste tests." News Staff, "Crown Cork CEO explains cutbacks," *Reading Eagle*, June 19, 2000, A13.

130   "Jefferson built two of his own vineyards." "The Vineyards," Thomas Jefferson's Monticello, accessed May 13, 2014, http://www.monticello.org /site/house-and-gardens/vineyards.

130   "patented a synthetic cork product dubbed 'Nepro.'" "McManus v. Margetts," Leagle Inc., accessed May 13, 2014, http://www.leagle.com/decision /19501286NJSuper122_1104.

130   "saved money by allowing crown caps to be made shallower and with less tin metal." "CrownCappers' Club," Crown Cap Collectors Society International, accessed May 13, 2014, http://www.bottlecapclub.org/docs /magazine/pdfs/ccsi2000_02.pdf.

131   "bought up cork companies on both coasts and built export facilities in Europe and North Africa." David Taylor, "The Great Cork Experiment," *Chesapeake Bay Magazine's Chesapeake Boating.net*, March 2008, accessed May 13, 2014, http://www.chesapeakeboating.net/Publications/Chesa peake-Bay-Magazine/2008/March-2008/The-Great-Cork-Experiment .aspx.

131   "By 1937, the company was producing more than 103 million bottle tops a day." "The Crown Cork Cap and Crown Soda Machine 1892 and 1888," op. cit.

131   "to provide in the United States a source for at least a part of the nation's cork requirement." William H. Brooks, "A Literature Review of California Domestic Cork Production," USDA U.S. Forest Service Gen. Tech. Rep. PSW-GTR-160, 1997, p. 480, accessed May 13, 2014, http://www.fs.fed.us /psw/publications/documents/psw_gtr160/psw_gtr160_04e_brooks.pdf.

131   "McManus successfully consolidated Crown's operations and boosted sales to $11 million." "Crown History," Crown Holdings, Inc., accessed May 13, 2014, http://www.crowncork.com/about/about_history.php.

131 "Crown Cork pioneered the aerosol can, adopted pull-tab pop tops, and expanded into household markets." Ibid.

132 "Painter's successors now manufacture high-speed stainless steel bottle- and can-filling machines that can fill two thousand cans or twelve hundred bottles per minute." "The Crown Cork Cap and Crown Soda Machine 1892 and 1888," op. cit., p. 4.

CHAPTER 6: "KEEP LOOKING": HOW PAINTER'S RAZOR-SHARP GENIUS INSPIRED KING GILLETTE

136 "continued to tinker on the side with his brothers on various improve- ments to barrels." Tim Dowling, *Inventor of the Disposable Culture, King Camp Gillette 1855–1932* (London: Short Books, 2001), p. 16.

136 "You'll hit upon something that a lot of people want." Walter Mon- fried, "Millionaire Ten Years Ago, He is Broke Now," *Milwaukee Journal*, August 15, 1942, A1.

136 "It was at [Painter's] solicitation that I joined the company." King Camp Gillette, "Origin of the Gillette Razor," *Gillette Blade*, Vol. 1, No. 4, Febru- ary 1918, p. 4.

137 "Mr. Painter was a very interesting talker." Ibid.

137 "[Y]ou are always thinking and inventing something." Ibid.

137 "Why don't you try to think of something like a crown cork." Ibid.

137 "but it won't do any harm to think about it." Ibid.

137 "[W]hen I started to shave, I found my razor dull." Ibid., p. 6.

138 "was looked upon as a joke by all my friends." Ibid., p. 7.

138 "The only way to do a thing is to do it." Painter, *William Painter And His Father Dr. Edward Painter: Sketches and Reminiscences*, op. cit., p. 28.

138 "But whatever you do, don't let it get away from you." King Camp Gillette, "Origin of the Gillette Razor," op. cit., p. 4.

138 "He is an inventor by nature." "Mr. William Emergy Nickerson," *Electricity*, Vol. V., No. 6, August 23, 1893, p. 70.

138 "I was a dreamer who believed in the 'gold at the foot of the rainbow' promise." King Camp Gillette, "Origin of the Gillette Razor," op. cit., p. 7.

139 "I am confident that I have grasped the situation and can guarantee, as far as such a thing can be guaranteed, a successful outcome." William E.

Nickerson, "The Development of the Gillette Safety Razor," *Gillette Blade*, Vol 2., No. 2, December 1918, p. 7.

139   "so crooked and crumpled as to be wholly useless." Ibid.

139   "'airtight instrument against infringers.'" Russell Adams, *King Gillette: The Man and His Wonderful Shaving Device* (Boston: Little, Brown, and Company, 1978), p. 39.

139   "In 1904, Gillette received his breakthrough patent." "Razor," King C. Gillette, U.S. Patent 775134 A, Nov. 15, 1904, Google Patents, accessed May 13, 2014, http://www.google.com/patents/US775134.

140   "'Smoothing' was the euphemism of choice." Russell Adams, *King Gillette: The Man and His Wonderful Shaving Device*, op. cit., p. 92.

140   "The fourteen-karat gold-plated razor came encased in a 'velvet and satin-lined French ivory case' of 'dainty size.'" "Milady Decollete Gillette," *Spokesman-Review*, July 18, 1915, A7.

141   "now employs nearly thirty thousand with sales topping $10 billion." "P&G Agrees to Buy Gillette In a $54 Billion Stock Deal," *Wall Street Journal*, January 30, 2005, accessed May 13, 2014, http://online.wsj.com/news/articles/SB110693197048439468.

141   "It is often true that invention involves underlying principles, purposes and questions of utility." Russell Adams, *King Gillette: The Man and His Wonderful Shaving Device*, op. cit., pp. 49–50.

CHAPTER 7: SEEING DOLLARS IN THE DIRT: THE WISDOM OF CHARLES E. HIRES

143   "I was not interested in farming and wanted to make my own way." Edna Marks, "Hires, Root Beer King, Comes to City to Fish," *Evening Independent*, February 2, 1929, A1.

144   "sweeping floors, cleaning out spittoons, polishing mirrors, cleaning mortars, and delivering medicines." For a description of the general duties of a drug-store boy, see *The Pharmaceutical Era* (New York), Vol. 17, May 13, 1897, p. 565.

144   "he attended open lectures and night classes at the Philadelphia College of Pharmacy." For more on the growth of the American pharmaceutical industry in the nineteenth century, see Glenn Sonnedeker, *Kremers and Urdang's History of Pharmacy* (Philadelphia: Lippincott, 1963), p. 181, and Gregory J. Higby, "Chemistry and the 19th-Century American Pharmacist," *Bull. Hist. Chem.*, Volume 28, Number 1, 2003.

145 "Laundries, dry goods, and other retail shops rose near churches, hospitals, medical publishing firms, tanneries, libraries, and homes." George R. Fisher, "Sixth and Walnut to Broad and Samson," Philadelphia Reflections, accessed May 13, 2014, http://www.philadelphia-reflections.com/blog/1222.htm.

145 "One day while walking out on Spruce Street, I noticed a cellar being dug." Charles Hires, "Seeing Opportunities," Charles Hires, "Seeing Opportunities," *American Druggist and Pharmaceutical Record* (New York), Vol. 61, October 1913, p. 28.

146 "I returned to the place the next day and saw the contractor and asked him if I could have some of this clay. . . . I filled the entire balance of the cellar, up to the ceiling, with this clay." Ibid.

146 "the brick clay was deposited in the region at the end of the last glacial period." Henry Carvill Lewis, "The Trenton Gravel and Its Relation to the Antiquity of Man," *Proceedings of the Academy of Natural Sciences of Philadelphia*, Volume 32, 1880, p. 297.

146 "The clay was also handy as a component in pharmaceuticals." "History of Fuller's Earth," HRP Industries, accessed May 14, 2014, http://www.fullersearth.com/about_fullers_earth/.

146 "Manufacturers also used the clay to bleach edible oils and decolorize petroleum used in medicinal products (such as Vaseline oils)." Charles L. Parsons, "Fuller's Earth," Department of the Interior, Bureau of Mines (Washington, D.C.: GPO, 1913), p. 19.

146 "It occurred to me that I might put up potter's clay in convenient-sized cakes that would be handy to retail and more convenient for people to use." Charles Hires, "Seeing Opportunities," op. cit., p. 28.

147 "an iron ring on which to stand their irons on ironing day . . . after "being charged very particularly to take care of them and return them in good order." Ibid., p. 28.

147 "He enlisted a metal-working friend to construct a crude stencil with die-cut lead letters spelling out 'HIRES' REFINED FULLER'S EARTH.'" Ibid.

147 "Smith, Kline & Co., founded in Philadelphia in 1830 as an apothecary." Mark Meltzer, "A Time-released Capsule How Small Phila. Shop Grew Into Pharmaceutical Giant," *Philadelphia Inquirer*, September 28, 1988, accessed May 14, 2014, http://articles.philly.com/1988-09-28/business/26229960_1_drug-store-product-line-kline-family.

148 "The side business made $5,000, which provided the starting capital for the root beer project that would bring him worldwide fame and fortune." Don Yates, "Charles E. Hires Company, 1870–present, Philadelphia, Pennsylvania," *Bottles and Extras*, Summer 2005, p. 50.

148 "doing business without advertising is like winking at a girl in the dark: you know what you are doing, but nobody else does." "Our History," Dr Pepper Snapple Group, accessed May 14, 2014, http://www.drpepper snapplegroup.com/brands/hires/.

148 "He used his fuller's earth profits to fund his research and development over the next five years." Don Yates, op. cit.

149 "You advertise in the *Ledger*, beginning right away, and I'll tell the book-keeper not to send you any bills unless you ask for them." Charles E. Hires, "Some Advertising Reminiscences," *Simmons' Spice Mill*, February 1915, p. 194.

149 *"Over fifty thousand pounds* of barks, roots, berries, and flowers went into the composition of Hires Root Beer Extract made last year." *The Illustrated American* (New York), Volume 7, August 15, 1891, p. 629.

150 "His personal and business motto was simply: 'Merit will win.'" Ibid.

150 "I have often thought when I have heard of the difficulties of a young man in getting along." Charles Hires, "Seeing Opportunities," op. cit., p. 28.

151 "SERVE." Ibid.

PART III

153 "But just buckle in with a bit of a grin." Edgar Albert Guest, "It Couldn't Be Done," Poetry Foundation, accessed May 11, 2014, http://www.poetry foundation.org/poem/173579.

CHAPTER 8: DEATH-DEFYING MAVERICKS OF GLASS: EDWARD LIBBEY AND MICHAEL OWENS

156 "Together, they created or fueled more than two hundred companies." Alan Schoedel, "Owens Centennial Observances Planned in 34 Cities to Honor Unschooled Genius of U.S. Glass Industry," *Toledo Blade*, August 30, 1959, p. 2.

156 "Owens's mechanical genius paved the way for lower production costs, higher output, and unprecedented uniformity of product quality and

size." Quentin Skrabec, Jr., *Michael Owens and the Glass Industry* (Gretna, La.: Pelican Publishing, January 31, 2007), p. 203.

157   "During the reign of Tiberius Caesar, unsurprisingly, the troubled emperor descended into depression, sexual debauchery, and vengeance." *Classical Weekly*, Volume VI, Number 20, March 29, 1913, p. 165.

157   "Ever-scheming Livia, the Roman Mom from Hell, is rumored to have poisoned several of Tiberius's rivals, including Germanicus, two of Augustus's grandsons, and perhaps even Augustus himself." Fagan, op. cit.

157   "The very first glass-makers came from ancient Egypt, Syria, and Palestine, but Roman conquerors and traders get the credit for adopting, adapting, and spreading early glass technology across Western Europe and the Mediterranean." "Wondrous Glass: Reflections on the World of Rome," accessed May 10, 2014, http://www.umich.edu/~kelseydb/Exhibits /WondrousGlass/MainGlass.html. See also House of Glass, "History of Glassblowing," accessed May 10, 2014, http://www.thehouseofglassinc .com/glasshistory.htm.

157   "'Glass was present in nearly every aspect of daily life,' a Roman art history specialist noted, 'from a lady's morning toilette to a merchant's afternoon business dealings to the evening *cena*, or dinner.'" Metropolitan Museum of Art, "Roman Glass," accessed May 10, 2014, http://www.met museum.org/toah/hd/rgls/hd_rgls.htm.

158   "The impact left nothing more than a small dent, which the emperor's guest miraculously repaired with a hammer (*matriolum*) he had brought along for the sales pitch." *Classical Weekly*, Volume VI, Number 20, March 29, 1913, op. cit., p. 102.

158   "If the invention were known, Tiberius feared, 'gold would become as cheap as mud.'" M. P. E. Berthelot, "Ancient and Mediaeval Chemistry," *Popular Science Monthly*, Volume 45, p. 117.

159   "Venice's secret police would be dispatched to hunt down escapees to the ends of the earth." Madeline Anne Wallace-Dunlop, *Glass in the Old World*, (Whitefish, Mont.: Kessinger Publishing, 2010 [1882]) op. cit. See also: thecultureconcept circle, "Glass a Magic Material—Pt 2 Venice, Verzelini & Vauxhall," accessed May 10, 2014, http://www.thecultureconcept.com /circle/glass-a-magic-material-pt-2-venice-verzelini-vauxhall.

159   "Many of the workers successfully escaped to Vienna, Belgium, France, and England." House of Glass, "History of Glassblowing," op. cit.

160   "'aboard moonlit gondolas by secret agents' to work for Colbert's Royal Company of Glass and Mirrors." Heyl and Gregorin, op. cit.

160   "Colbert and his operatives had gathered enough intelligence to continue mirror production on their own." Mark Pendergrast, *Mirror Mirror: A History of the Human Love Affair with Reflection* (New York: Basic Books, 2003). See also Melchior-Bonnet, *The Mirror: A History*, op. cit.

160   "The Liberty Song." Lydia Bolles Newcomb, "Songs and Ballads of the Revolution," *New England Magazine: An Illustrated Monthly*, Volume 13, Number 1, September 1895, p. 503.

161   "Chancellor of the Exchequer Charles Townshend (Britain's Chief Bagman), crusaded for a new set of onerous import duties and the creation of a tax compliance police squad headquartered in Boston—where resistance to the Stamp Act had been most virulent." USHistory.org, "The Townshend Acts," accessed May 10, 2014, http://www.ushistory.org/us/9d.asp. See also: Stamp Act, "1767—Townshend Acts," accessed May 10, 2014, http://www.stamp-act-history.com/townshend-act/townshend-acts/.

162   "Parliament enacted a package of four laws in Townshend's name in 1767." Massachusetts Historical Society, "The Townshend Acts," accessed May 10, 2014, http://www.masshist.org/revolution/townshend.php.

163   "The Boston selectmen, including John Hancock and Samuel Adams, added their clarion voices after a historic town hall meeting in October 1767 at Faneuil Hall." Historic Printed Letter Signed *"Joseph Jackson," "Samuel Sewall," "John Ruddock," "Wm Phillips," "Tim. Newell,"* and *"John Rowe"* as Select Men of Boston, dated October 31, 1767. *"To the Gentlemen Select-Men of Eastown,"* accessed from University Archives on May 10, 2014, http://www.universityarchives.com/Find-an-Item/Results-List/Item-Detail.aspx?ItemID=51597.

163   "The patriots drew up a target list of British goods." Ibid.

163   "The Boston leaders also agreed 'to promote Industry, Economy, and Manufactures' domestically." Ibid.

163   "British exports plunged from 2,378,000 pounds in 1768 to 1,634,000 in 1769." William R. Nester, *The Frontier War for American Independence* (Mechanicsburg, Pa.: Stackpole Books, 2004), p. 33.

163   "Defiant Americans, men and women alike, tarred and feathered the British tax collection squad." R. S. Longley, "Mob activities in revolutionary Massachusetts," *New England Quarterly*, Vol. 6, No. 1, March 1933, pp. 98–130.

163   "But it was too late and too little. The Revolutionary War die had been cast." Historic Printed Letter Signed *"Joseph Jackson," "Samuel Sewall," "John Ruddock," "Wm Phillips," "Tim. Newell,"* and *"John Rowe"* as Select Men

of Boston, dated October 31, 1767, op. cit. See also "Colonists Respond to the Townshend Acts," *Making the Revolution: America, 1763–1791*, America In Class, accessed May 12, 2014, http://americainclass.org/sources/mak ingrevolution/crisis/text4/townshendactsresponse1767.pdf.

163 "the glass armonica." "Franklin's Glass Armonica," History of Science and Technology, The Franklin Institute, accessed May 14, 2014, http:// learn.fi.edu/learn/sci-tech/armonica/armonica.php?cts=benfranklin -recreation.

163 "pulse glass." Joyce Chaplin, *The First Scientific American: Benjamin Franklin and the Pursuit of Genius* (Basic Books, 2006), p. 204.

163 "The industrious soap merchant-turned-forge owner had founded America's first profitable glass factory in the 1730s in Salem County, New Jersey." "Buttons to Bottles, Hadrosaurs to Rats, There's a Wistar," July 13, 2010, accessed May 10, 2014, http://footnotessincethewilderness .wordpress.com/2010/07/13/buttons-to-bottles-hadrosaurs-to-rats-there %E2%80%99s-a-wistar/.

164 "produced glass for the lab instruments of colonial Philadelphia math-ematician, astronomer, and inventor David Rittenhouse." Mark Haber-lein, "Glassmaking," in Thomas Adam, ed., *Germany and the Americas: O-Z* (Santa Barbara, Calif.: ABC-CLIO Inc., 2005), p. 452. See also William Barton, *Memoirs of the life of David Rittenhouse, LLD. F.R.S., late president of the American philosophical society, interspersed with various notices of many distinguished men: with an appendix, containing sundry philosophical and other papers, most of which have not hitherto been published* (Philadelphia: Edward Parker, 1813).

164 "As early American beer and whiskey makers multiplied, the demand for glass bottles grew. Beer-brewer and vineyard owner Thomas Jefferson courted glassmakers." Quentin Skrabec, Jr., *Michael Owens and the Glass Industry*, op. cit., p. 50.

164 "it is Jarves who 'is due the credit for perfecting and putting into practical use the art of pressing glass.'" Ruth Webb Lee, *Sandwich Glass* (Wellesley Hills, Mass., 1939), p. 91.

164 "Like other glass innovators before him, Jarves faced violent threats." Quentin R. Skrabec, Jr., *Edward Drummond Libbey, American Glassmaker* (Jefferson, N.C.: McFarland, 2011), p. 20.

164 "The glass blowers on discovery that I had succeeded in pressing a piece of glass, were so enraged for fear their business would be ruined by the new discovery." *Antiques*, October 1931, cited in Ruth Webb Lee, *Sandwich Glass*, op. cit.

165   "'I was born in Mason County, West Virginia,' in 1859, he recounted."
      Keene Sumner, "Don't Try to Carry the Whole World on Your Shoulders!"
      American Magazine, Volume 94, July 1922.

166   "Hobbs also brought in William Leighton, son of NEGC's Thomas Leigh-
      ton, who had patented the 'Boston silvered door knob' made of mercury
      glass for NEGC." U.S. Patent US 12265 A, accessed May 11, 2014, http://
      www.google.nl/patents/US12265. See also: Franklin Pierce Hall, "The
      American Doorknob," *Antique Homes*, accessed May 11, 2014, http://www
      .antiquehomesmagazine.com/Articles.php?id=14.

166   "Hobbs's son, John H., also joined the company and succeeded his father
      upon his retirement in 1867." Gordon Campbell, ed., *The Grove Encyclo-
      pedia of Decorative Arts*, Volume 1 (Oxford, UK: Oxford University Press,
      2006), p. 481.

166   "The company won industry renown for its perfection of lime glass."
      The Metropolitan Museum of Art, *In Pursuit of Beauty: Americans and the
      Aesthetic Movement* (New York: The Metropolitan Museum of Art, 1986),
      p. 440.

166   "Child labor was a staple of the glass industry. Girls worked in the pack-
      ing rooms, polishing and wrapping glass products." "Batch, Blow, and
      Boys: The Glass Industry in the United States, 1820s–1900," last updated
      January 3, 2012, accessed May 11, 2014, http://www.utoledo.edu/library
      /canaday/exhibits/oi/OIExhibit/Batch,Blow.htm.

166   "A shop of three skilled blowers and finishers would need three or four
      young boys." Ibid.

166   "The 'holding-mold boy' opened and closed iron molds for the glass-
      blower." E. N. Clopper, National Child Labor Committee, "Child Labor
      in West Virginia," Pamphlet No. 86, 1908, accessed May 11, 2014, http://
      www.wvculture.org/history/labor/childlabor05.html.

167   "At that time, bottles were made by hand. The workman would blow a
      bottle." Keene Sumner, "Don't Try to Carry the Whole World on Your
      Shoulders!" op. cit.

167   "By 1880, some six thousand boys between the ages of ten and fifteen
      (one-quarter of the glassmaking workforce) were putting in ten-hour
      days, six days a week, for as little as thirty cents a day." The American
      Society of Mechanical Engineers, *Designates the Owens "AR" Bottle Machine
      As An International Historic Engineering Landmark*, May 17, 1983, accessed
      May 11, 2014, http://www.utoledo.edu/library/canaday/exhibits/oi/oi
      exhibit/5612.pdf.

167 "'Work never hurt anyone!' he scoffed to a reporter." Keene Sumner, "Don't Try to Carry the Whole World on Your Shoulders!,"op. cit.

168 "Five years older than Owens, Edward D. Libbey got his first taste of the glass life as a 'chore boy' at the Cambridge, Massachusetts, headquarters of Deming Jarves's New England Glass Company." Jack Sullivan, "When Mr. Libbey Went to the Fair," *Bottles and Extras*, March–April 2010, p. 44, accessed May 11, 2014, http://www.fohbc.org/PDF_Files/When%20MrLibby%20Went%20to%20the%20Fair.pdf.

168 "He studied Greek and Latin, poetry, rhetoric, philosophy, and business." Quentin Skrabec, Jr., *Edward Drummond Libbey, American Glassmaker*, op. cit., pp. 31–32. See also "'Go West, Young Man,' The Early Years of Libbey Leadership, 1872–1893," p. 24, accessed May 14, 2014, http://libbeyhistory.com/files/Part_1.2.pdf.

168 "In 1874, as self-taught fifteen-year-old Mike embarked on his glass-blowing tenure at Hobbs, Brockunier, and Company, twenty-year-old Edward took a position as a clerk at the New England Glass Company." Fauster, *Libbey Glass Since 1818: Pictorial History & Collector's Guide*, op. cit.

169 "In 1883, his father died and Libbey inherited the company—along with its skyrocketing fuel, labor, and shipping costs." Jack Paquette, *The Glassmakers Revisited* (Xlibris Corporation, 2011), p. 16.

169 "One day a batch of glass came through that was merely amber instead of ruby in color." "How Toledo Became a City of Glass 100 Years Ago," *Toledo Blade*, August 14, 1988.

169 "Libbey 'created a market, and he had the genius to bring the market and the technology together.'" Quentin Skrabec, Jr., *Edward Drummond Libbey, American Glassmaker*, op. cit., p. 36.

169 "Libbey took out patents for other ornamental colored glass improvements and etched glass patterns as well" Ibid., p. 36.

169 "Skrabec noted, and this vigilant commitment to the 'defense of corporate intellectual rights was fundamental to the transformation of glassmaking from a craft to an industry.'" Ibid., p. 197.

171 "They enforced draconian employment rules to repress nonunionism 'that were stricter than those of almost any other national organization.'" United States Industrial Commission, *Reports of the Industrial Commission on Labor Organizations, Labor Disputes, and Arbitration, and on Railway Labor* (Washington D.C.: Government Printing Office), Volume XVII, 1901, p. 175.

171   "At its first convention in Pittsburgh in 1878, the AFGWU proposed uni-
      form production rates based on the 'output of the least productive plants
      and slowest workmen.'" Carroll D. Davidson Wright, U.S. Bureau of
      Labor, *Regulation and restriction of output* (Washington D.C.: Government
      Printing Office, 1904).

171   "Later, the union passed a radical resolution 'call[ing] upon the working-
      men of the world to unite under the banner of international socialism.'"
      Ibid. See also United States Industrial Commission, *Reports of the Indus-
      trial Commission on Labor Organizations, Labor Disputes, and Arbitration, and
      on Railway Labor,* op. cit.

171   "The glass industry, one Pittsburgh factory owner complained, was run
      by unions 'trying to do what the almighty did not see fit to do—prevent
      one man from making more than another man.'" James L. Flannery, *The
      Glass House Boys of Pittsburgh: Law, Technology, and Child Labor* (University
      of Pittsburgh Press, 2009), p.122.

171   "Owens's biographer Quentin Skrabec, Jr., notes that his commitment
      to the union 'seemed more pragmatic than philosophical.'" Skrabec, Jr.,
      Michael Owens and the Glass Industry, op. cit., pp. 86–87.

172   "Libbey, under siege by these outside agitators infiltrating his factory,
      called the national committee 'the wrecking squad.'" Skrabec, Jr., *Edward
      Drummond Libbey, American Glassmaker,* op. cit., p. 44.

172   "Mike Owens recounted when the industrialist came to town" Keene
      Sumner, "Don't Try to Carry the Whole World on Your Shoulders!" op. cit.

173   "While he rejected him for the superintendent's position, the New
      England capitalist took on the hot-tempered Flint as a glass-blower
      in 1888." "And Now Their Cashier Carries a Colt," *American Magazine,*
      Volume 94, January 1, 1922.

173   "The hard-driving Owens oversaw the seventeen-month, high-stakes job,
      which reaped life-saving profits for Libbey Glass." Quentin R. Skrabec, Jr.,
      Glass in Northwest Ohio (Charleston, S.C.: Arcadia Publishing, 2007), p. 43.

173   "Before the project, the firm 'was suffering from a deficit of $3,000,' glass
      historian Jack Pacquette found." Jack Paquette, *The Glassmakers Revisited*
      (Xlibris Corporation), op. cit., p. 21.

174   "Modeling it after the Gillinder & Sons glass exhibit." Gillinder & Sons was
      founded by English glass chemist, historian, and businessman William T.
      Gillinder, who originally had sailed to America to work for the New En-
      gland Glass Company. After several failed ventures, he established a glass
      factory in Philadelphia with partner/investor Edwin Bennett. Sons James
      and Frederick took over when the elder Gillinder died in 1871. The broth-

ers conceived the wildly popular glass house exhibit and paid a $3,000 concession fee to enter the fair; the annex building housing their display cost another $15,000. "Souvenir sales figures came to $96,000 with more than $14,000 paid to the Centennial Board of Finance as commission on the sales." WheatonArts.org, "1994 Gillinder Glass: Story of a Company," accessed May 11, 2014, http://www.wheatonarts.org/museumamerican-glass/pastexhibitions/90-99/1994gillinderglass/.

174   "Attendance was poor at first, until an employee suggested charging ten cents for admission (later raised to a quarter) and handing out souvenir stickpins decorated with Libbey glass bows." "How Toledo Became a City of Glass 100 Years Ago," *Toledo Blade*, op. cit.

174   "One enraptured reporter described it as a 'room lined with diamonds.'" Regina Lee Blaszcyk, *Imagining Consumers: Design and Innovation from Wedgwood to Corning* (Baltimore: Johns Hopkins University Press, 2000).

174   "A brilliant gamble, the lavish exhibit of glass-making manned by Owens and his team created white-hot buzz about Libbey Glass and sparked a craze in fashionable crystal." Jack Sullivan, "When Mr. Libbey Went to the Fair," *Bottles and Extras*, op. cit.

174   "The firm's cut-glass orders soared, as did its global reputation as the fair helped launch the 'Brilliant Period' of American cut glass." "'Go West, Young Man,' The Early Years of Libbey Leadership, 1872–1893," op. cit., p. 45.

175   "A poem by Edgar Albert Guest served as Mike Owens's office motivational poster. Tacked to his wall, the paean to persistence was titled 'It Couldn't Be Done.'" Poetry Foundation, Edgar Albert Guest, "It Couldn't Be Done," accessed May 11, 2014, http://www.poetryfoundation.org/poem/173579.

176   "Between 1811 and 1813, the so-called Luddites hacked away at thousands of wool-finishing machines." Anthony M. Orum, John W. C. Johnstone, Stephanie Riger, eds., *Changing Societies: Essential Sociology for Our Times* (Lanham, Md.: Rowan & Littlefield Publishers Inc., 1999).

176   "Big Labor devised multiple "antimechanization" strategies." James Flannery, *The Glass House Boys of Pittsburgh*, op. cit., p. 119.

177   "from about fifty cents." Ron D. Katznelson and John Howells, "Inventing-around Edison's incandescent lamp patent: evidence of patents' role in stimulating downstream development," May 26, 2012, accessed May 11, 2014, http://www.law.northwestern.edu/research-faculty/searlecenter/workingpapers/documents/Katznelson_Howells_Inventing_around_Edisons_patent_V17.pdf.

177   "He explained in his filing." United States Patent Office, "Apparatus for blowing glass," patent number US534840 A.

178   "It will be seen by the foregoing that in the use of mechanical means for carrying out the process of blowing glass the necessity of skilled labor is dispensed with." United States Patent Office, "Mechanical glass-blower," patent number US570879 A.

178   "A glob of molten glass would be picked up onto the pipe." "Owens the Inventor," last updated January 3, 2012; accessed May 11, 2014, http://www.utoledo.edu/library/canaday/exhibits/oi/oiexhibit/owens.htm.

179   By 'means of the absolute control of the air-pressure,' Owens wrote, 'the quality of the work done by the machine is superior to that heretofore produced.'" United States Patent Office, "Owens X," patent number US576074 A.

179   "Economists Naomi Lamoreaux and Kenneth Sokoloff point out." Naomi R. Lamoreaux and Kenneth L. Sokoloff, "Market Trade in Patents and the Rise of a Class of Specialized Inventors in the 19th-Century United States," *The American Economic Review*, Vol. 91, No. 2, Papers and Proceedings of the Hundred Thirteenth Annual Meeting of the American Economic Association, May, 2001, p. 39.

180   "When the fantastic idea of a towering, fully automated contraption of iron and steel that could blow glass bottles at high speed came to him." Alan Schoedel, "Owens Centennial Observances Planned in 34 Cities to Honor Unschooled Genius of U.S. Glass Industry," op. cit.

180   "From what you've told me, I could go out and have this machine built." Ibid.

180   "Team Owens built parts and prototypes whenever and wherever they could: at the office, in other Libbey-owned buildings, or in Bock's basement all hours of the day and into the midnight shift." Quentin Skrabec, Jr., *Michael Owens and the Glass Industry*, op. cit.

180   "You would laugh at the first device we made." "And Now Their Cashier Carries a Colt," *American Magazine*, op. cit.

181   "In 1904, Owens received his historic Patent No. 766,768." M. J. Owens, "Glass Shaping Machine," patented August 2, 1904; Patent No. 766,768, accessed online May 11, 2014, http://www.sha.org/bottle/pdffiles/Owens 1904patent.pdf.

181   "The usual obstructionists tried to prevent the spread of this efficient and astonishing technology, which, as the National Child Labor Committee acknowledged, had done more than any government regulation to end child labor abuses." Jack Paquette, *The Glassmakers Revisited*, op. cit.

181   "Union workers boycotted Toledo Glass and a new, Libbey-formed company, the Owens Bottle Company, which produced both the bottle-making machines and bottles." Quentin Skrabec, Jr., *Michael Owens and the Glass Industry*, op. cit., p. 139.

181   "Libbey acquired scores of businesses ranging from glass container plants to mold makers, to sand, paper box, and melting pot firms." Jack Paquette, *The Glassmakers Revisited*, op. cit.

181   "During the next decade, he would create adaptations to produce everything from glass prescription ware to gallon packers." The American Society of Mechanical Engineers, *Designates the Owens "AR" Bottle Machine as An International Historic Engineering Landmark*, op. cit.

182   "We are still finding new steps to be taken." Keene Sumner, "Don't Try to Carry the Whole World on Your Shoulders!" op. cit.

182   "While making profit for stockholders, the company's product has reduced the price of bottles from twenty five to fifty per cent. The world as well the stockholders has profited." "How the Bottle-Making Machine Came into Being," *Crockery and Glass Journal*, Volume 90, Number 1, July 3, 1919.

182   "By 1923, just twenty years after the first successful trial of his original automatic machine, ninety-four of every hundred bottles manufactured in the U.S. were being produced mechanically—either by the Owens machinery or by semiautomatic equipment made by others." Jack Paquette, *The Glassmakers Revisited*, op. cit.

182   "The extraordinary thing about it is that it does not break and fly to pieces like ordinary glass. Let me show you." Keene Sumner, "Don't Try to Carry the Whole World on Your Shoulders!" op. cit.

183   "The ancient, time-consuming, and unreliable techniques for producing window glass retained a problematic curve." Ibid.

183   "Colburn's inspiration came to him while eating pancakes." "Syrup Off the Roller: The Libbey-Owens-Ford Company," last updated January 3, 2012; accessed May 11, 2014, http://www.utoledo.edu/library/canaday/exhibits/oi/OIExhibit/Syrup.htm.

184   "Three years later, the company reported profits of $4.2 million and European sales exploded." Quentin Skrabec, Jr., *Michael Owens and the Glass Industry*, op. cit., p. 284.

184   "Libbey paid generous tribute to his partner" "Owens the Innovator," University of Toledo collections, accessed May 19, 2014, http://www.utoledo.edu/library/canaday/exhibits/oi/oiexhibit/owens.htm.

185 "That's the protective, shatterproof glass used at the National Archives in Washington, D.C., to seal and protect original versions of the Declaration of Independence and Constitution . . ." Julie McKinnon, "Pilkington preserves U.S. heritage under glass," *Toledo Blade*, July 27, 2001, accessed May 11, 2014, http://www.toledoblade.com/local/2001/07/27 /Pilkington-preserves-U-S-heritage-under-glass.html. See also "Syrup Off the Roller: The Libbey-Owens-Ford Company," op. cit.

CHAPTER 9: "PERFECT PARTNERSHIP": WESTINGHOUSE, TESLA, AND THE HARNESSING OF NIAGARA FALLS

187 "The 'War of the Currents.'" See Glenn Beck, *Miracle and Massacres: True and Untold Stories of the Making of America*, "Chapter 5: Edison vs. Westinghouse" (New York: Threshold Editions, 2013); Jill Jonnes, *Empires of Light: Edison, Tesla, Westinghouse, and the Race to Electrify the World* (New York: Random House, 2004); and Tom McNichol, *AC/DC: The Savage Tale of the First Standards War* (San Francisco: Jossey-Bass, 2013).

189 "The first impressions are those to which we cling most in later life . . . . A powerful frame, well proportioned, with every joint in working order, an eye as clear as a crystal, a quick and springy step. . . . Not one word which would have been objectionable, not a gesture which might have offended." "Death of Westinghouse," *Electrical World*, Vol. 63, No. 12, March 21, 1914, p. 637.

191 "Westinghouse patented nearly forty products." Quentin Skrabec, *George Westinghouse: Gentle Genius* (New York: Algora Publishing, 2006), pp. 68–75.

191 "The utility supplied power." "Philadelphia Company: List of Deals," Harvard Business School, Baker Library, Historical Collections: Lehman Brothers Collection—Contemporary Business Archives, accessed May 18, 2014, http://www.library.hbs.edu/hc/lehman/company.html ?company=philadelphia_company.

191 "Leyden jar." Make your own Leyden jar by following the instructions here: http://www.instructables.com/id/Make-A-Water-Leyden-Jar/, accessed May 18, 2014.

191 "electrocution studies on chickens and turkeys." American Physical Society, "This Month in Physics History: December 23, 1750: Ben Franklin Attempts to Electrocute a Turkey," accessed May 18, 2014, http://www .aps.org/publications/apsnews/200612/history.cfm. Franklin got quite a shock in one of the failed turkey tests. He wrote: "I have lately made an experiment in electricity that I desire never to repeat. Two nights ago,

being about to kill a turkey by the shock from two large glass jars, containing as much electrical fire as forty common phials, I inadvertently took the whole through my own arms and body, by receiving the fire from the united top wires with one hand, while the other held a chain connected with the outsides of both jars."

192   "My early greatest capital." Henry G. Prout, *A Life of George Westinghouse* (New York: The American Society of Mechanical Engineers, 1921), p. 5.

192   "He drove others." "Westinghouse, the Champion of Electrical Current," *Electrical World*, Vol. 79, February 4, 1922, p. 229.

192   "He was a great pioneer and builder." Nikola Tesla, "Tribute to George Westinghouse," *Electrical World & Engineer*, Vol. 63, No. 12, March 21, 1914, pp. 637–38.

192   "And the company paid." Gilbert King, "The Rise and Fall of Nikola Tesla and His Tower," Smithsonian.com, February 4, 2013, accessed May 18, 2014, http://www.smithsonianmag.com/history/the-rise-and-fall-of-nikola -tesla-and-his-tower-11074324/.

193   "Like Westinghouse, Tesla started tinkering." Nikola Tesla, "My Inventions," *Electrical Experimenter*, Volume VI, No. 71, March 1919, p. 776.

193   "'I have never since been able to touch a May-bug.'" Ibid.

193   "After seeing a photo of the famed Niagara Falls." Marc Seifer, *Wizard: The Life and Times of Nikola Tesla, Biography of a Genius* (New York: Citadel Press, 1996), p. 13.

194   "burst into tears." Nikola Tesla, "My Inventions: III: My Later Endeavors," *Electrical Experimenter*, Volume VI, No. 72, April 1919, pp. 864–65.

194   "persist despite all my efforts to banish it." Nikola Tesla, "My Inventions: II," *Electrical Experimenter*, Volume VI, No. 71, March 1919.

194   "the idea came like a flash of lightning." Marc Seifer, *Wizard*, op. cit., p. 22.

195   "Its efficiency too is higher." Nikola Tesla, "My Inventions: III: My Later Endeavors," *Electrical Experimenter*, Volume VI, No. 72, April 1919, p. 865.

196   "turned out to be a practical joke." Nikola Tesla, "My Inventions: IV: The Discovery of the Tesla Coil and Transformer," *Electrical Experimenter*, Volume VII, No. 73, May 1919.

197   "We have no crown jewels to pawn." "Tesla's Egg of Columbus," *Electrical Experimenter*, Volume VI, No. 71, March 1919, pp. 774–75.

197   "The egg represented the rotor." The Franklin Institute explains: "'Two-phase' motors use two sets of coils placed perpendicular to each other

surrounding the core. When alternating current is sent to the coils, they become electromagnets where polarity rapidly changes with each reversal of current flow. As the first coils are supplied with current, they create a magnetic field which starts the core turning. When the first coils' current supply reverses, the second coil set is at its maximum supply point and creates its own magnetic field; the core spins on. In effect the 'magnetization' amount never varies and a rotating magnetic field is created. The result is a smooth-running, commutator-free motor with the rotor as its only moving part." See The Franklin Institute, "Two-Phase Induction Motor," accessed May 18, 2014, http://learn.fi.edu/learn/case-files/tesla/motor.html.

197 "wild man of electronics." "Tesla Museum Campaign Exceeds Fundraising target," BBC News, August 22, 2012, accessed May 18, 2014, http://www.bbc.com/news/technology-19343855.

197 "greatest electrician of the world." Marc Seifer, *Wizard*, op. cit., p. 178. See also *Niagara Falls in Miniature* (Chicago: Rand, McNally & Co., 1890), p. 16.

199 "Tesla had harnessed months before him." "Nikola Tesla Becomes the Recipient of the Edison Medal," *Electrical World*, Volume 69, No. 20, May 19, 1917, pp. 980–81.

199 "$2.50 per horsepower on every motor." Quentin Skrabec, *Westinghouse*, op. cit., p. 115.

199 "Tesla split the proceeds." W. Bernard Carlson, *Tesla: Inventor of the Electrical Age* (Princeton, N.J.: Princeton University Press, 2013), p. 112.

199 "It is the most valuable patent." Quentin Skrabec, *Westinghouse*, op. cit., p. 125.

200 "that could be cast and machined efficiently." W. Bernard Carlson, *Tesla*, op. cit.

200 "to pass electrical currents through his body." See them online here: http://www.tfcbooks.com/tesla/1895-04-00.htm, accessed May 18, 2014.

201 "inspired the nickname 'the White City.'" "Explore the White City with Lisa Synder and Tim Samuelson," The Museum of Science and Industry, accessed May 19, 2014, http://www.msichicago.org/whats-here/events/explore-the-white-city/.

201 "As by a touch." *Appleton's Annual Cyclopedia and Register of Important Events of the Year*, Volume 18 (New York: D. Appleton & Company, 1878), p. 761.

202 "Westinghouse's and Tesla's breakthroughs firsthand." Quentin Skrabec, *Westinghouse*, op. cit., p. 169.

203   "epoch in industrial history." Henry G. Prout, *A Life of George Westinghouse*, op. cit., p. 193.

203   "Living on oatmeal." Richard M. Patterson, *Butch Cassidy: A Biography* (Lincoln: University of Nebraska Press, 1998), p. 21.

204   "first known heist." Douglas MacGowan, "Butch Cassidy and the Sundance Kid," crimelibrary.com, accessed May 19, 2014, http://www.crime library.com/gangsters_outlaws/outlaws/cassidy/3.html. See also "A Bank Robbery in Colorado," *Salt Lake City Herald*, June 25, 1889, A1.

204   "The mountain man's daring offer." Alan E. Drew, "Telluride Power Co.: Pioneering AC in the Rocky Mountains," *Power & Energy Magazine*, January/ February 2014, accessed May 19, 2014, http://magazine.ieee-pes.org /januaryfebruary-2014/history-11/.

205   "I'm willing to gamble that, gentlemen." Richard L. Fetter and Suzanne C. Fetter, *Telluride: From Pick to Powder* (Caldwell, Idaho: Caxton Press, 1979), p. 56.

205   "Three miles of bare copper wire." Alan E. Drew, "Telluride Power Co.," op. cit.

206   "for industrial use in the United States." Ibid.

206   "A plaque erected at the site." "Milestones: Ames Hydroelectric Generating Plant, 1891," IEEE Global History Network, accessed May 19, 2014, http://www.ieeeghn.org/wiki/index.php/Milestones:Ames_Hydro electric_Generating_Plant,_1891. The Ames Plant was also inducted into *Hydro Review*'s "Hydro Hall of Fame." See Alfred Huges and Richard Rudolph, "Ames Hydro: Making History Since 1891," *Hydro World*, Vol. 32, Issue 7, August 27, 2013, accessed May 19, 2014, http://www.hydroworld .com/articles/hr/print/volume-32/issue-7/articles/ames-hydro-making -history-since-1891.html.

206   "safe maximum voltage of forty thousand volts." "Provo High Voltage Insulators," *Journal of Electricity, Power, and Gas*, Volume 13, No. 1, January 1903, p. 115.

206   "generating enough power for a town of four thousand." "About Us," Xcel Energy, accessed May 19, 2014, https://www.xcelenergy.com/About_Us /Our_Company/Power_Generation/Ames_Hydro_Generating_Station.

207   "Tesla apparently never visited the Ames plant." Marc Seifer, *Wizard*, op. cit., pp. 214–19.

207   "thereby charging the earth with electricity." "Nikola Tesla in Colorado Springs," *Denver Eye*, September 17, 2012, accessed May 19, 2014, http:// www.thedenvereye.com/nikola-tesla-in-colorado-springs/.

207 "Cripple Creek, nearly fifty miles away." Ibid.

208 "After years of struggle." Quentin Skrabec, *Westinghouse*, op. cit., p. 170.

209 "necessary for operation and power transmission." "Electricity and Its Development at Niagara Falls," University at Buffalo Libraries, "Pan-American Exposition of 1901," accessed May 14, 2014, http://library.buffalo.edu/pan-am/exposition/electricity/development/.

209 "mighty power of the great cataract." "What Modern Genius Has Accomplished," *Sacramento Daily Union*, May 4, 1895, accessed May 9, 2014, http://cdnc.ucr.edu/cgi-bin/cdnc?a=d&d=SDU18950504.2.44#.

210 "personally supervised their installation." Quentin Skrabec, *The 100 Most Significant Events in American Business* (Westport, Conn.: Greenwood Publishing Group, 2012), p. 95.

210 "A diverse range of manufacturers." Jack Foran, "Introduction: Niagara Falls and Electricity," University at Buffalo Libraries, "Pan-American Exposition of 1901," accessed May 19, 2014, http://library.buffalo.edu/pan-am/essays/foran.html.

211 "A convention attendee explained." *Journal of the Society of Automotive Engineers*, Volume 20, 1927, p. 157.

211 "The success of Niagara Falls." Nikola Tesla, "On Electricity," Address on the Occasion of the Commemoration of the Introduction of Niagara Falls Power in Buffalo at the Ellicot Club, *Electrical Review*, January 27, 1897, accessed May 19, 2014, http://www.tfcbooks.com/tesla/1897-01-27.htm.

211 "humanity owes an immense debt of gratitude." Speech, Institute of Immigrant Welfare, Hotel Baltimore, New York, May 12, 1938, read in absentia, cited in James O'Neill, *Prodigal Genius: The Life of Nikola Tesla* (New York: Cosimo Classics, 2007), p. 83.

212 "payoff money to aldermen and regulators." Margaret Cheney, *Tesla: Man Out of Time* (New York: Touchstone, 2001), pp. 71–72.

212 "Tesla agreed to tear up the royalty agreement." Ibid., pp. 73–74.

213 "Wardenclyffe Tower in Long Island." Gilbert King, "The Rise and Fall of Nikola Tesla and His Tower," Smithsonian.com, February 4, 2013, accessed May 19, 2014, http://www.smithsonianmag.com/history/the-rise-and-fall-of-nikola-tesla-and-his-tower-11074324/.

213 "future ways Tesla could raise money." Jonathan Eisen, *Suppressed Inventions and Other Discoveries* (New York: Perigee Books, 1998), p. 422.

214 *"yield both food and shelter."* Goethe's "Hope," quoted in Nikola Tesla, "The Problem of Increasing Human Energy," *Century Illustrated Magazine*, June 1900, accessed May 19, 2014, http://www.tfcbooks.com/tesla/1900 -06-00.htm.

215 "useful and profitable employment." Henry G. Prout, *A Life of George Westinghouse*, op. cit., p. 303.

215 "at a certain point you have made enough money." Barack Obama, "Remarks by the President on Wall Street Reform in Quincy, Illinois," April 28, 2010, accessed May 19, 2014, http://www.whitehouse.gov/the -press-office/remarks-president-wall-street-reform-quincy-illinois.

PART IV

217 "The very first official thing I did, in my administration—and it was on the very first day of it too—was to start a patent office." Mark Twain, *A Connecticut Yankee in King Arthur's Court* (New York: Harper and Brothers, 1917), p. 68.

CHAPTER 10: SMART LIMBS: THE NEXT GENERATION OF AMERICAN TINKERPRENEURS

219 "He can walk and mingle with persons without betraying his loss; in fact he is restored to his former self for all practical purposes." From the author's collection of nineteenth-century newspaper advertisements.

219 "The company sold its patented products—which also included crutches and wheelchairs—by mail order." "Manual of Artificial Limbs Lays Blueprint for A.A. Marks Company," Healio Orthotics/Prosthetics Medblog, November 1, 2003, accessed May 16, 2014, http://www.healio.com /orthotics-prosthetics/prosthetics/news/online/%7B226963c-d779 -4273-a72e-efa65467cdd5%7D/manual-of-artificial-limbs-lays-blueprint -for-aa-marks-company.

219 "The company hailed the advent of indefatigable Charles Goodyear's vulcanization." "The Charles Goodyear story: The strange story of rubber," Goodyear Corporate, reprinted from *Reader's Digest*, January 1958, accessed May 16, 2014, http://www.goodyear.com/corporate/history /history_story.html.

220 "Goodyear probably never imagined." Ibid.

220 "He patented six important improvements in the design and manufacture of artificial limbs." A list of George E. Marks's patents is available

online at https://www.google.com/search?tbo=p&tbm=pts&hl=en&q=in
inventor:%22George+E.+Marks%22, accessed May 16, 2014.

220   "the *Manual of Artificial Limbs* and *A Treatise on Artificial Limbs*." George
Edwin Marks, *A Treatise on Artificial Limbs With Rubber Hands and Feet* (New
York: A.A. Marks, 1896).

220   "including a committee of the Franklin Institute, which honored the inventors with a prestigious medal." *Journal of the Franklin Institute*, Vol. 127,
No. 5, May 1889.

220   "no fewer than nine manufacturers of artificial limbs had assembled
on this occasion to display their wares." "Manual of Artificial Limbs
Lays Blueprint for A.A. Marks Company," Healio Orthotics/Prosthetics
Medblog, op. cit.

220   "Given the advances of today's prosthetics it might seem primitive, but
was typical for the time." Correspondence with the author, May 6, 2014.

221   "Winkley, now in its fifth generation of family ownership, is still in business today after more than 125 years." Franklyn Curtiss-Wedge, ed., *History of Rice and Steele Counties, Minnesota*, Volume 2 (Chicago: H.C. Cooper,
Jr. and Co., 1910), p. 1473.

221   "The overwhelming number of soldiers who lost limbs during the Civil
War—thirty thousand Union and forty thousand Confederate." Michael
MacRae, "The Civil War and the Birth of the U.S. Prosthetics Industry,"
ASME.org, June 2011, accessed May 16, 2014, https://www.asme.org
/engineering-topics/articles/bioengineering/the-civil-war-and-birth-of
-us-prosthetics-industry

221   "Engineering student James Edward Hanger led the pack." See Bob
O'Connor, *The Amazing Legacy of James E. Hanger: Civil War Soldier* (Infin-
ity Publishing, 2014).

221   "The Union doctor and his assistants removed Hanger's shredded limb
from above the knee with dirty saws and knives, then transported him to
a medical facility." J. H. Beers, *Commemorative biographical record of Wayne
County, Ohio* (Chicago: J.H. Beers, 1889), p. 47.

221   "No one can know what such a loss means unless he has suffered a similar catastrophe." "The J. E. Hanger story," Hanger.com, accessed May 16,
2014, http://www.hanger.com/history/Pages/The-J.E.-Hanger-Story
.aspx.

222   "I am thankful for what seemed then to me nothing but a blunder of fate,
but which was to prove instead a great opportunity." Ibid.

222 "With venture capital funding, Hanger made nearly one hundred acquisi-
tions." "Ivan Sabel's vision: Taking Hanger to new heights and frontiers,"
Hanger.com, accessed May 16, 2014, http://www.hanger.com/history
/Pages/Ivan-Sabel%27s-Vision.aspx.

223 "Thanks to Hanger's purchase of Blanck's patent rights . . ." "IDEO inventor joins Hanger Clinic," *The O&P Edge*, OandP.com, October 8, 2013,
accessed May 16, 2014, http://www.oandp.com/articles/NEWS_2013-10
-08_01.asp.

224 "Within a decade, Martino had patented a cushioned socket for thigh
legs using sponge rubber." Phillip A. Martino, "Rubber-cushion socket
for thigh legs," U.S. Patent 1497219 A, June 10, 1924, Google Patents, accessed May 16, 2014, https://www.google.com/patents/US1497219?dq
=martino+prosthetic&hl=en&sa=X&ei=wYJZU-R54c7JAYWYgPAJ&ved
=0CDwQ6AEwAQ.

224 "Four generations of Martinos have worked in the business, now based
in a two-story brick warehouse in Dorchester." Bill Forry, "The Martinos
of United Prosthetics embrace hope, and make it happen," *Dorchester Reporter*, September 11, 2013, accessed May 16, 2014, http://www.dotnews
.com/2013/martinos-united-prosthetics-embrace-hope-and-make-it
-happen.

225 "Harries used his machines to manufacture Purple Heart ribbons and
nearly six hundred other types of military decorations." Dan Shope,
"Bally Ribbon Mills has an innovative stripe," *Morning Call*, September
28, 2003, accessed May 16, 2014, http://articles.mcall.com/2003-09-28
/business/3481832_1_yellow-ribbons-bally-block-work-ethic.

225 "Bally workers spin nylon, polyester, aramid, graphite, glass, quartz,
ceramic, and silicon carbide." Diane Van Dyke, "Bally Ribbon Mills
weaves past and future," *Berks-Mont News*, February 3, 2006, accessed
May 14, 2014, http://www.berksmontnews.com/article/BM/20060203
/NEWS/302039991.

225 "Hundreds of employees use everything from original shuttle looms to
the most advanced software." Dan Shope, "Bally Ribbon Mills has an innovative stripe," *Morning Call*, op. cit.

226 "Our willingness to work and our openness to everything." Telephone
interview with the author, May 9, 2014, and correspondence with the
author, May 28, 2014.

226 "He spent 212 days in a hospital recovering." Universal Service, "Arbogast
has nerve of iron," *Pittsburgh Post-Gazette*, June 27, 1933, p. 24.

226 "The *Pittsburgh Post-Gazette* reported at the time." Ibid.

227 "Willow Wood made parts for the Navy's PT boats and the Army's B-17 bombers." "Our history," Willow Wood Company, accessed May 16, 2014, http://www.willowwoodco.com/about-willowwood/our-history.

228 "In addition to dozens of prosthetic sports attachments . . . such as well-known amputee and Boulder resident Aron Ralston, who made headlines after self-amputating one arm after a climbing accident in a slot canyon in Utah." Heather McWilliams, "TRS devices help amputees reclaim work, play skills," *Boulder County Business Report*, March 1, 2013, accessed May 16, 2014, http://www.bcbr.com/article/20130301/EDITION/130229930.

228 "He constructed an artificial leg of carbon graphite." "Van Phillips," *Documenting Invention*, Smithsonian.org, accessed May 16, 2014, http://invention.smithsonian.org/resources/popups/case_phillips.aspx.

228 "Anything you can think of, you can create." Martha Davidson, "Artificial Parts: Van Phillips," *Innovative Lives*, March 2005, accessed May 16, 2014, http://invention.smithsonian.org/centerpieces/ilives/van_phillips/van _phillips.html.

229 "One of them, tinkerpreneur Jeff Stibel, used money from the sale of his start-up Simpli.com." "About Braingate," Braingate.com, accessed May 16, 2014, http://www.braingate.com/intellectual_property.html.

229 "next generation of such key areas as auditory prosthesis, bladder control, pain, epilepsy, pharma research, and treatments for arrhythmia and heart failure." Business Wire, "Blackrock Microsystems Celebrates Public Opening of Expansive New Headquarters Facility," June 7, 2013.

229 "MIT described how his invention works." Rob Matheson, "Bionic ankle emulates nature," *MIT News*, April 17, 2014, accessed May 16, 2014, http://newsoffice.mit.edu/2014/hugh-herr-bionic-ankle-emulates-nature-0417.

230 "In 3.5 seconds, the criminals and cowards took Adrianne off the dance floor. In 200 days, we put her back." "A 200-Day Return Journey from the Boston Marathon Bombing," BIOM.com, accessed May 16, 2014, http://www.biom.com/about-us/company/.

230 "BiOm continues to develop new products with an estimated $50 million in grants and venture capital." "About us," BIOM.com, accessed May 16, 2014, http://www.biom.com/about-us/company/.

230 "I'm always thinking about minimizing the time and investment to get from bench to bedside." Rob Matheson, "Bionic ankle emulates nature," *MIT News*, op. cit.

230   "So that the record of history is absolutely crystal clear: There is no alter-
        native way, so far discovered, of improving the lot of the ordinary people."
        Travis Pantin, "Milton Friedman answers Phil Donahue's charges,"
        New York Sun, November 12, 2007, accessed May 16, 2014, http://www
        .nysun.com/business/milton-friedman-answers-phil-donahues-charges
        /66258/.

231   "I started looking into what phantom pain was . . . I decided to do some-
        thing about it." "Recent Intel ISEF Alum Katherine Bomkamp Now CEO
        of Own Company," *Society for Science and the Public*, November 8, 2012, ac-
        cessed May 17, 2014, http://societyforscience.typepad.com/ssp/2012/11
        /recent-intel-isef-alum-katherine-bomkamp-now-ceo-of-own-company
        .html.

231   "Bomkamp secured a patent on her invention and established her own
        company, Katherine Bomkamp International LLC." Ibid.

231   "Surround yourself with people who know more than you do." Correspon-
        dence with the author, May 13, 2014.

232   "He started his own company, called 'Re,' to manufacture the low-cost
        devices he calls 'ReHands.'" "About us," Reprosthetics.com, accessed
        May 17, 2014, http://reprosthetics.com/about-us/.

232   "'I think it would be cool if we had, like, our own company and then we
        made BOBs' . . . 'I hope to make lots of them'. . . . 'It's a really big deal to
        be getting a patent.'" John Donvan, Glen Dacy, and Enjoli Francis, "Girl
        Scouts' Prosthetic Hand Device to Get Patent," ABC News, June 16, 2011,
        accessed May 17, 2014, http://abcnews.go.com/Technology/girl-scout
        -team-patent-prosthetic-hand-device/story?id=13858959.

CONCLUSION

233   "based on the conviction that individual effort was stimulated by higher
        expected returns." B. Zorina Khan, *The Democratization of Invention: Patents
        and Copyrights in American Economic Development, 1790–1920* (Cambridge:
        Cambridge University Press, November 2013), p. 3.

233   "the 'fuel of interest' that stokes the 'fire of genius.'" Abraham Lincoln,
        "Lectures on Discoveries and Inventions," 1858, reprinted in Jason Emer-
        son, *Lincoln the Inventor* (Carbondale, Ill.: Southern Illinois Press, 2009),
        pp. 61–78 and also accessed May 17, 2014, http://www.abrahamlincolnon
        line.org/lincoln/speeches/discoveries.htm.

233   "to promote the Progress of Science and the useful Arts, by securing for
        limited Times to Authors and Inventors the exclusive Right to their re-

spective Writings and Discoveries." Article I, Section 8, Clause 8, of U.S. Constitution, art. I, sec. 8, cl. 8, accessed May 17, 2014, http://www.consti tution.org/js/js_319.htm.

233   "[t]he public good fully coincides . . . with the claims of individuals." James Madison, "The Federalist No. 43," *Independent Journal,* January 23, 1788, accessed May 17, 2014, http://www.constitution.org/fed/federa43 .htm.

233   "Congress and the early courts provided for expansive and generous protection of inventors' intellectual property rights." Adam Mosoff, "Who cares what Thomas Jefferson thought about patents? Reevaluating the patent 'privilege' in historical context," *Cornell Law Review,* Vol. 92, 2007, accessed May 17, 2014, http://cornelllawreview.org/files/2013/02 /Mossoff.pdf.

234   "Primary historical sources, congressional documents, and colonial-era courts—as well as early patent statutes and nineteenth-century patent case law—reveal that patents have been construed as *basic civil rights in property* since America's first days." For an excellent overview of the debate, see Adam Mosoff, "Who cares what Thomas Jefferson thought about patents? Reevaluating the patent 'privilege' in historical context," *Cornell Law Review,* op. cit.

234   "[T]he right of the inventor is a high property; it is the fruit of his mind." Daniel Webster, House floor speech delivered January 5, 1824, reprinted in *The Writings and Speeches of Daniel Webster Hitherto Uncollected* (Boston: Little, Brown, and Co., Vol. 2, national edition, 1903), p. 79.

235   "more clear than that which a man can assert in almost any other kind of property." Ibid., p. 438.

235   "the patent and copyright clause of the Constitution celebrates and encourages 'individual effort by personal gain [as] the best way to advance public welfare through the talents of authors and inventors.'" *Mazer* v. *Stein,* 347 U.S. 201 (1954), accessed May 17, 2014, http://www.law.cornell .edu/copyright/cases/347_US_201.htm.

235   "The miniature models, no larger than twelve inches by twelve inches by twelve inches, were required as part of the application process from 1790 to 1880." Two devastating fires at Patent Office buildings in 1836 and 1877 destroyed an estimated eighty thousand patent models. In 1908, Congress moved a total of two hundred thousand surviving models into storage warehouses. The Smithsonian Institute selected a few thousand of what it considered the most historically significant, abandoning the rest to auctioneers. Some patent models can be found on sale on eBay. Several collectors, including Alan Rothschild, have launched their own

museums. See http://www.patentmodel.org/about/history, accessed May 17, 2014, for more information.

235   *"Popular Mechanics* ran its own 'Patent Bureau' offering consultation and legal services to aspiring inventors." A typical example of a *Popular Mechanics* patent bureau ad can be found in *Popular Mechanics*, Vol. 7, No. 5, May 1905, p. 498.

236   "President Lincoln not only defended the intellectual property rights of clients, but personally encouraged technological innovation." See Jason Emerson, *Lincoln the Inventor*, op. cit., and also Owen Edwards, "Inventive Abe," *Smithsonian Magazine*, October 2006, accessed May 17, 2014, http://www.smithsonianmag.com/ist/?next=/history/inventive-abe-131184751/.

236   "The mechanically inclined pioneer was an early adopter of the telegraph." See Tom Wheeler, *Mr. Lincoln's T-Mails: How Abraham Lincoln Used the Telegraph to Win the Civil War* (New York: HarperBusiness, 2008).

236   "He tested the Henry and Spencer repeating rifles on the White House lawn." Chris Kyle, *American Gun: A History of the U.S. in Ten Firearms* (New York: William Morrow, 2013), pp. 34–42.

236   "He assisted weapons inventors George H. Ferriss, James Holenshade, Isaac Diller, and James Woodruff." Robert V. Bruce and Benjamin P. Thomas, *Lincoln and the Tools of War* (Indianapolis: Bobbs-Merrill Company, 1956), p. 208.

236   "Lincoln also delivered lectures on the history of discoveries, inventions, and patent laws." Jason Emerson, *Lincoln the Inventor*, op. cit.

236   "He took his young son to visit the Patent Office in Washington." Ibid., p. 9.

237   "He constructed a miniature model." Emerson notes that a second patent model of his invention has gone missing and was apparently lost after being given to Southern Illinois University. Ibid., p. 33.

237   "the U.S. Patent Office approved his invention and issued Patent Number 6,469 for his 'device for buoying vessels over shoals.'" Ibid., p. 18. See also Abraham Lincoln, U.S. Patent 6469 A, May 22, 1849, Google Patents, accessed May 17, 2014, https://www.google.com/patents/US6469.

237   "the president's ideas 'may have advanced the creation of modern ship salvaging and submarine construction.'" Jason Emerson, *Lincoln the Inventor*, op. cit., p. 18.

237   "The great American novelist Mark Twain—patent holder on three inventions." "Patent files hold Mark Twain story," *New York Times*, March 12, 1939, p. 58.

237   "The very first official thing I did, in my administration—and it was on the very first day of it too—was to start a patent office." Mark Twain, *A Connecticut Yankee in King Arthur's Court*, op. cit., p. 68.

237   "the patent office stimulated Americans to 'turn their thinking into things.'" "The Patent Centennial Celebration," *Scientific American*, Vol. 64, April 18, 1891, p. 244.

237   "From 1863 to 1913, an estimated 800–1,200 patents were issued to black inventors." Zorina Khan, *The Democratization of Invention: Patents and Copyrights in American Economic Development, 1790–1920*, op. cit., p. 125.

237   "Between 1790 and 1895, some 3,300 women secured more than 4,100 patents." Ibid., p. 132.

238   "Between 1870 and 1930, economist B. Zorina Khan's research shows." Ibid., p. 214.

238   "Fending off intellectual property thieves was vital to a budding tinker-preneur's survival." See Adam Mossoff, "Demand Letters and Consumer Protection: Examining Deceptive Practices by Patent Assertion Entities," Statement before the Senate Committee on Commerce, Science, and Transportation Subcommittee on Consumer Protection, Product Safety, and Insurance, November 7, 2013, pp. 5–8, accessed May 17, 2014, http://cpip.gmu.edu/wp-content/uploads/2012/08/Adam-Mossoff-Testimony-11.7.13.pdf.

238   "As part of his radical bid to 'fundamentally transform' America." Hayley Tsukayama and Liz Lucas, "Thousands cheer Obama at rally for change," *Columbian Missourian*, October 30, 2008, accessed January 8, 2014, http://www.columbiamissourian.com/a/107641/thousands-cheer-obama-at-rally-for-change/.

238   "the law was marketed as a job-creation vehicle that would relieve a backlog of an estimated seven hundred thousand patent applications and crack down on patent 'trolls' supposedly abusing the system through frivolous litigation against alleged infringers." "President Obama Signs America Invents Act, Overhauling the Patent System to Stimulate Economic Growth, and Announces New Steps to Help Entrepreneurs Create Jobs," White House press release, September 16, 2011, accessed January 8, 2014, http://www.whitehouse.gov/the-press-office/2011/09/16/president-obama-signs-america-invents-act-overhauling-patent-system-stim.

239   "These and other measures signed into law in 2011 by President Barack Obama threaten to drive garage tinkerers and small inventors." See, for example, John Duffy, "The Big Government Patent Bill," PatentlyO

blog, June 23, 2011, accessed May 17, 2014, http://patentlyo.com/patent
/2011/06/the-big-government-patent-bill-guest-essay-by-john-duffy
.html; Dana Rohrabacher, "'Patent reform' will hurt innovation," *National
Review Online*, June 22, 2011, accessed May 17, 2014, http://www.national
review.com/articles/270193/patent-reform-will-hurt-innovation-dana
-rohrabacher; Bernard Klosowski, "Will the new patent law kill the garage
inventor and startup?" *Entrepreneur*, November 21, 2013, accessed May 17,
2014, http://www.entrepreneur.com/article/230034#; and Kelli Proia,
"America Invents Act: Hurting startups, helping no one," *IP Made Simple*,
February 13, 2013, accessed May 17, 2014, http://ipmadesimple.com
/america-invents-act-hurting-startups-helping-no-one/.

239 "The US gets ten times the angel and venture capital of Western Europe—
which recently declared an 'innovation emergency.'" Skip Kaltenheuser,
"Patently ridiculous: Leahy Smith America Invents Act," *International Bar
Association News*, September 20, 2011, accessed January 9, 2015, http://
www.ibanet.org/Article/Detail.aspx?ArticleUid=a9debe56-3464-47d4
-a19a-1e3415b139bc.

239 "A large part of invention is trying out a vast number of ideas." Steve Perlman, "Why 'First-to-Invent' is Essential for America's Unique Process of
Invention," Letter to Senator Diane Feinstein, March 8, 2011, reprinted
in *State of Innovation*, accessed January 9, 2015, http://hallingblog.com
/inventor-on-why-first-to-file-is-bad-for-small-inventors/.

240 "It typically costs us $20,000–$30,000 to obtain a commercial-grade
patent." Ibid.

241 "University of Virginia law professor John Duffy points out that the law is
140 pages long, 'more than twice the length of the entire federal patent
statute' since its last recodification in 1952." John Duffy, "The Big Government Patent Bill," PatentlyO blog, June 23, 2011, accessed January 10,
2015, http://patentlyo.com/patent/2011/06/the-big-government-patent
-bill-guest-essay-by-john-duffy.html.

241 "Its sloppy drafting will result in 'cases interpreting the law going to the
courts for twenty years before lawyers really know how to advise clients,'
patent lawyer David Boundy predicts." Skip Kaltenheuser, "Patently ridiculous: Leahy Smith America Invents Act," op. cit.

241 "Also buried in the law: a new pay-for-play scheme, dubbed 'Fast Track
for Fat Cats' by indie inventors, which allows large companies to expedite
their applications by forking over a $4,800 fee." Bruce Burdick, "Michelle
Lee, what will you be?" *America Invents IP Blog*, December 12, 2014, accessed January 10, 2015, http://www.burdlaw.com/blog/?cat=26.

241   "Having to spend more money to speed up the process favors big companies, not small ones." Eilene Zimmerman, "Business owners adjusting to overhaul of patent system," *New York Times*, February 9, 2012, accessed January 10, 2015, http://www.nytimes.com/2012/02/09/business/small business/business-owners-adjusting-to-patent-system-overhaul.html ?pagewanted=all.

241   "Kappos then resigned from the White House to take a cushy lobbying job with New York firm Cravath, Swaine, and Moore, which Kappos had worked closely with when his former employer IBM retained them." Ashby Jones, "Cravath plucks former PTO chief David Kappos," *Wall Street Journal*, February 6, 2013, accessed January 10, 2015, http://blogs.wsj.com /law/2013/02/06/cravath-plucks-former-pto-chief-david-kappos/.

242   "civilizations die from suicide, not by murder." See Arnold J. Toynbee, *A Study of History, Abridgement of Volumes 1-6 by D.C. Somervell* (Oxford, UK: Oxford University Press, 1974).

242   "This revolutionary idea is a hallmark of American exceptionalism." For a great primer, see Charles Murray, *American Exceptionalism: An Experiment in History* (Washington, D.C.: AEI Press, 2013).

242   "French historian Alexis de Tocqueville reported that the doctrine of enlightened 'self-interest rightly understood.' . . . 'You may trace it at the bottom of all their actions, you will remark it in all they say. It is as often asserted by the poor man as the rich.'" Alexis de Tocqueville, *Democracy in America and Two Essays on America*, op. cit., p. 609.

242   "Author Charles Murray adds that the Founders promoted industriousness . . . 'the bone-deep American assumption that life is to be spent getting ahead through hard work and thereby making a better life for oneself and one's children.'" Charles Murray, *American Exceptionalism: An Experiment in History*, op. cit., p 18.

242   "He points to German social historian Francis Grund, a contemporary of de Tocqueville's." Ibid., p. 19.

INDEX

Page numbers in *italics* indicate photos and illustrations.